UTOPIAN
Legacies

UTOPIAN
Legacies

A History of Conquest and Oppression in the Western World

JOHN C. MOHAWK

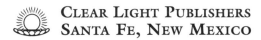

CLEAR LIGHT PUBLISHERS
SANTA FE, NEW MEXICO

This book is dedicated to the memory of
Ernest W. Mohawk and Elsie T. Mohawk.

First Edition
10 9 8 7 6 5 4 3 2 1

Library of Congress Cataloging-in-Publication Data

Mohawk, John, 1945–
    Utopian legacies : a history of conquest and oppression in the Western world /
    John C. Mohawk
        p. cm.
    Includes bibliographical references and index.
    ISBN 1-57416-034-6 (hardcover) – ISBN 1 57416-040-0 (pbk.)
    1. Imperialism—History. 2. Militarism—History. 3. Utopias—Religious aspects. I.
Title.
JC359.M575 1999
325'.32'09—dc21
                                                                99-038701
                                                                CIP

Cover design: Marcia Keegan and Carol O'Shea
Interior design & typography: Carol O'Shea
Cover photos: chain, The Stock Market/© Gerald Zanetti
Spanish shackles courtesy Museum of New Mexico, photograph © Marcia Keegan

Printed by Transcontinental in Canada

Contents

Acknowledgments

There are many whose encouragement, inspiration, and assistance made my own efforts possible. Professor Lawrence W. Chisolm was a founder of the American Studies Department at the State University of New York at Buffalo. He was also a mentor, colleague, and friend for nearly thirty years. For about ten of those years, he and I co-taught the Topics in Cultural History course, the two-semester core course in the American Studies graduate program. On every topic we discussed, Professor Chisolm offered gentle and persuasive insights infused with a love of learning and a profound appreciation of the tradition of transmitting such knowledge through books. I can never overstate how much he was an inspiration to my work as well as a personal friend. Professor Chisolm passed away in April, 1998.

I am also indebted to a long list of colleagues and acquaintances of whom I shall mention here but a few. Distinguished Professor Diane Christian gave me insights into ways of thinking about the history of Christianity that I found illuminating. Professor Robert K. Dentan offered excellent help with bibliographies in the anthropology literature. Conversations with Professor Charles Keil were critically helpful in sorting through how some group behaviors unfolded in the past. Professor Oren Lyons provided important support and access to people and institutions, as well as valuable insight into the causes of present world conditions.

I must also acknowledge the work of several people who were graduate students as this work progressed and provided assistance, insight, and encouragement: Lori E. Taylor; Patrick Ward, and Joseph Proegler and his wife Ghada.

There were many others to whom I owe a great debt for my own development. Some who were most inspiratonal were Chiefs

Irving Powless, Sr., Leon Shenandoah, and Irving Powless, Jr., of Onondaga. Among my closest friends were those who taught me about our world: Chiefs Bernard Parker, Corbett Sundown, and Harrison Ground of the Tonawanda Seneca. I owe a similar debt to former Chiefs Richard Cook, Jr. and Thomas Porter of the Mohawk Nation.

Paul Williams has been friend and conversation partner for more than twenty-five years and his skills as a negotiator and lawyer have been both instructional and inspirational. He is also one of the most knowledgeable social historians, especially about the Haudenosaunee, whom it has been my pleasure to know. Law Professor Howard Berman, a significant figure in the area of promotion and protection of the rights of indigenous peoples on the world stage, was a long-time friend and correspondent. He was far too young when he succumbed to brain cancer in 1997.

The individual who provided endless encouragement and thoughtful conversation as the book unfolded was my life partner and friend, Yvonne Dion-Buffalo. That she could abide my rantings across the full spectrum of topics offered in the book is testimony to her endurance, for which I am deeply grateful.

I cannot fail to acknowledge the individual whose example taught me the value and pleasures of reading. Ernest Mohawk was a mostly self-taught man who learned the skills of an electrician through books. His formal education went no further than the seventh grade, but he read about a wide range of subjects from plant biology to astronomy and, in addition, possessed a great knowledge of the culture and history of the Seneca people. He was my father, teacher, and friend, and no one could have asked for better in any of these categories. He passed away in September, 1993, but his presence is found in every page of my work.

No list of acknowledgements would be complete that failed to mention the editors at Clear Light Publishers. Valerie Shepherd provided both encouragement and thoughtful additions, and Sara Held worked tirelessly to add both clarity and cohesion to the finished product. This book would not have been possible without them, or without the support and encouragement of publisher Harmon Houghton.

ONE
Utopia and the Pursuit of the Ideal

The Garden of Eden, the Republic, the Workers' Paradise, and similar utopian visions have existed since antiquity in most if not all of the world's cultures and have played a very important role in the history of Western civilization. Most utopian ideologies have been marginal to the mainstream of Western thought and belief systems, but a few have provided background and context for some of the culture's defining moments. These ideologies propose that there has existed, now exists somewhere, or could exist in the future a perfect society, an existence in which all human needs are satisfied, all problems are solved, and everyone's life is fulfilled. Utopian ideologies are by definition subjective and require significant exercise of imagination because they propose societies that cannot be seen or experienced and that have never existed and arguably cannot exist.

The "pursuit of the ideal"—a theme in Western culture—is a similar tradition. Although distinct from utopianism, it articulates a belief that all reasonable human beings who have access to an adequate base of information will pursue an identical concept of what is ideal or good. The pursuit of the ideal arises from the received assumptions and beliefs of Western culture, many of which are related to past utopian visions. It could more properly be termed the "pursuit of the cultural ideal" since the ideal is socially constructed, and its elements have roots in the culture's ideological history. An individual who was not familiar with the history of these ideas and who had no reason to embrace its assumptions would be at a serious disadvantage both in trying to understand how it works and in participating in its life.

The ideal is defined in terms of Western culture: it is the pursuit of that which is popularly accepted by the mainstream of Western culture as good and desirable. The fact that the pursuit of the ideal is defined as being both popular and mainstream in Western culture is important because it separates the historic phenomenon from individual efforts to do good work. When we speak of the pursuit of the ideal, we are speaking of cultural phenomena that span generations and even centuries. The ideals of individuals, however, may diverge in varying degrees from those of the culture. Even within cultures with highly developed socialization processes, some individuals will be skeptics.

The history of ideas in the West is dominated by a certainty that an ideal world is possible, that such a world would be in the best interest of all human beings, and its conception and production will inevitably be the product of Western thought. At least three distinct disciplines have addressed aspects of these phenomena: philosophy, anthropology, and history. Philosophy has tended to pay more attention to Western civilization's pursuit of the ideal, and anthropology has developed an understanding of social movements by which utopian ideas are pursued through political, spiritual, and/or military strategies. History has produced versions of how the record has unfolded. The history of Western civilization in the context of all three—utopian social movements, the pursuit of the ideal state of existence, and the historical record—has not been fully explored.

The utopian ideas that are of most interest in such an exploration are linked to social movements that have left an indelible mark in the historical record. Although there have been many utopian-inspired movements, relatively few, such as Christianity, Islam, and Marxism, have changed the course of Western history. In these instances, the beliefs of a small or isolated group became the driving ideas that inspired people who had political or military power at their disposal. Often they commanded an army, coercive police force, or other civil authority that could be used with a heavy hand.

The pursuit of utopian goals requires resources, both material and nonmaterial, and its achievement is such a splendid objective that its followers are inclined to believe nothing should stand in the way of securing those resources. Whatever the utopian justification, the practice of acquiring these resources by force or other forms of coercion is simply an act of plunder. Utopian ideologies enable plunderers to claim—even to believe—that they are in pursuit of noble goals. There is no reason to doubt that people are capable of embracing an imaginary perfect world while pursuing materialistic objectives. In such a pursuit, it is important to note that the utopian vision is the primary goal, while plunder, although attractive, is a secondary objective.

In most instances the time envisioned in utopian ideology is the future. "Utopia," a word meaning, literally, "no place," has usually been imagined to exist in the future. The origins of utopian movements, however, are embedded in a much more concrete and knowable past that can be examined for clues to what motivated people and how their dreams and expectations played out in the real world. This examination requires us to view Western utopianism in the context of Western history and culture and not as a series of isolated movements that can be dismissed as aberrations. They are not aberrations. These movements are so woven into the fabric of the culture that to consider them in isolation from the conditions that produced them would not only diminish their importance but would deprive us of information critical to an understanding of the world we inherit.

The major utopian movements came into existence in specific contexts. They later became transformed into successive movements that influenced culture, often in destructive ways, and they remain important in the production and reproduction of contemporary cultures. The role of the ideologies is of critical importance because long after the movements have altered or lost their energy, the ideologies may persist, preserved in the memory of the culture in an honored position and capable of reemerging at a later time. In fact, elements of a utopian ideology born in one age and context are known to persist and may be pursued by future generations in completely different contexts. Therefore, this story is not a series of episodes of utopian movements but rather chapters in the larger history in which these movements are born or played out.

Utopian ideologies contain within them two compelling characteristics. First, if a group expects that their utopian story will culminate in the production of a perfect world, everything they do to create or react to the conditions that will bring this about acquires enhanced importance. Second, the utopia does not actually arrive; it is always in the future. The utopia imagined by the ancient Greek philosophers illustrates the charged importance of human agency in utopian thinking. Beginning with Socrates, the Greeks came to believe they had discovered a path to knowledge that would lead to making the world a better place. Socrates was so dedicated to the idea that he gave up his life rather than renounce it.

People who are engaged in utopian projects tend to envision the world in a state of being that precedes another state of being. The common wisdom among the converted is that things are progressing in a positive way toward the realization of the utopia. Inherent in true utopian thought, therefore, is a notion of progress. While the members of the group are awaiting its arrival—sometimes over very long periods of time—they are urged or coerced or terrorized in myriad ways to continue to believe that it will in fact arrive. When the supernatural is expected to deliver the utopia, this trust or confidence is defined as faith, but that term is not inappropriate when applied to secular utopianism. The Christian's belief in the utopian Kingdom of God on earth is an article of faith, but so is the Marxist's belief in the inevitable triumph of socialism. To deviate from this expression of faith is to invite reprisal, especially when those who guard the faith have the power to mobilize such reprisal.

People who believe that they are acting on a plan to solve all of humankind's problems think they are on a kind of sacred mission, even when the origin of their inspiration is secular in nature and makes no claim to intervention by a higher power. Although adherents may have only a vague idea about how the utopia will come about or what it will be like when it arrives, utopian movements often stimulate high levels of enthusiasm and a widely shared sense of being a "chosen people" with a special destiny. People caught up in such movements tend to be intolerant of others who are not part of this projected destiny, who do not believe in the same things, and are not expected to share in the future benefits. One reason for the popularity of these movements is that they exalt the importance of the group, praise their imagined superior qualities and future prospects, and urge that, relative to other peoples, they are special and more deserving. This pattern of self-aggrandizement has often proven popular and energizing. It contains a message that others who are not special or chosen are without significant value and may be treated accordingly. This kind of intolerance can result in the denial of rights, including the right to live, to hold property, to vote, or to hold professional licenses, if the inspired group has the power to do these things. A scornful indifference to these unbelieving and unentitled others can manifest as racism and/or ethnocentrism. Such intolerance has been known to lead to crimes against humanity, including systematic acts of genocide.

Anthropologists have described a phenomenon among oppressed peoples that can spark movement for cultural change. While most cultural change happens unconsciously and gradually over time, people occasionally make conscious efforts to improve their culture. Such an effort, when it mobilizes significant numbers to action, is termed a revitalization movement. Adherents of revitalization movements imagine their improved society or future utopia as a condition that must be created through their own vision and efforts. Revitalization movements may be characterized as generating a high level of enthusiasm around unrealistic expectations, often with tragic results. Some revitalization movements have produced visions of utopia but did not leave much of a mark on history. The ideas of the Amana and Oneida communities, for example, were certainly utopian-inspired movements, but did not change the course of history to a significant degree.

Revitalization movements are far more common and their legacies far more intricately interwoven into the fabric of contemporary cultures than is generally recognized. Sometimes the crisis that triggers the desire for change occurs when a group is not actually oppressed but feels disrespected by a culturally dominant group. A series of reactions may develop. If the culturally dominant group suggests that these people are illiterate and backward, they may respond that their enemies are decadent and immoral. If they are said to be impoverished because of their lack of ambition and talent, the responding group may assert that wealth is of little importance to them, or they may adopt dangerous strategies in seeking to acquire wealth for themselves. Their reaction may contribute to the development of aggressive nationalism. The German reaction to French cultural domination in the nineteenth century may be an example of this. During the nineteenth century, when many Germans felt dominated by French pretensions to high culture, they reacted by exalting everything German and essentially inventing a cultural history to support nationalist sentiment. Echoes of this movement played into the agenda of the Nazi revitalization movement, which promoted its own utopia, the Third Reich, and a claim to German biological, moral, and cultural superiority over all other peoples of the world.

In another type of revitalization movement, the emphasis is upon a return to the past. We find revival movements in which the group seeks to reconstruct itself in a cherished image of the past. As much a product of imagination as history, the image idealizes the lives and privileges of glorified ancestors and claims that they lived a kind of utopian existence. The group seeks to identify with those things deemed positive and desirable in their contemporary existence—an existence under real or perceived stress—and to eliminate impediments to a better life while emulating behaviors and values of their ancestors. Their hopes of achieving a more successful culture are often unrealistic not only because of incorrect or incomplete information about the actual lived experiences of their ancestors but also because their own culture has imported values and other elements of culture from foreigners—often the people responsible for the stress. The introduction of these elements is usually unintentional and unconscious and therefore largely invisible to the reformers.

Another type of revitalization movement produces the phenomenon of cargo cults, which attempt to abandon the past and remodel the culture on a vision of an ideal foreign culture. The experience of the people making the attempt is limited by the fact that almost everything they use to conceive of the alien culture, from language to technology and social customs, is based on a mixture of indigenous traditional culture and impressions of a foreign culture with which they are imperfectly familiar. To outside observers of such cultural phenomena, it is clear that the absence of realism comes from the attempt to create a culture from nothing, as well as from lack of information about how to go about such a task.

Some South American Indian revitalization movements reflect the conditions of their oppression. These Indians were often brutally enslaved or subjected to conditions of serfdom very close to slavery in the mines and plantations of the Spaniards. For them, utopia would be a remote place that contained no Spaniards and that the Spaniards could not find. Here we find the idea of the promised land that exists in legend or prophesy to which a people can be delivered. North American Indians, on the other hand, were generally not enslaved or subjected to crippling economic demands except in areas settled by the Spanish. Otherwise, North American Indians were, with few exceptions, coerced or driven by military force from their ancestral lands. These Indians saw the fowl, fish, and animals of their homelands driven to near extinction; their people decimated by disease; and their land made off limits to them by a relentless invader. For them, utopia would be a place where all things lost would be restored and the material culture of their ancestors could be enjoyed. Revitalization movements among these peoples tend to emphasize the revival of the ancient and traditional culture, often through moral purification and the renewal of ceremonies that had once been central to their lives. There have been many such revivalist movements among the North American Indians, but the Ghost Dance religion of the late nineteenth century is perhaps the best known. People believed that through ritual they could revive the buffalo herds and bring departed ancestors back to life. They reportedly believed that bullets would not penetrate the spiritually purified shirts they wore. The project generated intense enthusiasm around expectations that were obviously unrealistic to any outside observer but absolutely real to those seized by its promises.

Revitalization movements are not limited to tribal societies or even to groups traditionally recognized as oppressed, but are among the most widely experienced phenomena in world history. Such movements have impacted virtually every society and every individual on earth. As cultural phenomena they have sometimes blurred the lines between Western and non-Western cultures. The Taiping Rebellion in China (1850–1864), for example, was led by a fundamentalist Christian peasant, Hung Hsiu Ch'uan, who thought he was a son of God and preached that all property should be held in common. His rebellion carried the utopian name "Heavenly Kingdom of Great Peace." The movement's followers smashed Buddhist, Confucian, and Taoist temples and attacked a coalition of the Qing Dynasty and Western military occupiers. Eventually fielding an army of a million disciplined troops, the movement occupied the Yangtze Valley and the city of Nanjing and waged one of the most destructive civil wars in world history. An estimated 20 to 30 million people were killed before Hung's forces were decisively defeated.

In order to create and sustain the idea that the group is somehow a chosen people, history is often rewritten in a way that confirms this idea. Coupled with historical invention is a tendency among such movements to seek and find scapegoats who are not part of the culture or not believers in the movement and are considered responsible for obstructing it. For example, the fantasy of the victimization of Germany by a conspiracy of Jewish bankers played a major role in the massacre of Jews during World War II. Given the opportunity, such movements often appropriate to themselves permission to clear away anything perceived as an obstacle in their path—including peoples who are located at a lower level in the hierarchy of power and unable to protect themselves.

The British philosopher Isaiah Berlin discussed the relationship between utopian ideologies and mass violence in *The Crooked Timber of Humanity*. He stated that while it is widely perceived that utopian thought is in decline in the West, it is also true that powerful examples of its continued presence abound. In *The Sense of Reality* he described a tendency at the heart of Western culture to pursue a specific "ideal" way of life. This pursuit can be traced at least as far back as classical Greece and has continued to inspire Western philosophical concepts about the nature of the ideal and to reinforce a set of assumptions with far-reaching implications:

> At some point I realised that what all these views had in common was a Platonic ideal: in the first place, that, as in the sciences, all genuine questions must have one true answer and one only, all the rest being necessarily errors; in the second place, that there must be a dependable path towards the discovery of these truths; in the third place, that the true answers, when found, must necessarily be compatible with one another and form a single whole. (Berlin 1998, 5–6)

There is a certainty to this line of thought that is seductive but ultimately flawed. Berlin asserts this way of thinking cannot be universally applied in light of the diversity of human aspirations found among the world's peoples. For some kinds of questions, especially those involving the physical world or mathematics, some justification can be made for this line of thought, but among diverse human cultures it cannot be applied in discussions about values. Asked to define the ideal world in terms of values, Amish farmers and Japanese industrialists can be expected to give vastly different answers. Given the differences in language and culture, it is possible that a person whose experience is limited to Amish culture could not even conceive or express the concept of an ideal world as imagined by a Japanese industrialist, and vice versa. To the question about what the ideal world would be, there is, quite obviously, more than one correct answer. Since there are four to five thousand cultures in the world, there is no way of knowing how many such correct answers there might be.

Berlin added that the concept of the ideal was fundamentally flawed because people's ideas about what would solve problems keep changing as problems and conditions that create them keep changing. Indeed, the efforts to bring about change help create unexpected conditions that alter ideas about what constitutes the ideal. In short, the ideal is impossible to achieve even with a specific society because people will always experience new sets of problems the original visionaries did not anticipate.

This difficulty is further complicated by the fact that even within a specific society people do not agree about the definition of the ideal (or what is good) that can and should be created. The world, indeed the neighborhood, has never been and will never be of one mind about this subject. If those who have a vision of the ideal world use coercion and force to intimidate or terrorize nonbelievers into compliance, their effort at enforcement necessarily destroys freedom of choice and human dignity for some and thereby destroys the possibility of creating an ideal society for all. Berlin thought that the best that could be done would be to strive for a pluralistic society in which people would be socialized to accept that there exist different and sometimes competing ideas about the ideal, and to remember the record of devastation and horror brought on by efforts to suppress or destroy those differences.

Many of the historical texts recounting the evolution of Western civilization echo the story of the pursuit of the ideal because previous generations of historians believed Western civilization was on a path to the perfection, or near perfection, of humankind. The assumptions underlying Western history are problematic and underscore how subtle these tendencies can be. For example, although there is a nod to the histories of the ancient civilizations of the Fertile Crescent, the Nile, and Crete—civilizations in existence for thousands of years prior to the rise of classical Greece—Greek culture is commonly presented as a phenomenon that arose more or less mystically from the land. By doing this, historians have separated Greek and therefore Western history from the stream of ancient history and made it appear distinct and special in ways more consistent with utopian ideologies than with its rightful place among the world's cultures. Ancient civilizations existed as remotely in time from the Golden Age of Greece as does that age from the twentieth century, and Greece inherited far more from those civilizations than many historians of Western civilization have been inclined to admit.

The evolution of culture was anything but linear and its outcome anything but certain. The history of the ancient world's civilizations, including that of Greece, is a record of civilizations that rose and declined. There were successive empires born of conquest that suffered under tyrants. There were natural disasters, plagues, invasions, and any number of events that might challenge the idea that the triumph of civilization was inevitable. Bleak living conditions were often the lot of the conquered, and both urban and rural peoples at times shared a sense of hopelessness born of oppression. To find within that record an unbroken story of cumulative improvements in the human condition requires an exercise in creative history that previous generations of historians felt compelled to endorse.

Most of us would like to believe our world is one fundamentally different and distinct from ancient worlds with their superstitions and dogmas, more liberated from traditional metaphysics, more dedicated to rational existence, and therefore consciously contemporary. We want to believe we live in an age that is beyond the irrationalities of revitalization movements or the quest for an unattainable ideal. We consider ourselves sophisticated pragmatic people, tolerant of difference and cautious about embracing destructive ideologies. We consider ourselves fully modern, not simply in the sense of that term used by historians or philosophers, but in the sense that we are contemporary beings, aware that our world is complex, and skeptical about simple answers to complex issues.

This view is consistent with the ideas of philosophers who have framed modernity as beginning with the age of conquest and colonization and ending with the age of "decolonization," proposing a new consciousness under which the old ideas of European hegemony and white supremacy are considered out of date. Some writers have designated this new and gentler age as the era of "postmodernity," a period following the domination and repression that were the political and economic reality of the process of the creation of modernity for so much of the world.

Twentieth-century philosophers have energetically tried to discount, discredit, and reject the utopian ideas of the past. Although such ideas continue to exist and to attract followers—the Second Coming is confidently awaited and some still yearn for the Workers' Paradise—it is no longer universally acceptable or academically legitimate to embrace most of these ideologies uncritically. Although utopian movements may not have the power to effect dramatic social change at the moment, the belief that an ideal human condition is possible—and that the West possesses the only legitimate version of what that ideal world would be—continues to exist. In contemporary mass societies, it is perpetuated in part through the kind of propaganda familiar as advertising. Jerry Mander's 1978 book, *Four Arguments for the Elimination of Television*, argues that television has produced a major transformation in the way people receive and interpret information. In his 1991 book, *In the Absence of the Sacred: The Failure of Technology and the Survival of the Indian Nations*, Mander provides some important insights into the trends of American (and all of Western) culture. He proposes that starting around 1940 American culture took a radical turn.

Exhibits at the World's Fair in Flushing, New York, in 1939 introduced for the first time a corporate message that technology offered humankind a future life without disease and free from the drudgery of the workplace. The combination of machinery, chemistry, electrical engineering, and other technological wizardry would create a world that met all human needs and solved all human problems. Humanity, according to this message, stood at the doorstep of utopia, and every aspect of life was on the verge of being transformed. The concept of the ideal is alive and well in the West. It proposes that the modern age possesses a vision of how human beings should live their lives that is compelling and progressive and that all human beings, given enough information, should want to embrace this ideal. Those who resist are thought to do so out of ignorance or superstition.

Often the pursuit of this ideal existence—generally embodying the Western middle-class standard of living—requires that natural resources such as coal and water be used to generate electricity. People are often displaced by these plans. Whether or not the goals can pragmatically be achieved, the pursuit of the ideal is often relentless and, to its victims, heartless. In this pursuit, regional economies are sacrificed; forests plundered; animal habitats destroyed; species of animals and plants rendered extinct; and low-intensity warfare is waged against indigenous and peasant populations. Even in contemporary times the pursuit of the ideal, like the pursuit of utopia, is usually destructive.

In Western culture, such destruction has not generally been opposed by most of the people. Leaders who accomplish feats identified with the pursuit of the ideal are almost universally popular even if their methods are dishonorable. Some of history's most celebrated figures—Alexander the Great, Julius Caesar, Charlemagne, Napoleon—remain popular for that reason. Adolph Hitler's popularity has never been surpassed in German history. He ceased being popular among the German people only when the Nazi revitalization movement was destroyed and a new generation of Germans could not and would not embrace his vision or his methods. As long as the idea of the Third Reich was alive, Hitler remained a hero of godlike stature to many Germans. The ideals that are pursued by those in power rarely concern such matters as harmonious relations among peoples or the regeneration of the ecology of a distressed region. They are almost always ideals that, if pursued, involve some level of dispossession, removal of populations, exploitation, pollution, economic devastation, or other evil.

These tendencies have not existed in every culture in the world or at every moment of history, but it is important to acknowledge that they are major themes—perhaps the characterizing themes—in Western culture. Revitalization movements have energized people and given them permission to commit horrible crimes against humanity in the pursuit of utopia. The pursuit of the ideal has provided a stream of rationalizations that justified plunder, racism, and oppression in the name of a better future. The fact that conquests and their reward were acceptable and continue to be celebrated in Western history is a key to the story of how the world came to be the way it is.

Bibliography

Berlin, Isaiah. *The Crooked Timber of Humanity: Chapters in the History of Ideas.* Princeton, N.J.: Princeton University Press, 1990.

Dowd, Gregory Evans. *A Spirited Resistance: The North American Indian Struggle for Unity, 1745–1815.* Baltimore: Johns Hopkins University Press, 1993.

Jacob, H. E. *Six Thousand Years of Bread: Its Holy and Unholy History.* New York: Doubleday, Doran & Co., 1944.

Mander, Jerry. *In the Absence of the Sacred: The Failure of Technology and the Survival of the Indian Nations.* San Francisco: Sierra Club Books, 1991.

_____. *Four Arguments for the Elimination of Television.* New York: William Morrow, 1978.

Wallace, Anthony F. C. "Revitalization Movements." *American Anthropologist* 58 (1956): 264–281.

Welch, Claude E., Jr. *Anatomy of Rebellion.* Albany: State University of New York Press, 1980.

TWO
Gardens of Eden

All problems depend to some degree upon the ways in which people think and act; but the external universe and men's relations to it, although they have no doubt changed throughout historic time, have altered less than ways of thought and of language, whose inner history is in part the history of those [problems] which are properly called philosophical.

Isaiah Berlin, *The Sense of Reality: Studies in Ideas and Their History*

All societies have had their utopian dreams, and in many ancient societies, utopias were envisioned as located in a distant past when human beings and nature existed harmoniously in blissful unity. Are such utopias pure fantasy, or do they contain some seeds of truth about the lives of our oldest human ancestors? Was the past once a place of innocence and delight where human beings cavorted with the spiritual representatives of the natural world in perfect harmony and balance? Or was it, as many European philosophers have imagined it, a brutish existence of each against all competing at a near-starvation level for survival at its basest definition? How do the ideals expressed in early visions of utopia differ from later ideologies that expected the conditions for utopia to be created by society? A comparison of ancient utopian legends with what is known of the lifeways of early peoples suggests some interesting answers to these questions.

The accepted story of the origins of the modern West usually begins with a discussion of the Greeks as founders of the tradition. The ancient Greeks saw little value in ancient and nomadic cultures, which they termed barbarian. To the Greeks, only people who lived in cities and took part in civil government could be viewed as true human beings. The writings of philosophers such as Aristotle elaborated Greek beliefs about civilization, including the view that all other peoples were inferior.

This characterization of ancient peoples and even contemporary peoples who do not live primarily in cities is a prejudice of many civilized societies, and it permeates the body of Western literature. By imaging the past as a hellish place devoid of human virtue and the basic necessities of life, modern civilized peoples rationalize their own existence as flawed but the best thus far possible, asserting that a better place could exist only in the future. In this way the conversation about the capacity for productive change is limited to experiences of civilized people documented in civilized societies. If our accepted version of the ancient past cannot provide us with clues about humankind in a kinder, gentler world, people will turn to the only available alternative: the future.

Ancient peoples imagined the idealized past in the same way civilized peoples have imagined the utopian future, and these differences have created tremendous obstacles around cultural expectations. Can human beings create societies where human needs are met, wants are satisfied, and nature's powers are controlled for the benefit of humankind? Or does the future hold a world increasingly out of balance with nature; a world of diminishing human access to natural resources; a world barren of birds and fish and trees; a world battered by horrific weather patterns of flood and drought, growing deserts, rising seas, starvation, and hopelessness? In the largest sense, these are the questions over which competing visions—of worlds that have vanished and worlds not yet created—seek the allegiance of humankind.

Contemporary speculation and research about the lives of the earliest humans throws doubt on demeaning stereotypes that have been accepted for centuries. Careful examination of what is known about the lives of ancient peoples shows how poorly these cultures have been understood. Cultures that trace their roots to immeasurably ancient times often viewed the past as a time not only of innocence but also of grace. Seeking patterns that inform them of the rules that govern their lives, traditional peoples have always explored ways of seeing the future through the experiences of the past. Many ancient cultures viewed the past as a time of discovery, of the acquisition of the "original instructions," as some modern Hopi express this idea. Some cultures have stories about a past during which human beings conversed with God or gods or spirits of nature and the spirits of the animals. The Iroquois (Haudenosaunee), for example, have stories of the past depicting a time when people were clear about the desires of the spirits who created life on the earth, and found a sense of security and grace in that knowledge. Among the Iroquois myths is a story of human beings becoming forgetful of their obligations for the great good fortune of the gift of life; when this happened, unhappiness, misfortune, and anomie befell them. Therefore ceremonies of thanksgiving are given by the people to the Creator of Life so they will always remember to be grateful. But, the story continues, someday in the future people will once again become forgetful, the earth itself will grow old, and life will change.

Iroquois cosmology is in a sense utopian, but the utopia—the perfect world—is in a shrouded and very ancient past during which the relationship between human beings and the spirits who support life was very strong and cooperative, and even the animals and birds participated along with human beings in the continuous drama of life. As time passed, according to this myth, things changed and continue to change. Even before the European expansion at the end of the fifteenth century and long before the beginning of the Age of Extinction at the end of the seventeenth century, Iroquois storytellers described a perfect age in the distant past and urged the necessity of carrying on traditions to preserve as much of the relationships and knowledge of those times as possible in a present that was becoming ever more distant from that utopia. This version of utopia is clearly intended to motivate people to preserve Iroquoian spiritual and ritual practices and oral traditions.

The Hopi have a similar relationship to utopia. In their stories, things are fine in the beginning, but human weaknesses such as greed and aggression run contrary to the laws by which nature is stabilized. Disharmonious human activities create conditions that cause nature to take revenge through catastrophes that destroy whole worlds. New worlds are subsequently formed, and the same experiences are repeated in a cycle that reflects human weaknesses until these worlds are also destroyed. Once again, a reverence for balance in nature and attention to maintenance of tradition are the only antidotes to impending disasters. The Hopi utopias are located in an ancient past, and the morals of their stories are that human beings are collectively responsible for maintaining delicate balances with the spiritual powers that support life on earth, and there are consequences if these balances are not preserved.

Since the beginning of human time, peoples have traversed the earth in search of food, safety, and comfort. The earliest human societies, the hunting and gathering cultures, lived on every continent except Antarctica over profound periods of time. These cultures were primarily organized around an endless and, if the word can be used in such circumstances, enlightened quest for food. Although these cultures were extremely diverse, several things can be said about them. They were nomadic, moving across large areas in a pattern that took maximum advantage of the bounties of the land. They kept moving to avoid exhausting the food supply and to find desirable wild foods in different places during different seasons. Knowing where and when to travel to find food is a key to survival. If longevity is any indication of success, this was a successful form of culture.

Some environments, such as deserts, present severe challenges, but we find peoples who have adapted to them over very long periods of time. The rain forests were very difficult places. In spite of their great biological complexity, food is not plentiful in such environments. Although rain forests make up only 2 percent of the world's surface, they hold more than 60 percent of the world's species and in many areas are incredibly biologically diverse and delicately balanced. The rain forests were the second to the last environment to be inhabited by human beings.

The last place was the most obvious challenge: the Arctic. To survive in the Arctic, human societies must have lived on its fringes for a long time, learning techniques to enable them to survive as they moved ever deeper into the most forbidding habitable environment on earth. Early human beings accomplished this with no possibility of airlifts, no insurance policies, and no radio communication. The material cultures of the Inuit people of Alaska, northern Canada, Greenland, and Siberia are marvels of human adaptability. In an impressive variety of microenvironments within the Arctic Circle, they learned to hunt whales, caribou, and seals and to fish successfully. It is worth noting that although the Arctic appears a frozen, barren wasteland to the uninitiated, it is in fact endowed with substantial resources. Indeed, except in rare instances, people generally prospered in these environments until modern times, when Western expansion inadvertently invaded even their remote homelands.

Modern human beings owe much to the ancient peoples who subsisted on the land through hunting and gathering. It is speculated that gathering is one of the significant activities that differentiate human beings from other primates. Early on, ancestors of human beings learned to use a piece of bark or other material as a vessel into which berries or other edibles could be placed and carried back to the group. The invention of the carrying vessel distinguished human beings from other animals in some important ways. A gorilla or chimpanzee will usually eat food where he or she finds it and often will not share with others. Sharing meant that early proto-humans were motivated to establish a hearth—a base of operations from which to organize foraging more efficiently—and to develop group behaviors that favored cooperation and community. In hunter-gatherer communities, human beings would live their entire lives in small, intimate communities in which people probably had no words for loneliness, and the cruelest punishment that could befall an individual would be banishment from the group.

Someone who returned with a harvest of wild edibles might want to recruit the rest to return to the same spot to gather more. The need to give directions and to divide up the treasure may have helped stimulate the very early development of language. The ancient tradition of cooperation was undoubtedly motivated by the long period from birth to adulthood—of their young. This long period between birth and self-sufficiency helped to shape early human cultures. There are cultures in the world in which the adults do little to attend to the needs of their young, but these cultures are unusual, and most societies would tend to view them as not typically human.

Cooperation vastly improved the group's and by extension the species' long-term chances of survival. Human beings, more than most primates, depend on other members of the group for their survival and comfort. Human "social services" are very ancient. From very early times, child care was shared, and the sick, infirm, and injured were cared for. It was common practice to share food so that no one in the group would go hungry as long as food was available. When there was no food, everyone went hungry, although in emergencies, the hunters may have been fed as a first priority so they would be strong enough to secure more food. The practice of sharing food so no member of the group died of starvation while other members ate heartily appears to go back to a time before human beings took on the appearance of modern people, and we know that it continued into the late stone age in many cultures.

This kind of culture was successful for a very long time in a wide variety of environments. Although modern fiction writers and some motion picture producers have imagined stone age peoples living very harsh lives, a good deal of evidence supports the position that even in challenging environments stone age peoples could live reasonably comfortable lives. Studies of surviving stone age cultures indicate that hunting peoples have plenty to eat almost all the time, plenty of free time, and a generally pleasant life. At most times and in most places they experience little hunger, enjoy plenty of good food, exercise, good company, and free time. It therefore seems unlikely that, except in times of natural calamities, ancient stone age people were condemned to lives that were, in the words of seventeenth-century English philosopher Thomas Hobbes, "nasty, brutish, and short." (Hobbes was commenting on another matter entirely, but his quote is often taken out of context and applied to ancient peoples.) Except for their material culture, they were, in many essential ways, much more like us than we have been taught to believe.

Among people who consider themselves modern, there is a tendency to denigrate and stereotype cultures of the past, on the assumption that although things might be very bad in our time and culture, life now is the best it has ever been. We cannot know whether that assumption is correct, however; and we cannot rule out the possibility that, in essential ways, ancient peoples could have been as happy as, or even happier than, contemporary peoples.

Although ancient humans were undoubtedly fiercely territorial and, like other primates, probably carried on occasional feuds with their neighbors, two elements necessary for the development of a highly organized military tradition were largely lacking: motive and opportunity. There was little accumulated wealth to stimulate the desire for plunder, and the alien group was likely to be similarly armed and able to defend itself quite well. Thus, very ancient cultures—the Paleolithic—were probably not very warlike. This appears to have changed during the Neolithic period, when advances in tool-making seem to have led to the development of more sophisticated weapons.

Ancient human cultures engaged in both intertribal and intra-tribal violence, but contemporary people are well advised to be careful about making sweeping generalizations about violence in their societies. Scientists who study chimpanzee behavior find that some chimpanzee societies attack their neighbors, and human societies have undoubtedly engaged in some intertribal violence since the beginning of time. Their motives are difficult to know because we have no concrete accounts from very ancient peoples, but accounts from modern tribal peoples who are for the most part Neolithic, or "new stone age," indicate that violence is a product of revenge for injuries suffered or for harm believed to be caused by sorcery.

It is very difficult to characterize the violence of Neolithic groups as a whole, since some engaged in very little intratribal rivalry of any kind, while others appear to have spent much of their energy doing little else but fighting. Deadly blood feuds and even primitive versions of organized warfare were commonplace in some cultures. Like contemporary cultures, most Neolithic groups fought back when their territories were invaded. Ancient peoples had little to tempt them to plunder, and booty taken on raids during this period consisted mostly of captives, often women and children, who could be held as slaves, as human currency for negotiating the return of captives, or to replace by adoption members who had been captured or killed.

A characteristic of ancient cultures that is evident in more recent cultures is the practice of seeking dreams or visions. If we were able to time-travel back hundreds of thousands of years to study our ancient forebears, we might name them the "Dreaming Apes." Our ancestors sought visions and evolved a brain peculiarly well adapted to dreaming and, ultimately, to the invention of myths. The size of the modern human brain and its complexity are a mystery. It is large enough that its functions cannot be explained in what we think of as practical terms. The human brain evolved not only the ability to perform complex problem-solving activities but also an enormous imaginative capacity that enables it to interpret the world, to envision and create, and to call on powers that today might be described as paranormal or mystical.

The long period of hunter-gatherer culture, originating at least as far back as when some ancient ancestor climbed down from a tree and ventured into an African savannah, created and cultivated the conditions that brought forth the modern human brain. Evolutionists and others might argue that the development of such an organ was the result of biological selection, that the human brain serves a purpose in the struggle for survival.

It has been argued that it is the brain that gave modern humans an advantage over those cousins of our species that became extinct. Except as a statement of human vanity, however, we do not know whether the development of the human brain was an evolutionary step of profound dimensions, or another dead-end trail of evolution destined for extinction sooner than most.

What is clear is that the modern human brain is a fairly recent invention and that the results have been mixed. The modern brain was probably responsible for the enormous adaptability of our species across a wide range of ecological environments to which people have become intensely emotionally attached. Human cultures have taught themselves to embrace and identify with various environments as part of the capacity of adaptation.

It is thought that many of the myths that serve as cosmologies for societies may have originated as dreams that were determined to be of special significance and were remembered and memorialized in ritual. It is possible and even likely that these formed the basis of early revitalization movements that eventually evolved into religions or communal practices resembling religious practices. These grand myths have enabled people to interpret and adapt to the environments they have inhabited. Myths have enabled cultures in remote and almost featureless places to live lives informed by powerful spiritual forces that were part of the ecology. Such movements probably account for the elaborate stories and ceremonial lives of peoples who live in relatively difficult environments such as deserts, grasslands, and arctic seashores. Revitalization movements probably played an important role in the cultural adaptations that enabled peoples to inhabit environments of seemingly limitless complexity.

Human beings have lived with plants and animals since time immemorial and through all that time have interacted with both and with other geologic and mineral entities. Peoples inhabiting specific ecological environments over long periods of time came to know the living and nonliving features of their world very well. They came to know, for example, which plants and animals were edible, and which could be adapted to provide shelter, decoration, and all the other uses to which people put the materials of their world. Plants, which often inhabit specific ecological niches, cannot escape predators. Their defense mechanism involves producing organic compounds that potential predators cannot or would not prefer to eat. In essence, plants produce poisons in order to survive, but some of these compounds are useful to treat human health problems and are part of a traditional search for medicinal plants—a quest that is probably older than our species.

New environments provided challenges and opportunities and the necessity of engaging new plants as well as new landscapes. Ancient and natural peoples accomplished this through dreams and visions in which the power of a plant or an animal to heal disease or injury was revealed to one or more people. Sometimes the story of the receiving of this information is preserved and reenacted, complete with a song and/or a dance that was part of the revelation. People quite often experienced cures as a result of this ritual. The healing powers of herbs and animal material made the patient, at least symbolically, indebted to the entities in nature that effected the cure.

Certain plants became sacred in the sense that their powers could be invoked through careful observance of rules and by repayment through sacrifice. Because healing was such a serious matter, and because the cures were extremely valuable, the knowledge and practice of curing were often kept secret. These mystery belief systems contributed enormously to the capacity of people to adapt to ecological environments and represented a system of cultural production with almost limitless applications. It was almost certainly this process that first identified and then validated the use of many of the curative herbs used today. Ancient horticulturalists undoubtedly used a similar approach to choose plant species that later evolved into some important foods—corn being but one of these. Such adaptations are ongoing among traditional cultures around the globe.

One of the universals among all human cultures is the need to find meaning in their world. Dreams and revelations enabled people both to become psychologically rooted to the land and to establish connections with an enormous array of beings that enabled them to create not only identity but also meaning. A vast number of culturally specific entities—represented by thunderbird spirits, white buffalo calf spirits, medicine masks, and sacred mountains—serve in part as the people's adaptation to place.

This type of cultural production produced revitalization movements that are certainly very ancient and date back at least as far as the Paleolithic or old stone age. Their elements are often symbolic and poetic because they articulate subtle relationships between people and elements of nature that impart wisdom about both the vulnerability and powers of humankind. These movements transformed what might otherwise be seen as uninviting landscapes into places inhabited by the dynamic beings that represented the faces of nature, giving meaning to both landscape and the human society that inhabited it. They were so intertwined with people's existence that it is difficult to estimate the total impact they have had on culture—from architecture to irrigation to language and art. The creative energy of cultures finds its roots in such movements; and they have been part of the tool kit that enabled peoples to survive. As long as these movements defined the dynamics between human societies and nature, revitalization movements expanded the potentials of humankind. This phenomenon, when triggered among oppressed peoples against their oppressors, however, has produced very different results.

Human beings have developed remarkably adaptive cultures, and this quality has set fully modern humans apart from proto-humans. Although many cultural adaptations have been successful in the sense that they contributed to survival for long periods of time—in the case of hunter-gatherers, sometimes tens of thousands of years as distinct cultures—there have been instances when individual cultures have failed. "Failure" has not always meant total annihilation; it is a very subjective term. The term is used here to mean that at some time the particular culture expressed a definition of success that it was able to enjoy, which at a later time was no longer viable and in that sense had failed.

In the ancient Middle East we find stories from pre-biblical times that tell of a utopian past when nature provided food and apparently the luxury of at least some idleness. The Garden of Eden, whatever its origin among the cultures of the Middle East, is an example of one of the earliest utopias. It may represent a view backward to a distant memory of a period when human beings did not face hunger and were not forced to work as hard to get food. Is it possible that over the centuries these people retained oral traditions that described their world in the distant past? It seems likely that the stories originate from before a time when people expected conditions to be created by society, in an era when people thought of nature or spiritual forces as possessing power over their lives.

Judeo-Christian tradition has long interpreted the story of Eden in the context of the search for definitions of good and evil. Christian theologians have given it endless interpretations around such diverse issues as gender qualifications and the definitions of "original sin." In the Christian tradition, expulsion from utopia sets the framework for a discussion about the definition of sin.

Around 5000 B.C. (or perhaps earlier), the grasslands of eastern Europe, now the steppes of Russia, were inhabited by nomadic herdsmen. These peoples were proto-Indo-Europeans, whose languages would evolve into modern European and various other languages. Centuries later these nomads would sweep out of their original homelands into western Europe, the Near East, and India and form cultures that continue to flourish in those places.

A classic type of patriarchy developed among these nomadic cultures. Small tribes or clans defined by male descent managed herds of goats and sheep and horses on the grasslands. A single male—a patriarch—owned the herd. Around the herd was organized a band consisting of the patriarch's children and grandchildren and often relatives such as his brothers and wives and their children and grandchildren. When a patriarch died, custom did not allow the herds to be divided among the children; only the eldest male inherited the family herd.

Patriarchy is an extremely ancient and powerful cultural impulse that originated thousands of years ago. It was originally characterized by power derived from an ability to use coercion. Indeed, the person who owned the herds the clan depended on had coercive power over everyone in his entourage. It was a very different kind of existence from that of the hunter-gatherer, whose coercive powers were probably more limited because no one owned property that everyone depended upon for their livelihood. Under patriarchy the traditions that dictated whom one could marry became those of male domination based essentially on property rights. A significant step for human societies, patriarchy appeared in many herding cultures in other parts of the world. Except in periods of severe drought or other calamities, it is likely that herdsmen rarely starved and the group enjoyed relative safety in the period prior to the development of organized warfare. Hunter-gatherers and nomadic herdsmen probably raided one another, just as hunter-gatherers are known to raid other hunter-gatherers for such purposes as procuring their women or for revenge.

Agriculture was probably a product of some kind of change, most likely climatic, which rendered hunting and gathering less viable in some geographic locations. Neolithic people began to plant and cultivate the crops they formerly gathered. Agrarian societies were, for the most part, socially stable and at the same time mobile since they combined hunting, gathering, and herding with more settled modes of life. Over a long period of time, however, the population of game within reach declined and people were forced to concentrate on planting. Seasonal mobility increased in environments that required yearly migration for herding or hunting. Following the Neolithic era, intensified agricultural production and other technological developments enabled people to create larger settlements, nations, and empires, to which we give the name "civilization."

Neolithic peoples made great contributions to modernity for which they are rarely adequately credited. In addition to domesticating herd animals, these early agriculturalists nurtured virtually every edible grain, green, tuber, or other kind of cultivar in use today. Some foods, such as rice and wheat, are descendants of wild grains that they simply collected and planted for greater harvests. Other plants, such as tomatoes and corn, began as plants that bore little resemblance to modern foodstuffs and evolved into modern forms through plant selection by Neolithic peoples over many centuries.

In South America, the Andean peoples plant some 3,600 cultivars, the vast majority of which are unfamiliar to contemporary peoples outside the Andes. Their ancestors and other mountain peoples learned to grow crops effectively on higher, drier, and colder land than is possible through modern agriculture. Their legacy may acquire dramatic significance as global climate changes and the quality of agricultural land declines in future centuries.

Ancient and contemporary traditional cultures have left a body of knowledge that is broad and deep. Modern people, bound by habitual stereotypes that blind them to the value of cultures they view as unsophisticated or primitive, have little or no awareness of the endangered knowledge of traditional peoples or how important it may become to the survival of humanity and the welfare of the planet.

Bibliographical Essay

An account of the Hopi creation story is found in Frank Waters, *The Book of the Hopi* (New York: Penguin Books, 1963, 1977). The Iroquois cosmology is covered in J. N. B. Hewitt, "Iroquoian Cosmology, Part 2," *Annual Report of the Bureau of American Ethnology for the Years 1925–1926,* Vol. 43:449–819.

Some interesting thoughts on the origins of the human species are found in Richard E. Leakey and Robert Lewin, *Origins: What New Discoveries Reveal About the Emergence of Our Species and Its Possible Future* (New York: Dutton, 1977), especially chapter 5.

A study of stone age cultures that supports the view that such cultures enjoyed an ample diet and also free time is Marshall Sahlins, *Stone Age Economics* (Chicago: Aldine, 1972, 1974), especially chapter 1. His findings are based on studies of contemporary stone age peoples who were observed to enjoy relative affluence and rarely experience hunger.

A work that questions the assertion that male dominance is the normal condition of the human species is Eleanor Leacock, *Myths of Male Dominance: Collected Articles on Women Cross-Culturally* (New York: Monthly Review Press, 1981). See especially "Women's Status in Egalitarian Society: Implications for Social Evolution" (133–183). This article was reprinted from *Current Anthropology* 19, 2 June 1978, 247–275.

An interesting and informative view of the roles of men and women in preliterate societies is found in Richard Lee, "Politics, Sexual and Nonsexual, in an Egalitarian Society," in Eleanor Leacock and Richard Lee, eds., *Politics and History in Band Societies* (New York: Cambridge University Press, 1982), 37–39.

Stanley Diamond's *In Search of the Primitive: A Critique of Civilization* (New Brunswick, N.J.: Transaction Books, 1974) urges that the word "primitive" be understood in a positive way in terms of the root word "prime."

Bernard Nietschmann, in "The Third World War," *Cultural Survival Quarterly* 11, no. 3 (1987):1–16, proposes that since the end of World War II much of the violence in the world that involves organized armed combatants in the field is directed at indigenous people who were living on the land long before the creation of the nation states now in competition for land and other resources.

The issue of an absence of violence in some preliterate societies is discussed by Colin Turnbull, "The Politics of Non-Aggression," in Ashley Montagu, ed., *Learning Non-Aggression: The Experience of Non-Literate Societies* (New York: Oxford University Press, 1978). Robert Knox Dentan affirms this tendency in "Notes on Childhood in a Non-Violent Context: The Semai Case," in the same volume. See also Robert Knox Dentan, *The Semai: A Nonviolent People of Malaya* (New York: Holt, Rinehart & Winston, 1968); and Colin Turnbull, *The Forest People* (New York: Simon & Schuster, 1961, 1987).

A book that surveys the legacy of American Indian peoples for world civilization is Jack Weatherford, *Indian Givers: How the Indians of the Americas Transformed the World* (New York: Crown, 1988).

José Ortega y Gasset's book, *History As a System and Other Essays Toward a Philosophy of History* (New York: Norton, 1941, 1961), includes a chapter, "The Sportive Origins of the State," which also offers significant information on the origins of the marriage ceremony in Western culture.

Reference

Berlin, Isiah. *The Sense of Reality: Studies in Ideas and Their History.* New York: Farrar, Straus & Geroux, 1996, 1997, 69.

THREE
Civilization, Plunder, and Greek Philosophy

> The tame animals are better in nature than the wild ones, and it is better for the former to all be ruled by human beings because thus they are preserved. In addition, the relation of male to female is by nature that of better to worse and ruler to ruled. . . . Things must also hold in the same way for all human beings. Thus, all those who are as widely separated from others as are soul and body and from whom such work is the best there is—are slaves by nature. For them, it is better to be ruled over by a master.
>
> Aristotle, *Politics*

Early agricultural settlements produced a revolution in food production, and the deployment of organized armed force arose in the wake of the development of agriculture. Agricultural settlements evolved into small cities with defensive fortifications built to ward off raids by herdsmen and hunter-gatherers. Agricultural cultures made available that for which organized warfare was invented—loot. Military social organization is as ancient, or nearly as ancient, as civilization itself because the concentration of wealth produced in settlements, including food stores but also trade wares, invited raids by passing nomadic peoples. The original purpose of organized armed force was the acquisition of plunder, which gave rise to a secondary purpose: defense against the plunderers.

Armed force was with us long before the rise of civilizations and has been an inherent part of the history of civilization. The ancient civilizations of the Nile and Mesopotamia were profoundly influenced by their military cultures. Thousands of years ago in the semi-arid regions of what we think of as the Cradle of Civilization, where agriculture and fortifications developed, people raised armies and recorded their conquests in stone and clay.

Civilizations in the ancient world were influenced by both military culture itself and the military-style planning and organization that made possible construction of elaborate defenses. For centuries, most population centers were surrounded by walls, the most effective fortifications prior to the invention and military use of gunpowder. Walls would come to signify the presence of civilization, and some civilizations built huge walls to keep raiders and invaders at bay. The only human construction visible from space is such a structure, the Great Wall of China.

Some early civilizations relied heavily on hydraulics to store and deliver water. The earliest builders of settlements were undoubtedly reacting to crisis and opportunity relative to the food supply, and they settled in places where wild grains grew well and could be cultivated. People in arid regions soon learned their crops benefited from water management during periods of drought, and this led to the invention of irrigation canals and holding ponds.

The building of dams, canals, roads, and bridges required the mobilization of significant amounts of labor—the same organizational skills that were applied to the creation of fortifications and the mobilization of armed force. We find cities with walls 20 feet high, surrounded by moats 10 feet wide and 3 feet deep, in settlements dating back to 7000 B.C. These military defenses arose almost as early as permanent settlements and long before the development of metallurgy.

The organization and technology needed to extract the ore and process metal into useful objects appeared around 3500 B.C. One of the earliest uses of metals was for weapons of war, including body armor, axes, arrow points, and shields. Metal weapons had great advantages over stone weapons, particularly durability in battle and malleability in fashioning such objects as shields and armor. In a remarkably short time following the development of the technology to create it, bronze was fashioned into swords that could be used to stab or slash an opponent.

These advances occurred thousands of years before the emergence of the more familiar Mediterranean cultures such as that of Greece. A military culture quickly developed as weapons became more efficient. Leaders learned to appreciate the advantages of practice, training, tactics, and discipline in combat. Armies were generally organized into fighting units of ten, and tens of tens. This kind of organization was readily transferred to civilian life, which in some of these civilizations was not very different from military.

Surviving texts on stelae and the great monuments of the ancient world are testimony to the fact that for most ancient agricultural civilizations, warfare was central to their histories in their own eyes. Ancient civilizations were not usually modest about their accomplishments and military conquests. The histories written by civilizations in the Near East, the Mediterranean, Asia, Central America, Asia Minor, North Africa, Southeast Asia, and other areas are often lists of dynasties and celebrations of conquerors, great battles, and sieges. Stripped to essentials, the story of civilizations is a record of organized violence for the purpose of armed aggression in pursuit of plunder, and for the purpose of defense against this aggression by rival powers.

The physical circumstances of urban life have in some circumstances made aggression a necessity. Cities are, for the most part, dependent on the countryside for almost everything they need, including raw materials, food, and people to provide fresh sources of labor. As settlements grew more crowded, the possibilities of systematic exploitation of resources at the periphery grew more inviting, and those who had once been the target of attacks became instead the aggressors. Civilizations sent armies in search of goods such as mineral deposits, fishing grounds, slaves, wood, agricultural produce, tribute, and any number of other sources of wealth. Plunder on such a scale gave rise to what we term imperialism: the form of organized theft practiced by civilizations with the capacity to apply military force to peoples less powerful than themselves. When civilizations grew sufficiently wealthy, population usually increased and there was less wealth to go around. Excess population provided both motive and opportunity for unleashing colonizers on distant lands.

Nineteenth-century German scholars seeking Aryan roots for Western civilization promoted the idea that Greek culture arose without cultural antecedents—as if metaphysically from the hills of Greece. Like other cultures, however, Greek civilization was a product of a time and place and was not simply invented out of nothing. Greek culture inherited elements from early settlers in the area as well as from Mesopotamia and other civilizations around the Mediterranean.

People speaking an Indo-European language that eventually evolved into classical Greek invaded Greece from the north around the beginning of the second millennium B.C. (circa 2000-1900). The invaders, known as Mycenaeans, conquered and displaced the original inhabitants, some of whom eventually fled to other areas of the Mediterranean. Over a period of centuries, the Mycenaean Greeks dominated the Aegean. They colonized the region and in about 1450 B.C. are believed to have conquered the Minoan civilization, which had risen on the island of Crete. According to the great Greek poet Homer, the Mycenaeans conquered Troy around 1250 B.C.

When the Mycenaean Empire declined in the twelfth century B.C., Greece fell into what later writers would call a dark age— although it is not at all clear that the ancient civilizations actually disappeared—and for several centuries writing was lost. The designation "dark age" tends to overlook the tremendous changes that took place in Greece during that time. At least as early as the eleventh century B.C., Greece entered an early Iron Age.

Following the decline of Mycenaen power, it is thought that the earlier political cohesion completely disintegrated. Monarchy eventually disappeared to be replaced by a system of locally independent Greek communities that evolved into city-states. By around 900 B.C., city-states were generally dominated by local landowners, an aristocracy that formed a Greek governing oligarchy and came to define much of Greek political culture for several centuries. Around 750 B.C., the development of Greek city-states reached its peak—we know of 600 of them, but there were probably more than twice that number. At about the same time, a new alphabet was adapted from Phoenician script. This date also corresponds with the rise of what is described as a second Iron Age, during which the availability of iron and the technology to use it improved dramatically.

This technological change had tremendous impact, transforming Greece from a primarily pastoral culture to an intensely agricultural one. The Greeks had long since abandoned primogeniture— the practice whereby an eldest son inherits the father's estate intact—and during this period landed estates were divided among the male children of the landowner. With the division and redivision of land, the landholdings became too small to produce the wealth desired, and there arose a demand for some kind of land reform. Technological innovations led to availability of tools that enabled more intensive cultivation of the land and fewer people to produce food, thus creating a surplus of laborers. The increased food supply stimulated an increase in the population (some writers say up to sevenfold), which gave birth to a period of Greek colonization. Greek colonies sprouted up around the ancient Mediterranean and beyond the Bosporus. Colonies supplied Greece with more raw materials, including metals and metal ores, and brought increased prosperity to the aristocracy.

The culture of independent city-states produced the hoplite, the fabled Greek warrior. Hoplites were landowner-warriors who could assemble to defend their properties against invaders or could organize to conduct invasions of their own. They went on campaigns that usually lasted only a few days, specialized in hand-to-hand fighting, and personified the Greek ideal of heroism on the battlefield. Hoplites formed a heavily armored infantry. They wore bronze helmets and face guards, breastplates fashioned of a quarter-inch of bronze, and shin guards. Carrying heavy shields and short swords, they fought cooperatively in a formation called a phalanx.

The Greeks did not actually invent any of the elements of hoplite warfare. The phalanx had been used for centuries in Asia

Minor, the body armor had been likewise invented much earlier, and even their tactics of warfare were familiar. A distinction between the Greeks and the armies of the despots of Asia Minor centered on who was doing the fighting, and why. The armies of Asia Minor were composed of a monarch or similar head of state, a limited number of warriors, and much larger numbers of peasants who did the necesssary physical work to support the light infantry and archers during battle.

In ancient warfare, great battles were fought until one king or the other was killed or captured. When that happened, a winner was established and the battle was over. This rather abrupt and single-objective style of war meant that dynasties that had existed for decades, even centuries, could disappear in a single battle. The game of chess is modeled after this type of warfare.

During the classical period of hoplite warfare, Greek armies clashed in great battles involving adult male combatants, while the older people, women, and children remained safely behind city walls until the battle was over. The Greek city-state of classical antiquity waged war almost every year in order to acquire enough wealth and power to maintain its independence and self-sufficiency in the face of rival city-states. The motivation for Greek attacks on other city-states was completely uncomplicated: plunder and defense against other plunderers.

The frequent battles rarely resulted in the annihilation of a city-state, however, and rarely produced significant civilian casualties or even heavy casualties among the military. The Greeks adopted rules that were intended to perpetuate this kind of warfare and discouraged the use of more lethal combatants such as archers, who were deemed cowards.

In 490 B.C. Persia invaded Greece. In a series of battles, some of which are legendary, Greece repulsed the Persian armies. Persia could commit huge numbers to the battlefield, but its light cavalry was unable to keep the Greek hoplites from charging the unarmored Persian archers and slaughtering them at close range.

The Greeks had invented the most effective warship to that time, the trireme. These vessels were fashioned from Greece's great pines, and warfare at sea came to be a major reason for the decline and virtual disappearance of the Greek forest. Greek citizen-warriors practiced vigorously at rowing these ships, said to be the fastest in the Mediterranean, with up to 170 oarsmen powering the vessels at around ten knots. Greek triremes devastated the Persian flotilla and established Greek domination in naval warfare. The superweapon of Mediterranean warfare, the triremes were responsible for raising Athens to an ancient world superpower. Warfare was an integral part of Greek culture—both as an ideal of heroism and the chief mechanism for increasing wealth. Despite a population that included the greatest poets, philosophers, and other intellectuals of the era, no one seems to have questioned the ethics of warfare or proposed a philosophy of peace.

Had Athens not prospered through its military conquests to become an empire, it is unlikely it would have attracted men of intellect from around the Greek world who set the stage for the most famous Greek philosophers, Socrates, Plato, and Aristotle. If Alexander the Great had not forged an army that conquered most of the known world, it is unlikely that Hellenic culture would have spread as far, taken roots as deep, and produced influences as long as it did. For the movement that began with Socrates to inspire Western thought, his and other Greek ideas had to persist through conquest by the Romans, the division of the Roman Empire into east and west, the flourishing of Christianity in Byzantium, and the conquest of the Crusaders until, finally, in the fourteenth century, it reemerged and made its way to Italy and modernity.

A turning point in intellectual history was the rise of the philosopher Socrates (470?–399 B.C.) and the development of classical Greek philosophy. Greek philosophic thought traces its roots to Ionia, the areas of Asia Minor occupied by Greeks. Among its earliest noted practitioners was Thales, a wealthy merchant who lived about 600 B.C. He is credited with formulating the first reasoned effort to explain how the world works. His explanation sounds somewhat simplistic today, but the emphasis on reasoning was a significant innovation in its time. The influence of his method spread around the Mediterranean through

Italy and Greece over the course of the following two centuries, slowly accumulating knowledge and, as a result, changing the received ways of thinking about the world. Reason was winning a battle against superstition if not against mythology. One result of this revolution in thought was a gradual decline in dogmatic belief in the ancient gods.

During the fifth century a group of professional teachers known as the Sophists proposed a profound skepticism that intensely questioned the values of Greek political life, religion, and even patriotism. One of the early Sophists, Protagoras of Abdera (d. 410 B.C.) was a successful teacher in Athens. Unlike the Ionian philosophers who had concerned themselves with the cosmos, the Sophists focused their work on the lived experiences of humankind. At least some of them elevated individualism to a virtue and cast doubts on previously accepted ideas of individual morality. They taught that truth is illusory, that the world was inconsistent and therefore relative, and that morality was not a product of reason.

Socrates revolted against the Sophists because he rejected the idea that the individual could live a good life without clear knowledge of what constituted the "good." In a long dialogue, he used his method of inductive argument to produce definitions of absolutes such as the "Good," as well as guides on character and conduct that could be considered correct and applicable in all circumstances at all times. Socrates believed that knowledge of the "idea of the Good" was the necessary condition of virtue, happiness, and well-being—whether individual or national—and that only through logical examination could true values be defined and then used to develop the individual's moral nobility:

> Socrates thought that if certainty could be established in our knowledge of the external world by rational methods . . . the same methods would surely yield certainty in the field of human behavior—how to live, what to be. This could be achieved by rational argument. (Isaiah Berlin 1998, 4)

Using his method of logical debate, Socrates tirelessly instructed students in his method of reaching supreme knowledge and promoted his view of ethics, virtue, and truth. In the process, he tore down some of his contemporaries' most cherished beliefs, embarrassing important fellow citizens and predictably making some powerful enemies.

Socrates became embroiled in the politics of Athens when two of his own followers ran afoul of the democratic oligarchy in power at the time. He was charged with vague offenses: being "a maker of novel gods" and corrupting youth. These charges masked political motives: Socrates was being accused of association with enemies of the Athenian state and was suspected of inspiring those enemies' criminal behaviors. Certainly his teaching of the sons of the ruling elite had political implications.

In a speech that became the foundation for Plato's *Apologia*, Socrates denied both charges. In his defense, Socrates stated,

> [T]he young who follow me of their own accord—those who have the most leisure, the sons of the wealthiest— enjoy hearing human beings examined. And they themselves often imitate me, and in turn they attempt to examine others. And then, I suppose, they discover a great abundance of human beings who suppose they know something but know little or nothing. Thereupon, those examined by them are angry at me, not at themselves, and they say that Socrates is someone most disgusting and that he corrupts the young. And whenever someone asks them, "By doing what and teaching what?" They have nothing to say, but are ignorant. So in order not to seem to be at a loss, they say the things that are ready at hand against all who philosophize. (West and West 1984, 72)

In his speech Socrates recounts a message from an oracle that declared him to be the wisest of men. He believed he had been entrusted with a message from God concerning the "care" or "tending" of one's soul: it was one's duty "to make one's soul as good as possible," to make it "like God." Socrates' mission was to teach and spread this truth. He believed that to abandon his mission would be a rebellion against God. He considered that democracy posed a problem in that it put society in the hands of those without the expert knowledge of the "Good" that made them capable of governing.

Socrates left no written record. His history, as well as most of what we know of his philosophy, survives because his student and disciple Plato preserved his memory in the *Crito* and the *Phaedo*, as well as in the *Apologia.*

The classical school of Greek philosophy founded by Socrates created a radical new direction in Western thought that can be considered a revitalization movement within Greek philosophy itself and would eventually create a movement that would have a profound influence on Western civilization. Unlike many such movements, this radical intellectual movement was not created by the downtrodden and oppressed at the bottom of society but by a privileged intellectual elite who had access to democratic participation, which was itself based on their elite status. Socrates was a fully accepted member of the Greek citizenry and a former hoplite who had served bravely in battle.

Given the political implications of his activities, Socrates was duly placed on trial for his life and found guilty as charged. Friends and even enemies urged him to avoid death by recanting his words and disavowing his actions. He refused to avoid the death sentence and eventually took hemlock because to recant would have refuted the meaning of his life.

The two best known Greek philosophers who followed Socrates—Plato and Aristotle—built a body of work that was inspired by their predecessor but were generally careful to avoid the kinds of conflict that could bring them the same fate as Socrates. Most of what is known about Socrates was related by Plato, who is credited with founding the tradition of philosophical discourse in the West and who was the most successful and popular teacher of his time. Plato established a school in Athens that attracted one of the most respected men of ideas of all time, Aristotle, whose work on many subjects would become the ultimate authority for Western scholarship and scientific thought many centuries later. Plato himself was so successful that the school he established was open for more than nine hundred years.

For Socrates, "goodness of soul" meant knowledge of good and evil, and in that sense he believed "all virtue is knowledge." Plato developed his Idea or Form of the Good into a theory of Forms that exist in a higher spiritual realm apart from matter, space, and time. He argued that these Forms constitute the true realities. Each Form is the master pattern of corresponding things existing in the world that are imperfect copies of the Form. Man has indirect experience of the Forms through his pursuit of knowledge of the Good. The highest Form, the Form of the Good, is the source of the reality of all things—and thus "being" implies the union of matter and ideas.

Plato's version of an ideal existence, expressed in the *Republic* and in later writings, was inspired by Socrates' teaching. The *Republic* was the first book to propose a planned ethical society and is one of the most famous utopian projections of all time. It would inspire and influence Western thinkers far into the future, including Karl Marx, Marxists, and other utopianists of the nineteenth century. The *Republic* describes elements of a "perfect" society that would inspire later generations of Europeans: an authoritarian state, marriages designed to favor children with desirable (inherited) traits, state censorship, the abolition of private property for the masses, and state-controlled and -manipulated education of the young. This utopian society was to be governed by those with the most elevated minds—philosophers:

> No one must have any private property whatsoever, except what is absolutely necessary. Secondly, no one must have any lodging or storehouse at all which is not open to all comers. . . . They must live in common, attending in messes as if they were in the field. . . . [Philosophers] of all in the piety dare not have any deal-

ings with gold or silver or even touch them or come under the same roof with them. (Lavine 1989, 9. Republic, Book III, 415 E)

Only philosophers could be considered adequately trained in the pursuit of the Ideal and therefore be qualified to rule the state.

Plato thought that the existence of the Ideal, a state of being in which Truth, Beauty, and Justice were realized, was obscured to the individual by the senses and could only be achieved through rigorous application of reason. In this view, the bodily senses were obstacles to the realization of the Ideal. This was an idea that would resonate for future generations of Christian European thinkers, including Augustine and the authors of Puritanism.

Operating out of his school in Athens, Plato was apparently less confrontive than Socrates in presenting his views, and the opposition he encountered was confined mostly to philosophical circles. Nevertheless his ideas proposed changes that constituted a radical challenge to the political patterns of the time.

Radical movements intended to bring about cultural change almost always encounter resistance. It is inherent among such movements that its adherents find not only something fundamental and correct about how they see the world, but something flawed and even immoral in the views and often in the persons of those who do not see it the way they do. Very often individuals and groups engaged in this kind of conscious cultural change movement tend to lose sight—to varying degrees—of reality. In exploring their ideas and attempting to give them more substance, they often create an elaborate prospect of an idealized future resulting from the realization of their ideas. The focus on an idealized future is readily visible among religious movements, but in the case of the movement inspired by Socrates we have an example of a movement of this type that did not call upon the supernatural and was not allegedly inspired by a vision or other kind of visitation except, perhaps, his reflections on statements made about him by an oracle.

In virtually every culture in the world, revelation had been and would continue to be a dominant source of the received wisdom through which people interpreted reality. The shift of emphasis from revelation to reason as a source of such information would create a tension that would cause profound schisms in Western culture and would continue to be played out to the present time.

The Greek philosophical tradition created a platform and a context for Greek, and later for Western, ethnocentrism. Thinkers who followed the Greek philosophical tradition after Socrates' time magnified ethnocentrism around the issue of knowledge by their own method of acquiring it. If one's thinking successfully repudiates other peoples' ways of thinking, and one defines other peoples' thinking as mythological in nature and their thought as relying on intuition and other unreliable ways of knowing, it will follow that other people have no reliable way of coming to knowledge. From this it follows that the cultures of such people exhibit an inherent inferiority. Carried to its logical extreme, this claim to an exclusive way of knowing would suggest that before Socrates and the foundation of Greek philosophy, no knowledge existed in the world, an obviously outrageous claim.

Socrates would have been amazed at what his teachings would inspire. Some sixteen centuries later, around the middle of the thirteenth century, western Europe would be reintroduced to Greek philosophy following a long absence during which the Greek works were unavailable in most of Western Christendom. It would be difficult to overstate the fervor with which Greek thought would eventually be embraced. At one point, the only accepted sources of knowledge in some Western courts were the Holy Bible and the teachings of the ancient Greeks and Romans. One would not be exaggerating to state that the latter had been elevated to the status of divinely inspired works.

It was during the earlier period of the development and evolution of Western philosophy that King Philip II of Macedon organized one of history's most efficient military machines. In a generation he and his son Alexander the Great conquered the known world, bringing Greek culture to peoples as far away as India and setting in place a Greek cultural hegemony that lives on to this day. Then, at age thirty-two, Alexander died. Despite his accomplishments, Alexander's empire soon disintegrated and the Greek cities resumed their traditions of incessant internecine warfare until, exhausted, they fell to the armies of Rome.

The Hellenistic world created by Alexander's conquests gave rise to Greek-speaking cities throughout the empire. These societies produced advances in the study of science that represented a departure from philosophy. Archimedes, a Greek who lived in Sicily (d. 211/212 B.C.), is credited with both scientific theories and inventions. He proposed a hydrostatic principle using the amount of water displaced by an object to measure its mass, and invented the Archimedes screw, a device useful for raising water from the bottom of ships. The first thinker to apply logic combined with observation to solving problems, he was a founder of Western science. Rather than applying revelation or pure reasoning, modern science has accumulated knowledge about the physical world through tests and experiments that can be repeated with identical results.

During the following centuries, Greek culture began a long slow decline, and by the third century A.D. the pseudosciences of alchemy and astrology had become popular in the West. Alchemy, which may have its roots in Hellenistic Egypt, was strongly influenced by philosophy. When it was rediscovered during the Renaissance, alchemy inspired utopian pseudoscientific projects such as the search for the fountain of youth.

The Western world continues to be influenced by the Greeks, albeit indirectly. The Greek philosophers postulated that knowledge was attainable. They proposed that for every answerable question there was one and only one correct answer, that a method existed to arrive at that answer, and that the answer would be consistent with any set of other correct answers. These teachings were a significant departure from that of the Greek past.

In addition, the idea of the one correct answer implied the ability to solve problems through correct answers. Logically it would be possible, if one had enough information, to solve any problem. It was but a short step to the idea that all the problems of humankind were solvable if enough information and the correct thinking were applied, an idea that has powerfully utopian elements.

A further tendency in this kind of thinking is the absolute value that the ability to solve problems confers. If one follows a plan to solve all the problems of humankind, no price is considered too high to pay to advance that plan to its goals. That form of utopian thinking incorporates a criterion for logical projection. Plato proposes that a perfect society, one best able to deal with the problems of mankind, would be ruled by enlightened people, those most able to solve all problems through their knowledge: that is, philosophers. Philosophers were enlightened in what can only be called the secular religion proposed by Socrates, Plato, and their followers. Such enlightened people would be able to apply the principles and knowledge of the world to solve any of its problems. It is a very seductive idea, and a logical one. If intelligent and knowledgeable people could be expected to manage society better than unintelligent and ignorant people, should not the most knowledgeable and intelligent be allowed to rule?

Although this proposal gained ground in philosophy, it was rarely successful in politics. Most people would agree that it would be better to have the most intelligent and culturally wise people as rulers, but no cultures have been able to agree on basic definitions, priorities, or the people most suited to rule. Most people would also agree that peace is a more desirable condition than war, but pacifists, like philosophers, are at a distinct disadvantage in politics. Politics is not logical. Politics is political and is therefore subject to passions such as greed and lust for power. It is perhaps best described as an expression of a kind of chaos theory based on fortune and happenstance. People who have power to make decisions most often make decisions based on their interpretation of what is in their own best interests, and more often than not, such people have decided that what is in their own best interests happens also to be in the interest of society.

Secular as well as religious societies have the ability to construct utopian ideologies that rationalize activities that will do great harm to others. This potential, as we will see, becomes a tendency that will plague Western civilization.

Bibliography

Aristotle. *The Politics of Aristotle*, trans. Peter Simpson. Chapel Hill: University of North Carolina Press, 1997.

Berlin, Isaiah. *The Crooked Timber of Humanity: Chapters in the History of Ideas*. Princeton, N.J.: Princeton University Press, 1998, 4.

De Colange, Fussel. *The Ancient City: A Study on the Religion, Laws and Institutions of Greece and Rome*. Garden City, N.Y.: Doubleday, 1956 (1894).

Grant, Michael. *The Rise of the Greeks*. New York: Scribner's Books, 1987, 1988.

Hamilton, Edith. *The Greek Way*. New York: New American Library, 1942, 1948.

Hanke, Lewis. *The Spanish Struggle for Justice in the Conquest of America*. Boston: Little, Brown & Co., 1949, 1965.

Harrison, Paul. *The Disenchantment of Reason: The Problem of Socrates in Modernity*. Albany: State University of New York Press, 1994.

Hollister, C. Warren. *Roots of the Western Tradition: A Short History of the Ancient World*. New York: John Wiley & Sons, 1966.

Lavine, T. Z. *From Socrates to Sartre: The Philosophic Quest*. New York: Bantam Books, 1984, 1989.

Lucas, Henry S. *A Short History of Civilization*. New York: McGraw-Hill Book Co., 1943.

Nussbaum, Martha. *Cultivating Humanity: A Classical Defense of Reform in Liberal Education*. Cambridge, Mass.: Harvard University Press, 1997.

Simpson, Peter L. Phillips (trans.). *The Politics of Aristotle*. Chapel Hill: University of North Carolina Press, 1997.

Stone, I. F. *The Trial of Socrates*. New York: Anchor Books, 1989.

Taylor, A. E. *Socrates: The Man and His Thought*. Garden City, N.Y.: Doubleday Anchor Books, 1953.

Wallace, Anthony F. C. "Revitalization Movements." *American Anthropologist* 58 (1956): 265.

West, Thomas G., and Grace Starry West. *Four Texts on Socrates*. Ithaca, N.Y.: Cornell University Press, 1984.

FOUR
Rome and the
Christian Conquest

> If we are to hope to understand the often violent world
> in which we live . . . we cannot confine our attention to
> the great impersonal forces, natural and man-made,
> which act upon us. The goals and motives that guide
> human action must be looked at in the light of all that we
> know and understand; their roots and growth, their
> essence, and above all their validity, must be critically
> examined with every intellectual resource we have.
> Isaiah Berlin *(The Crooked Timber of Humanity)*

Ancient Rome was a pagan world not unlike other civilizations
that arose in the eastern Mediterranean, emerging from city-
states with distinct local traditions and combinations of local
gods and gods appropriated from other cultures. It became the
dominant empire of the ancient world, and the institutions
that evolved in the Roman Empire set the stage for the age of
Christian Empire that would follow. Rome was not a utopian
empire, but Greco-Roman culture created conditions that
would give rise to utopian movements and a cultural foundation to Christian Empire.

During the eighth century B.C. the Latins were wedged
between the Etruscans and the Gauls at Naples—the two civilizations that had arisen in Italy. According to legend, Rome was
founded in 753 B.C., and its early development was dominated
and influenced by Etruscan architecture and religion. The Roman

Republic was founded in 509 B.C. when the last Etruscan king of Rome, Tarquin the Proud, was driven from power.

The Republic was initially an oligarchy under which patricians (landowners) elected two chief magistrates called consuls. The senate (from a word meaning elders) of some 300 patricians served as a consulting body to the consuls. Two governing bodies were formed: the Senate, representing the interests of the patricians, and the Tribal Assembly, which ostensibly represented the commoners. The Senate dealt with foreign affairs and became an increasingly powerful body.

In 493 B.C. Rome joined a defensive alliance with other Latin communities to form the Roman Confederation. During the fifth and fourth centuries B.C., the Roman Confederation fought and won numerous local wars, and in each case forced the defeated opponent to join this confederation. Early Roman history is a story of expansion through conquest, although at this point it would have been considered unlikely to be the city-state destined to unify Italy. In 327 B.C. Rome entered into a long and bitter war with a mountain people called the Samnites, who were allied with the Etruscans and Gauls of northern Italy. Rome's eventual success forced these peoples into the Roman Confederation. By 262 B.C. the entire Italian peninsula was united under Roman control.

Rome fought a twenty-three-year war against Carthage, which was the greatest power in the Mediterranean. The war ended in a Roman victory in 241 B.C. Rome received war indemnities from Carthage, including the island of Sicily, and several years later seized the Carthaginian islands of Sardinia and Corsica. By 222 B.C., when Rome defeated the Gauls in northern Italy, the Roman Empire extended to the Alps.

Carthage recovered rapidly and rebuilt its army. The Carthaginian general Hannibal assembled a solid mercenary army in Spain. When Rome declared war, he marched through the Alps into northern Italy and in a lengthy campaign repeatedly defeated Roman armies. For the next thirteen years Hannibal, considered one of the great military geniuses of all time, traversed Italy at will, cutting down orchards, slaughtering sheep, and creating havoc.

This war proved to the Romans that sharing authority between two consuls was not an effective way of managing a military machine, and they placed the army under the control of a single commander they called the proconsul. The first of these, Scipio, invaded Spain and forced the Carthaginians there to retreat to Africa. Scipio defeated Hannibal in 202 B.C. With victory over Carthage, Rome gained the territory of Spain and the elimination of Carthage as a competitor in the region.

In the next fifty years, Rome moved to expand its empire, annexing Illyria and Macedonia and through diplomacy adding various Hellenistic states to the empire. Great wealth flowed to Rome from its provinces. Some of the wealth was used to build roads, aqueducts, and bridges, but more typically it flowed into the hands of the few wealthy landowners, widening the gap between the poor and the wealthy. The provincial governors controlled both civil and military affairs and often wielded their power in the pursuit of personal gain. When there was war on the frontier, the governor and his lieutenants profited handsomely from loot and from the sale of captives as slaves. During peacetime they taxed the provincials mercilessly and profited from bribes and various forms of extortion.

The Romans exhibited a genius for empire-building rarely matched in world history. Although Alexander treated the people of his provinces as conquered peoples, the Romans offered citizenship to its former enemies, and with citizenship came a stake in Rome's fortunes. The Romans constructed an impressive array of aqueducts and cisterns in some provinces and turned parts of North Africa into productive wheat-growing areas.

Ancient Rome maintained its conquest of the Mediterranean world by keeping units of the Roman army stationed in most of the provinces. The Roman genius centered on an attention to the arts of war and on skill at governing an empire. Throughout much of its history, Rome's military strength lay in the training and efficiency of its heavy infantry. Roman soldiers were intensively trained in swordsmanship and close-quarter combat and sometimes used fighting techniques of the gladiators. Each man in the front line of the Roman phalanx was responsible for an area six feet by six feet, and Roman soldiers performed very effectively and in a very disciplined fashion in that formation. In the history of the Republic and the Empire, Rome was defeated more or less decisively on the battlefield only twice, once at the hands of mounted archers and once in the thick forests of Germany.

Inevitably, conquest and empire-building brought changes to Roman society. Aristocrats used their wealth and power to amass great estates, worked by gangs of slaves acquired during military campaigns. Much of the land that composed these estates was leased from the government, which the aristocrats controlled. To get more land, they undersold the small independent farmers, who could not compete with slave labor and were soon forced off the land, leaving the countryside for the city. The great estates continued to grow, dispossessing small farmers and creating urban poverty and powerful social conflicts that threatened the stability of the Republic.

Many of the residents of the cities were provincials who had obtained Roman citizenship but who knew little of Rome's traditions. Unemployment was high and the numbers of urban poor were growing. By the second century B.C., the legacies of conquest included a huge rural slave population and a growing underemployed urban population that depended on the government for food and entertainment. Most of the adult male Roman population had been independent small farmers who made up the bulk of the armies that built and defended the empire; they were now reduced to a mob of urban poor.

Efforts were made to correct this situation. Tiberius Gracchus, a young aristocrat elected tribune in 133 B.C., proposed what amounted to a redistribution of land from wealthy landowners to the urban poor. When the Tribal Assembly tried to enact this plan, a group of senators and their allies attacked and killed Gracchus and three hundred of his followers. In 121 B.C., when his brother Gaius tried to introduce even more radical reforms, he and some three thousand of his followers were attacked and killed by the same forces. A land bill did go into effect, and some people were assigned lands previously leased to aristocrats, but many of these people had lost their incentive to farm and were accustomed to life in the city. They sold their lands to the aristocrats and moved back to town.

Rome's ancient customs stipulated that only property-owning men could serve in the army. Since the expansion of the great estates had reduced the numbers of small property owners, there were fewer and fewer men available for military service. In 107 B.C. the consul Marius broke with tradition and encouraged landless volunteers to join the army, promising them booty and pensions in exchange for a sixteen-year enlistment. Large numbers rushed to sign up. Marius' new army won victories in Africa and against barbarians invading Italy from the north—and changed the political realities of Roman society forever. Henceforth armies no longer depended on the Roman state but on the general who provided them with pensions, land, and plunder. They owed the general loyalty and provided a de facto private army that enabled him to pursue his career in Roman politics.

Rivalries among leaders soon eroded Roman political institutions and produced bloody civil wars that imperiled the Republic, and Rome came under the control of a series of strong men. In 60 B.C., Julius Caesar, Pompey, and Crassus formed the first ruling triumvirate. Julius Caesar was to become the most famous of the Roman emperors. Understanding that the Roman masses supported conquests, he provoked war with the Gauls, conquered them, and invaded Britain. The empire now included lands bordering the North Sea and the English Channel and east to the Rhine.

These conquests made Caesar enormously popular in Rome and extended Roman rule for the first time into northern Europe. Fearing his popularity and his expanding power, the Senate declared him a public enemy in 49 B.C. Caesar took the offensive, leading his army across the Rubicon River and to Rome. Caesar defeated Pompey and went on to lead a series of brilliant military campaigns in Asia, Africa, and Spain, returning to Rome in 45 B.C. a hero.

Caesar was made a virtual king. He began a series of reforms that included distributing land to Roman citizens, forcing owners of estates to hire nonslave labor, and removing corrupt governors of provinces. He reformed the calendar ("July" derives from his name and "August" from his successor's) and even named provincials to the Senate. His rule did not last long. He was assassinated in the Senate building by a conspiracy of senators on March 15, 44 B.C. This act set into motion a civil war in which Mark Antony and Octavian, Caesar's great-nephew, united against Brutus and other leaders of the Senate who had killed Caesar. Octavian and Mark Antony defeated Brutus in 42 B.C. and divided the empire into east and west precincts. Mark Antony became the consort of Cleopatra, the queen of Egypt, and when they began dividing up the eastern part of the empire among their children, Octavian declared war. Octavian's forces were victorious in 31 B.C. Antony and Cleopatra committed suicide, and Octavian emerged as emperor of the Roman Empire. With the acquisition of Egypt, Roman domination of the Mediterranean was complete.

Octavian received the honorific name Augustus, became consul and tribune, was named governor of all the provinces where Roman armies were stationed, had the power to appoint people to the Senate, and was given a body guard of nine thousand men. He was, in effect, the military and civil dictator of the Roman Empire. With Augustus' reign, which ended the Roman Republic, there began a period of some two centuries of relative peace known as the Pax Romana.

Rome had come a long way. It had begun as a city-state in which landowners served as a warrior class of heavy infantry and owed their allegiance to Roman society; it became an empire peopled by volunteer mercenaries who owed allegiance to one military leader. The path to empire was strewn with massacres, repression, looting, corruption, and slavery, much of which served the purpose of funneling wealth into the hands of those who controlled the government or the military or, in the end, the military government.

Augustus proved to be an able ruler and enacted many of the reforms envisioned by Julius Caesar. When Augustus died in 14 A.D., he was succeeded in power by his adopted son Tiberius. In 96 A.D., after a period of turbulence over the question of succession, there began the reigns of the "Five Good Emperors," (96–180 A.D.), a period that has been called the Golden Age of Rome. The last great Roman conquests took place under the emperor Trajan (98–117 A.D.) and included parts of Romania and Armenia, Mesopotamia, and Assyria. This period marked the greatest extent of the empire; later emperors abandoned these areas as indefensible.

At its height the Roman Empire was truly remarkable. Its population was around 50 million, and it stretched across territories now occupied in whole or in part by forty modern countries. Across all that vast land a traveler could be comfortable speaking one language, carrying one kind of coin, and doing business under a single system of law. Above all, and an element much remembered in later years, the Roman Empire provided a period of internal safety and stability for most of the people most of the time, even though there were periods of political conflict.

The behavior of Roman legions in the provinces, however, could be marked by startling cruelty even during periods of stability in Rome. One of the most famous examples is the Romano-Jewish War in 66 A.D. Roman management of the provinces produced great poverty in its conquered territories. It has been said that a slave in Italy lived a more prosperous material life than a free peasant in Judea. In addition, the Jewish people found Roman rule to be unjust. When the people of Judea at last revolted, the Romans attacked with such ferocity that all the inhabitants of one town committed suicide rather than fall into Roman hands. The Jewish historian Josephus reported that at the end of the war there was little timber to be found in Judea because so much had been consumed in the crosses used to crucify Jewish survivors of the war. The Jewish people were eventually dispersed throughout the empire, where they were destined to be treated as conquered peoples.

Before the revolt, the Jews of Galilee lived in a society in which Roman soldiers were for the most part kept at a distance from the population and were used primarily to threaten retaliation against invaders and to quell serious rebellions. Average citizens of Galilee probably saw Roman soldiers rarely. Because they lived under

Jewish laws and customs, they probably did not feel their religion, national traditions, or way of life threatened by Rome (Sanders 1995, 21).

King Herod the Great had ruled Judea and Galilee for more than thirty years. When he died in 4 B.C., armed uprisings throughout his country were extinguished by the Roman legions stationed at Syria. After about 6 A.D., Judea came under the control of a Roman governor, Pontius Pilate. Although there were tensions and occasional riots, there is no evidence that Jews were incensed to the point of rebellion during the reign of Pilate. Of more consequence to the Jews was the fact that the empire was in the process of bringing modernization in the form of commercialism to the rural peasantry. This development mobilized dissatisfaction.

> Commercialization . . . makes it terribly clear that things can change, and are, in fact, changing—for the worse . . . . Peasants who have accepted subsistence living and appropriated surplus for centuries smell the whiff of doom in commercialization and reach not just for the restoration of traditional exploitation but for radical, utopian, and egalitarian visions of an ideal world. (Crossan1998, 159)

Although many in Judea and Galilee chafed under Roman rule, the Jews saw little chance that a military leader would rise up who could defeat the Roman legions. If there was to be deliverance, many believed, it would be at the hand of God. There may not have been a clear idea of the form that deliverance would take, but the hope was alive. Jewish history to that time included stories of divine intervention by the supernatural, the most central of which was the story of the deliverance of the Jews from slavery in Egypt under Moses. According to tradition, the followers of Jesus of Nazareth believed the God of Israel would deliver his people a second time.

Jesus was baptized by the popular prophet John the Baptist. The prophet was executed by Herod's son Antipas, who was provincial governor of Galilee under Pilate, ostensibly because the

Baptist had voiced his objection to Antipas' marriage to a niece who was already married. The historian Josephus reported that the real reason for his execution was that Antipas feared the prophet's opposition might stir up a revolt (Sanders 1995, 29, 93).

For most of the first two centuries of its existence, the Christian movement was a sect of Judaism. Jesus began his mission at Capernaum, a small town on the shore of the Sea of Galilee about seventy-five miles north of Jerusalem, where one of his disciples, Peter, had a house. Jesus was a peasant from a rural area where the literacy rate was probably around 3 percent, and it is highly unlikely that he could read or write (Crossan 1998, 235).

According to convention, Jesus and his twelve apostles traveled from town to town proclaiming the gospel to people like themselves and living on charitable donations, dining at the homes of friendly locals, and probably living off money given them by women who were their supporters (Sanders 1995, 109). Jesus preached and performed healings, especially faith healings, and his reputation and popularity grew. He was joined by Mary Magdalene and by a collection of male disciples (the traditional number emerged as twelve). According to the Gospel of Mark, Jesus was very popular in these towns and had an enthusiastic following that grew into a movement, albeit a modest one.

Some religious movements of the region—notably Zoroastrianism in Persia—described the history of their world in terms of ages, epochs, or "kingdoms." According to the standard gospels, the historic Jesus proclaimed the power of God and foretold a divine intervention by God that would deliver the Jewish people from their oppression. The instrument by which this would happen was something he called the Kingdom of God, or the Kingdom of Heaven. The gospels are somewhat vague about exactly what was meant by the Kingdom of God/Heaven, but Jesus' promise rang with hope:

"He that believeth in me hath everlasting life." (John 6:47)

Although volumes have been written about Jesus, official records of the time provide little information about Jesus' life or trial and execution. The movement demonstrated a classic revitalization pattern: it claimed a charismatic leader who had special knowledge of truth or the supernatural, who had the capacity to forecast the future, and who knew how the people needed to prepare for the expected event. Although almost all the accounts of what Jesus said or did have been questioned by scholars, the information available is persuasive that Jesus' followers at first thought the cosmic intervention—the arrival of the Kingdom of God or Kingdom of Heaven—would happen in their lifetimes or at some point in time relatively soon. According to the Gospel of John, Jesus had told them

> [F]or the hour is coming, in the which all that are in the graves shall hear his voice, And shall come forth; they that have done good, unto the resurrection of life; and they that have done evil, unto the resurrection of damnation. (John 5:28–29)

This expectation, as often happens in prophetic movements, became problematic when the expected event did not occur in the decades after Jesus' death.

Although some modern scholars question New Testament versions of the events surrounding Jesus' trial and condemnation, it is fairly universally accepted that Jesus was executed and buried and that several days later some of his followers reported that he had been resurrected and had appeared to them and had conversed with them. People, especially beloved people, often appear to their loved ones shortly after death, and both Jewish and Greco-Roman traditions include stories reflecting a belief that this can and does happen. The reappearance of Christ, however, was considered miraculous because some of his followers insisted that he had been resurrected in the flesh. It was this element—the resurrection of Jesus' physical body—that rendered the event a miracle. Two of the fundamental elements of Christian belief were present almost immediately following Jesus' death: the expectation of the arrival of the Kingdom of God and the story of his reappearance—albeit fleeting—alive and in the flesh.

Jesus' followers reported this resurrection as proof that people could return from the dead and expressed confidence that their leader would initiate a mass miracle and would beckon all true believers from their graves—in the flesh—to a new life. When Jesus returned to his followers and the Kingdom was established on earth, death would be conquered and there would follow a millennium during which deceased Christians would rise from their graves and rule the earth. At some point all the non-believers would be summoned from their graves; and on the Judgment Day, they could be consigned to death, or nonexistence, forever.

Christianity was posited on a belief in miracles and would become a religion of miracles. The Christian utopia or heaven is a promise that, in exchange for true faith or belief, one will achieve individual salvation and life everlasting in the Kingdom of God, and that the punishment for a lack of faith or even imperfect faith is consignment to oblivion. A miracle, by definition, is an event that happens in defiance of the laws of nature and requires some supernatural agency to accomplish it. The element of rebellion against the natural order—against death—symbolized by the Resurrection was woven into the fundamental articles of Christian belief almost from the beginning.

The first two centuries following Jesus' execution saw a flourishing of sects that embraced various interpretations of the meaning of Jesus' life and death. Indeed, there were probably more distinct versions upheld by religious groups who identified themselves as followers of Jesus during those centuries than there are today. Several early Christian sects known as gnostics produced gospels that stopped short of asserting that Jesus had been resurrected in the flesh, and, in time, the gnostic gospels would be suppressed and would nearly disappear.

The earliest known followers of Jesus—the disciples—were to the best of our knowledge, illiterate Jewish peasants who could not have written the story (Crossan 1998, 234–235). A revitalization movement will simply vanish unless there are people who are able and willing to find a way to preserve it and pass it on. The written word is not the only way this can be done, but in the case of early Christianity, it was scribes and not peasants who most permanently preserved a tradition of Jesus' life and death, and it was they who were the primary interpreters of those events. Interestingly, the Gospel of Mark tends to be somewhat disdainful of the original apostles because they lacked a perfect faith in the Resurrection; the writer seems to be designating an unnamed woman who anointed the risen Jesus with burial herbs as the first true believer in the Resurrection—in other words, the first Christian (Mark 14:3–9, Crossan 1998, 558). The people who wrote the books of the New Testament were, for the most part, men who came to the faith after Jesus' death.

The Christian idea of salvation was perfectly utopian because it offered a solution to all of humankind's problems through divine intervention in conjunction with human agency (faith in the Resurrection of Jesus and the Kingdom of God, together with submission to Church authority). In the interest of achieving its goals, this movement would often be intolerant of other peoples' rights, and its followers were willing to appropriate and exploit the practices of rival religions as a necessary step toward achieving their goals.

The movement that Jesus inspired was a conscious effort to bring about changes intended to create more satisfying conditions of life for the understandably disgruntled peasant population of Judea. Initially a reform movement within Judaism, it broke out of that mode when successive generations of followers acted to universalize the themes of the movement to reach out to non-Jews. Similar movements form the basis of many of the world's religions. The movements are characterized as messianic when the leader is a human being who takes on supernatural characteristics, as revivalist when the movement seeks to recover some benefits thought to be enjoyed by previous generations, or even as cargo cults when the movement expects intervention in the form of an event that brings desired benefits to the believers. The promises of a perfect future often induce intense enthusiasm among believers; this enthusiasm enables people to ignore normal skepticism and accept ideas they might otherwise find implausible.

The movement's belief system often overturns normal logic and tends to distance the group from commonly experienced versions of reality. Utopian movements, with their religious fervor, are frequently produced among oppressed groups, such as the peoples of Judea and Galilee. Such movements, however, are forced to change over time if they are to survive. If they predict some kind of millennial event, like the Second Coming, and the predicted event fails to occur, they must change their expectations or the expected time period to accommodate reality. In fact, reality is always a threat to such belief systems, and the ability to adapt to new or changing conditions is a primary requirement if the group is to avoid extinction.

Early Christians needed not only to adapt to changing expectations, they had to respond to radical differences among themselves in matters of belief. The Christian creed, or statement of faith, in the first century was a short statement of belief in the Resurrection of Jesus and not much more; but soon questions arose. Did Jesus truly reappear in the flesh, or the spirit? Was Jesus a human being, or a manifestation of God? These and other questions created schisms among the believers, and soon the creed grew in length to reflect how various "heresies" were resolved by the Church authorities.

The period of internal peace within the Roman Empire—the Pax Romana—lasted until 180 A.D. Following the assassination of two emperors, chaos ruled Roman politics for over fifty years. Hundreds of generals were declared emperor. Twenty-six achieved enough stability to be recorded as real emperors, and of these twenty-six only one died of natural causes; all the rest either died in battle or were assassinated.

Paul, the most influential and successful of the early Christian missionaries, arrived in Rome in 62 A.D. During the decades of chaos, the new religion quickly came to the attention of the Roman state because its members refused to bow to the emperor as a god, according to Roman custom, and for this they were perceived as troublemakers at best and potential traitors at worst. Some Romans believed that Christianity was a pernicious superstition. Christians experienced a period of persecution during which some were thrown to the lions and others were martyred, undergoing the most horrible tortures. An especially memorable period of persecution occurred under Emperor Nero, who reportedly accused Christians of setting fires that devastated Rome. The Church leadership found that these acts of brutality generated sympathy for and interest in the Church, and membership was actually growing in spite of the tortures and murders. The Church made heavy demands on its members and encouraged martyrdom as a guarantee of salvation.

> Discipline in the early church was severe. Confession often was public, and absolution for sins was withheld until all imposed penances had been fulfilled. Martyrdom was regarded as the supreme proof of faith, and many eagerly hoped to be crucified, torn by beasts, or burned to death as an evidence of their faith. (Lucas 1943, 242)

The persecution and martyrdom of Christians, carried out for little more than their refusal to renounce their faith, produced a discussion about how the suffering of the martyrs was related to that of Jesus. If Jesus were the son of a divine spirit, it was argued, he may not have suffered on the cross. Some of the voices who were destined to support the emerging orthodox belief urged that the martyrs suffered as Jesus had suffered because Jesus was a flesh-and-blood human being while on earth.

> Tertullian . . . speaking for the majority, defines the orthodox position: as Christ rose bodily from the grave, so every believer should anticipate the resurrection of the flesh. He leaves no room for doubt. He is not, he says, talking about the immortality of the soul. . . . What is raised is "this flesh, suffused with blood, built up

with bones, interwoven with nerves, entwined with veins (a flesh) which . . . was born, and . . . dies, undoubtedly human." (Pagels 1979, 4–5)

The struggle between rival Christian teachers and groups to define the set of orthodox beliefs to be embraced by "true" Christians was one of the important processes that determined the direction of the Christian movement in the second century. While the New Testament is ambivalent, for example, about whether Jesus appeared as a spirit or in the flesh following the Resurrection, the issue became pivotal to the movement:

> [W]hen we examine its practical effect on the Christian movement, we can see, paradoxically, that the doctrine of bodily resurrection also serves an essential political function: it legitimizes the authority of certain men who claim to exercise exclusive leadership over the churches as the successors of the apostle Peter. From the second century, the doctrine has served to validate the apostolic succession of bishops, the basis of papal authority to this day. (Pagels 1979, 7)

The very early Church had been somewhat egalitarian and exhibited an ability to respect women, nature, and people of varying cultures. It began, as we have seen, as a reform movement in Judaism and was growing and accepting converts at the time of the Romano-Jewish War. The Christian Church in Rome, however, found itself in competition with many sects and religions, including a Roman adaptation of Persian Mithraism, which had become widely accepted in Rome. That religion revolved around worship of the sun god, Mithras, whose temple was associated with caves on Vatican Hill and whose birthday was celebrated on December 25, near the time of the winter solstice. According to mythology, Mithras ascended to heaven around the time of the spring equinox. The head of this religion carried the title pappas, a title that survives in Italian as papa, meaning "pope." Adopting a strategy designed to make Christianity more universally acceptable and to attract converts in Rome, the early Church incorporated aspects of Roman pagan traditions such as those of Mithraism. As Christianity spread, this strategy would be extended to other peoples and traditions around the world.

By the middle of the third century A.D., Rome was in economic decline. This trend has been ascribed variously to pestilence and resulting depopulation, a decline in productivity of the mines, debasement of the coinage, a shortage of firewood, declining fertility of the soil, and a balance of trade problem with the eastern parts of the empire. Life in the towns became less prosperous. An absence of conquests on the frontiers meant that fewer slaves were being imported into Italy, and free Romans were now recruited to work on the great estates. As power gradually devolved from Rome, the western parts of the empire, including Gaul, Spain, Italy, and parts of North Africa, were becoming more rural, and the great estates that enjoyed good management were becoming more prosperous and self-sufficient. Small farmers could not compete under these conditions, and great numbers had no choice but to become tenants on the estates.

Civil wars had brought the empire to the verge of collapse, and barbarians and even Persia attacked the Roman frontiers. In 285 A.D. General Diocletian united the armies and drove the barbarians and Persians back. He strengthened the powers of the emperor at the expense of what remained of civil government and created an absolute monarchy supported by a huge bureaucracy. Diocletian divided the empire into two parts, roughly corresponding to a Latin Roman Empire and a Greek Roman Empire. He established the capital of the Eastern Empire at Nicomedia on the Black Sea straits, and Maximian, who became emperor of the Western Empire, established the western capital at Milan.

Persecutions of Christians continued sporadically. In 303 A.D., when Diocletian was told during a consultation with an oracle of Apollo that the appearance of false oracles was caused by Christians, Diocletian launched a harsh persecution. In addition to the killing of Christians, the persecution included desctruction of churches, seizure of bibles and other materials of Christian worship, and the criminalization of Christian worship (Chadwick

1993, 121). Persecutions were carried out with particular intensity in the Eastern Empire.

Diocletian had appointed Constantius, a Roman army officer, to the position of "Caesar," or deputy emperor, of Gaul and Britain. Constantius' son Constantine, whose mother, Helena, later became a saint of the Church, was raised in the Eastern Empire at the court of Diocletian after his father and mother separated. Exposed to Christian influence in his family, Constantine also encountered Christianity in court circles and in the cities of the East.

Following the abdication of Diocletian, Constantine lived as a virtual hostage at the Byzantine court of Emperor Galerius. Constantine escaped and joined his father in 305. When Constantius died in 306, the army immediately acclaimed his son Constantine as Caesar. After five years of involvement in civil wars with a shifting cast of allies and rival emperors, Constantine led an army into Italy and attacked the current Western emperor, Maxentius, at Rome. The latter unwisely abandoned his fortifications to fight with the Tiber River at his back, and Constantine won a stunning victory that he thought could have only happened through divine intervention. (Chadwick 1993, 126)

Tradition holds that on the eve of this battle—arguably the most important in Christian history—Constantine had a dream or vision that his forces would emerge victorious under the symbols of Christianity. He ordered his soldiers to adorn themselves and their shields with the Christian cross and, in a battle that can be described as something of a military miracle, emerged victorious.

Constantine seized Rome and was proclaimed emperor of the Western Empire. From that time forward he considered himself a Christian and he privileged Christianity above all other religions. The following year he and his co-emperor, Licinius, issued the edict of Milan, which lifted the persecution of Christians. A period of tension between the two emperors was exacerbated when Licinius reversed himself and began a persecution of Christians in Armenia. Constantine attacked Licinius and by 323 had become the sole emperor of the Eastern and Western empires. In 331 he moved the seat of the Roman Empire to the new capital he ordered built at Byzantium, which he renamed Constantinople.

It would be impossible to overstate the importance of Constantine's conversion for the development of Christianity. Constantine not only lifted the persecution, he gave the Church exemption from taxes, gifts of property (especially in Rome), and took a personal and authoritative role in settling internal doctrinal disputes. His involvement was critical to the Church's future prospects and was the first instance during which state power was used to advance the interests of Christianity. Church doctrine was fashioned to meet the needs of the state, and eventually Christianity was "normalized" throughout the empire. Constantine's patronage rescued the early Church from the status of one of many competing cults and transformed it into the wealthiest and most politically powerful institution in the Roman world, in the process insuring its long-term survival.

Throughout the early centuries, bickering in the Christian ranks among bishops and presbyters over doctrinal questions continued. Constantine called the first worldwide ecumenical council at Nicaea to settle all issues of Christian doctrine. The Nicene Creed, which emerged from the council, was to be the unquestioned statement of faith until Constantine's death in 337 A.D. Shortly thereafter, bickering resumed. After Constantine's death, his son Constantius, now emperor, tried to engineer a compromise to a dispute about whether the Son of God could be the same as God. By this time it was clear that doctrinal issues within Christianity were matters of state interest, and emperors treated them as such.

In 361 the emperor Julian, who had been raised as a Christian but tutored in the tradition of the ancient Greek philosophers, announced his support for paganism and initiated a pagan revival. The revival faded after Julian was fatally wounded in battle in 363. Christianity had become the religion of many of Roman society's elites; under Emperor Theodosius, late in the fourth century, it became the only legal religion of the Roman Empire. Thus the movement that had originated among Jewish peasants in Galilee in reaction to Roman oppression had evolved over less than four centuries to become the religion of that empire.

Following the guidance of emperors in practically every question of doctrinal choices, orthodox Christian leadership ultimately chose an authoritarian path. The official view came to be that all authority was vested in the hierarchy of the priesthood, and the egalitarian nature of the early congregations was suppressed. Over time women came to be viewed as unclean, and their sexuality was deemed a temptation that took men's minds from spiritual matters. Eventually orthodox Christians would declare the physical world the playground of the devil, and all pleasures, even such simple pleasures as bathing, would be seen as temptations of the flesh. The idea of Satan as a trickster or figure who put obstacles in the path of the righteous to test their faith was exhumed, and Satan was transformed into a personification of evil.

Peoples of other faiths, especially pagan cults, were demonized as agents of Satan whose objectives were the destruction of Christianity and the conquest of the minds of all people. This latter notion was particularly disturbing because Christianity had arrogated to itself an exact equivalent of that mission. As orthodox Christianity became ever more the official religion of the empire, it also became more important as a tool for keeping order among the masses. As the interests of the Church and those of the empire became as one, the combination proved as intolerant as any predecessors in either the Church or the state. Church authorities turned their energies to oppression of pagan and other religions, eventually outlawing the practice of these religions upon penalty of death.

Persia regained Armenia from Rome in 350, Huns invaded Europe in 360, and Emperor Valens was defeated and killed by Visigoths at a battle at Adrianople in 378. Roman legions began to evacuate Britain in 383, and Theodosius the Great, the last emperor to rule both East and West as such, died in 395. The invasion of the Visigoths reached Italy in 401, and their leader, Alaric, captured and sacked Rome in 410. The Visigoths conquered the Vandal kingdom in Spain in 416, and in 418 Franks settled in parts of Gaul. The Roman Empire, once the most powerful institution in the world, was disappearing:

> Even when reinforced by the supernatural sanctions of the Christian church and sustained by a rapid acculturation of German mercenaries and frontiersmen, the late Roman Empire lacked resilience in the face of disaster, since most of its subjects found the government oppressive, rapacious, alien. In the fifth century, therefore, local defeats in the western provinces could no longer be made good, and Roman power disintegrated in the Latin-speaking half of the empire. (McNeil 1963, 388)

In 425 barbarians settled in various Roman provinces: Visigoths and Suevi in Portugal and northern Spain, Huns in Pannonia, Ostrogoths in Dalmatia, and Vandals in southern Spain. In 455 the Vandals sacked Rome. In 542 a plague, imported by rats from Egypt and Syria, struck Constantinople and for the next five years spread throughout Europe. It is the worst plague ever recorded in human history. At one point, 10,000 people a day perished in Constantinople, and overall an estimated 100 million died—almost four times as many as during the plague of the fourteenth century. The Roman Empire never recovered.

The Eastern, or Greek, Roman Empire would survive for more than a thousand years after Rome was sacked by barbarians in 410. Probably the most important and durable contribution of Greek Christendom to later western European societies was Roman law. Codified during the sixth century by Justinian, emperor at Constantinople, it was destined to have enormous influence on the development of law in the West. Justinian also reconquered much of North Africa and Italy and reunified much of the Roman Empire under Byzantine rule.

The memory of the ancient Greek philosophers was almost completely lost in the lands of the Latin Church, although those philosophers' writings had been preserved in the Greek Roman Empire. In the Eastern Empire, however, Justinian began the process of officially suppressing secular knowledge. In 529 A.D., he closed the school that had been founded by Plato in Athens in 387 B.C., as well as all other non-Christian schools.

Few Western conquerors since Roman times have failed to adopt the symbolism and even sometimes the tactics of the ancient Romans. In somewhat the same way that the *Odyssey* and the *Iliad* had served as master narratives for the Ancient Greeks, the idea of the Roman Empire has served as a master narrative for the West, which has at various times copied its military and imperial culture and reimagined itself in the image it has created of ancient Rome.

The Roman Empire left a remarkable legacy that continues to be expressed in many areas of Western culture, including most of the alphabet, language, legal codes, styles of art, engineering skills, traditions of medicine, and sports. The most historically significant legacy of imperial Rome, however, was Christian orthodoxy, which reproduced Rome's dedication to unquestioned authority, its willingness to extend membership to converts, much as Rome bestowed citizenship on its provincials, its drive for world domination, and an intolerance for difference that would be, at times, more intense than that of its imperial ancestor. In the centuries following the collapse of the central secular authority in the Latin west, the Church grew immeasurably wealthy as it accumulated properties while paying no taxes. At one point the Church owned between a quarter and a third of the land in western Christendom. The concentration of money, land, and power in the Church proved a breeding ground for corruption, intrigue, and murder. The relationships between secular and Church authorities would evolve to almost breathtaking complexity, with popes coming to power through money and influence, and the lines between religion and politics becoming at times hopelessly blurred.

For more than a thousand years, beginning with its acceptance as the state religion of the Roman Empire, the Church dominated thought in the Christian world. In 381, the Second Ecumenical Council granted to the bishop of Constantinople jurisdiction over the Christian bishops in most of Asia, Asia Minor, and the Balkans and recognized Greek-speaking Constantinople as "the new Rome."

At first administratively, and eventually culturally, Christianity was divided into East and West, Greek and Latin. Although Latin would survive in Constantinople for some centuries, the Greek language virtually disappeared from western Christendom by the sixth century. This was a major source of the increasing alienation and distrust between Latin and Greek Christendom, although there also existed substantial differences in outlook in other areas. In terms of religious doctrine, a major point of disagreement was the issue of whether priests were to be allowed to marry.

In North Africa, in reaction to the opulence of the Roman Church, ascetics engaged in heroic acts of self-deprivation, renouncing material possessions and pleasures, including sex. The ascetics inspired monastic movements devoted to the idea that priests dedicated to God did not pursue earthly delights. The Greek Church, however, did not adopt these ideas, and Greek Orthodox priests were permitted to marry.

The Latin Church had never been much interested in preserving the knowledge or philosophy of the Greco-Roman world, and the important works of the ancient Greeks had largely disappeared from the Roman world by the second century. Aristotle's writings were already rare after the first century, and it is uncertain how much of Plato's writing was available in the West after that.

Christianity and Greek philosophy represented distinct and different ways of seeing the world. Just as Greek philosophy had been hostile to the supernatural religions of the ancient world, the legacy of Socrates was potentially equally hostile to Christian dogma. Socratic thought described a natural universe that was knowable, orderly, moral, and purposeful. Classical Greek philosophy focused on the accumulation of knowledge and the development of the powers of logic and rational thought in its pursuit of the ideal. Christianity did enter into lengthy discourses, such as the controversy on the nature of good and evil, but such arguments were self-referential, taking place entirely within the context of the Christian belief system. Christian beliefs encompassed divine revelation, resurrection and an afterlife, a divine trinity, and, in time, a whole list of related doctrines on sacrifice,

sin, repentance, and salvation. Greek philosophy, with its powerful emphasis on logic, reasoning, and worldly knowledge, was in
many respects its potential enemy.

One of the greatest Christian theologians, St. Augustine
(354–430), lived in what is now Algeria during a period of recur-
rent crisis in the Latin West. He wrote one of the most important
books of early Christianity, *The City of God,* in an attempt to explain
the disastrous sack of Rome in 410. Critics of Christianity were
pointing to the decline of Rome's pagan religion as a major cause of
the weakening of the empire that made the sack of Rome possible.
The City of God was written, in part, to counter this notion:

> God is the unchangeable Governor as He is the unchange-
> able Creator of notable things, ordering all events in His
> providence until the beauty of the completed course of
> time . . . shall be finished, like the grand melody of some
> ineffably rare master song. (Epist. 138, Figgis 1963, 40)

Augustine provided much of the intellectual framework for
Church doctrine. In *The City of God* he asserts that worldly events
such as the sack of Rome represent the unfolding of God's plan,
which will lead inevitably to the Second Coming, Resurrection of
the believers, and Judgment Day. If God's plan is inevitable and
manifest in the events of history, it is the will of God and not the
immorality, irrationality, weakness, or corruption of the Church
that brings about disasters such as the sack of Rome. His view of
the world includes elements of the theory of predestination and a
philosophy of history that would dominate Christian thought for
more than a thousand years. *The City of God* shows the influence
of either Plato's works or writers who echoed Plato and is considered the first work to synthesize elements of Plato's philosophy with
Christian dogma.

As a young man, Augustine had led a promiscuous life and
had fathered and abandoned a child out of wedlock. Later in life
he came to believe that sex was evil and that human beings are
powerless to control their own lust. He claimed that the sin of

Adam illustrated the fact that human beings had lost the ability to choose good over evil. According to Augustine, human beings were subject to a predestined fate and only God's choices determined individual salvation.

Pelagius, a monk who is believed to have come from Britain, arrived in Rome at the beginning of the fifth century. He taught that individuals possessed freedom of will and preached that people should take responsibility for their own actions. A person who lived a pious life would then be on the road to salvation. Augustine sharply disagreed and successfully lobbied to have Pelagius excommunicated from the Church. Augustine was aware that the idea that individual free will could lead to salvation would diminish the Church's power. He urged that people were inherently evil and in need of the Church's authority. The possibility of salvation was acquired not from pious acts springing from free will but simply by embracing Jesus Christ, and God had predetermined which individuals among those would achieve salvation. The only road to salvation was defined by submission to the authority of the single human agency with power to influence the outcome—the Church.

Pelagius attacked the idea of predestination articulated by Augustine in *Confessions* because, if it were true that God had already selected those destined for salvation and morality was not a factor in the process of selection, people would not be motivated to live moral lives. The points of this debate would echo across the centuries. Although Augustine eventually triumphed against Pelagius, by the sixteenth century the Church had reversed its stand. Church doctrine came to support the notion that moral behavior was a factor in eligibility for salvation, while certain Protestant sects embraced Augustine's ideas about predestination.

Other heresies were also settled in a fashion designed to enhance the power and authority of the Church. When the African Donatists insisted on higher standards of behavior for priests, Augustine responded by invoking Theodosian laws against heresy and urging the Church to use force to crush the movement. The Church had become a repressive agency with access to military force to protect and extend its authority and its wealth. The idea that the Church, in facilitating a quest for a utopian afterlife for the individual, was justified in compelling people to follow its authority has continued far into the modern era.

Augustine's belief that God had a plan and that history was the unfolding of that plan on earth furthered the notion of progress, an idea that can be traced at least as far back as the Persion religion of Zoroastrianism. The belief in the events of history as God's will unfolding toward a positive end has shaped the philosophy and theology of history in the West until the modern era. For many it remains valid to the present time (Kelley 1991, 142–156).

Among the targets of early Christian intolerance were the tradition and writings of the ancient Greek philosophers. Civil wars and barbarian invasions caused significant turmoil and the incidental destruction of institutions such as academies and libraries, but the Church purposely suppressed classical Greek knowledge. Christian zealots were responsible for book burnings and the destruction of ancient libraries. Pope Gregory the Great ordered the library of the Palatine Apollo burned and forbade laymen to read even the Bible. Jerome, an early father of the Church, boasted that classical authors were being ignored; in 398 A.D. the Fourth Council at Carthage forbade Church leaders to read them. Young monks bragged of their ignorance of classical writings, and books and libraries were systematically destroyed. John Chrysostom, a father of the Greek Church, declared his satisfaction that all trace of the writings and philosophy of antiquity had disappeared under the early hegemony of the Christian Church.

As both Church and state turned their attention away from the tradition of accumulating knowledge of the world, western Europe gradually fell into a religion-dominated dark age in which not only philosophy but other secular subjects such as technology and mathematics were practically abandoned as proper avenues of learning. Works of art were destroyed. The monasteries became repositories of books and carried on a tradition of reading and writing, but most of their activity was restricted to religious materials.

The West fell into a prolonged economic depression that was intensified by a pervasive hostility—fostered by the Church—toward trade and lending money at interest. The Church sometimes involved itself in disputes around debts and released debtors from their obligations, a practice that tended to discourage commercial loans. The physical legacy of the Roman Empire, including its baths, aqueducts, and roads, was neglected and allowed to fall into ruin; and parts of Europe did not recover from the attack on knowledge until the nineteenth century.

The event that probably administered the coup de grace to the old Latin Empire was the plague that swept Europe in the sixth century, arguably the most terrible plague in all of human history. People fled to the Church in terror, partly because the Church had convinced them that the plague was a punishment from God for improper attention to spiritual matters. When Greek medicines and medicinal practices were shown to be ineffective against the plague, the Latin Church emerged to dominate all formal practices in the field of medicine. The Church, which had promoted a cultural retreat from careful sanitation and hygiene, ironically benefited from a disastrous plague that could only be fought in those centuries with scrupulous attention to exactly those issues.

Although the Roman Empire in the west declined and its administrative capacities as an empire disappeared, it was not forgotten. For centuries, indeed until today, Rome has remained a symbol of glory, wealth, stability, and power that has inspired people to emulate what they imagined to be the Roman legacy. Its wonders are whatever the viewer most desires them to be. In that way, its images continue to have power over the imaginations of human beings who find their own society inadequate, and Rome's fall is often ascribed to weaknesses actually found in a contemporary world. Its real legacies seem, in retrospect, less visible and less well known than its imagined ones. In that sense, Rome represents a true utopia of the past.

Bibliography

Berlin, Isaiah. *The Crooked Timber of Humanity: Chapters in the History of Ideas.* New York: Alfred A. Knopf, 1991, 2.

The Bible, the King James Version.

Carmichael, Joel. *The Birth of Christianity: Reality and Myth.* New York: Hippocrene Books, 1989.

Chadwick, Henry. *The Early Christian Church.* New York: Penguin Books, 1967, 1993.

Crossan, John Dominic. *The Birth of Christianity: Discovering What Happened in the Years Immediately After the Execution of Jesus.* San Francisco: Harper Collins, 1998.

Eisler, Riane. *The Chalice and the Blade.* San Francisco: Harper & Row, 1987.

Ellerbe, Helen. *The Dark Side of Christian History.* San Rafael, Calif: Morningstar Books, 1995.

Figgis, John Neville. *The Political Aspects of St. Augustine's 'City of God.'* Peter Smith: Gloucester, Mass.: Peter Smith, 1921, 1963, 40.

Haught, James A. *Holy Horror.* Buffalo, N.Y.: Prometheus, 1990.

Karlsen, Carol E. *The Devil in the Shape of a Woma*n. New York: Vintage Books, 1987.

Kelley, Donald E., ed. *Versions of History: From Antiquity to the Enlightenment.* New Haven, Ct.: Yale University Press, 1991.

Lucas, Henry S. *A Short History of Civilization.* New York: McGraw-Hill, 1943.

McNeil, William. *The Rise of the West.* Chicago: University of Chicago Press, 1963, 388.

Nigg, Walter. *The Heretics,* trans. and ed. Richard Winston and Clara Winston. New York: Alfred A. Knopf, 1962.

Pagels, Elaine. *Adam, Eve, and the Serpent.* New York: Random House, 1988.

_____. *The Gnostic Gospels.* New York: Random House, 1979.

Sanders, E. P. *The Historical Figure of Jesus.* London: Penguin Books, 1993, 1995.

Smith, John Holland. *The Death of Classical Paganism.* New York: Charles Scribner's Sons, 1976.

FIVE
Imperial Christendom in the Middle Ages

> The new children of Israel slaughtered everyone they
> found. They set fire to the great synagogue where the
> Jews had gathered and burned them alive. Tancred
> smashed his way to the Dome of the Rock and looted it.
> The next day, all the Moslems they could find were
> slaughtered.
>
> ("The Crusades," BBC documentary)

Subsequent historians would give the name "middle ages" to the
period from the disintegration of state power in the Western
Roman Empire in the fifth century to the rise of the Renaissance
in the fourteenth century. The term implies that it was a time
defined by other more distinct ages, a kind of hiatus in history. In
fact it was a separate era characterized by distinctive institutions
and history that would leave their mark on future eras.

Although the experience of conquest and often enslavement by
the Romans had traumatized European populations, memories of
Rome had softened in time. Living with poverty, violence, and
hunger, western Europeans could look back on the Roman Empire
as the greatest and noblest state that had ever existed. Throughout
the Middle Ages it came to be regarded with nostalgia as a past, or
lost, utopia.

In the fourth century, the Eastern Roman Empire (Byzantium)
ruled areas in southern Europe and the Middle East bordering the
Persian Empire (including Palestine) between Egypt and Anatolia

(present-day Turkey). Under constant pressure from potential invasions, the Byzantine Empire continued to tax and otherwise ruthlessly exploit its provinces as it had done before the disintegration of the Western Empire.

About two hundred years following the appearance of Augustine's *City of God*, events in the Middle East were to take center stage in world history. Sometime around 613 a merchant of Mecca, Muhammad, who was to prove to be a great and respected poet, began to have visions in which he heard the angel Gabriel. The angel inspired him to embark on a mission to bring the word of Allah to his fellow humans. Muhammad's teachings reflect the Old Testament of the Hebrews and some Christian beliefs but were relentlessly monotheistic, rejecting the trinity of Christianity. His followers asserted there was but one God, Allah, and Muhammad was his prophet. Submission to Allah was designated "Islam." Muhammad's sacred revelations were soon written down as the Quran, the holy book of Islam. The revelations acknowledged some of the sacred texts of both Judaism and Christianity, finding that Moses and Christ were legitimate prophets but asserting that Muhammad was the final prophet and carried the true word of God. The new religion had many elements familiar to Christianity: belief in heaven and hell, salvation, resurrection, and a judgment day. It differed from Christianity around some critical issues, including who was to represent the heavenly kingdom on earth, technicalities about predestination, and whether Jesus was a divine figure.

Muhammad and his movement soon came into conflict with Arab factions and authorities at Mecca. The prophet personally led armies into battle against the movement's enemies and thus established the permissibility of the use of armed force to spread the word of Islam. At Medina, Muhammad had 600 Jews killed because they refused to convert to Islam (Hoffman 1995, 193).

Originating with a charismatic leader who was believed to experience revelations from God, the Islamic revitalization movement, like the Christian movement, was organized in an effort to extend the benefits of those revelations to peoples far and wide, and its followers created institutions that perpetuated its beliefs. Islam spread to southern Asia and as far as western Africa within a few generations of its founding, beginning a dramatic rise to the status of a world religion. It is and will probably always be shrouded in mystery because of the absence of detailed records from Muhammad's day and the fact that his earliest biographer wrote more than a century after his death.

Following Muhammad's death in 632, his followers embarked on a period of conquest. In 634 the Byzantine and Persian Empires were exhausted from a recently concluded war, and there was considerable unrest in Egypt and Syria because of excessive taxation and religious oppression by the Byzantines (Hoffman 1995, 194). These circumstances gave an advantage to the energized and rising Islamic movement, which initiated one of the most surprising periods of military conquest in history. From humble beginnings, the armies of Islam experienced repeated successes.

In 636 Khalid ibn al-Walid orchestrated a surprise defeat of a Byzantine army at Yarmuk. Arab armies had conquered Mesopotamia, Egypt, and Persia by 651. The ancient Middle East was united once more, this time as an Arab empire with an expansionist agenda. The early Muslim military victories against Byzantine and Persian armies helped to advance the belief that Allah favored their cause. By 711 Islamic armies had swept into Spain. This first burst of Islamic conquest arose primarily among territories that had comprised the cultures of the ancient Middle East, many of which had been overrun and devastated by the armies of Alexander the Great nearly a thousand years earlier. The Islamic forces suffered their first serious defeat in 718, when a Muslim army mounted a siege of Byzantium.

Muslim armies won a series of victories until 733, when Frankish emperor Charles Martel defeated a raiding party of Moors in France outside Poitiers. Martel's victory may have been, in an unexpected way, one of the most important battles in European history. Muslim success had been virtually assured by the fact that their armies consisted of mounted swordsmen, and European fighting forces lacked sufficient numbers of mounted warriors to defend against their attacks. Martel had taken some land from the

Church and placed it in the hands of knights, who used the land and serfs to raise war horses, which were then expected to arrive at the battlefield bearing armed warriors. Some Western historians have credited Martel's creation of a mounted army with halting the Islamic conquest of the whole of western Europe. In any case, he set the stage for the rise of the knight-landowner class and the pattern of vassal relationships, landholding, loyalties, and obligations that came to define European feudalism.

The rise of Islam precipitated a contest of cultures in which Islam was to emerge as a counterbalance to Christianity, but the Arabic world became a great civilization in its own right. Baghdad, founded in 750, became a center for the manufacture of rugs, silks, jewels, weapons, precious metal objects, and fine cloths. It became wealthier than Constantinople and as populous. The religion founded by a merchant produced a culture that reveled in trade and prosperity. Basra, Samarkand, Damascus, Cairo, and other Muslim cities blossomed during a period of peace and prosperity that may have been the greatest in the history of the world to that time. The Islamic Empire spread not only the religion of Muhammad but also the Arabic language and Islamic law. As with many empires born of conquest, it was not to last as such. After about a century of conquest the empire fell to factionalism in much the same way Alexander the Great's empire disintegrated after his death. Islamic culture, however, took firm root, and the religion continued to spread, more through proselytizing than military conquest. Across a vast expanse of Islamic civilization stretching from North Africa to India and eventually to parts of Eastern Europe, a traveler could enjoy the benefits of everywhere encountering the same religion, the Arabic language, and Islamic law.

The Islamic and Christian religious empires were sometimes characterized by rigidity and rejection of cultural modes other than their own, although they treated "others" differently in different places and times. Both civilizations were built around submission to orthodoxy and the acceptance of a single cultural model. Islam was often relatively tolerant of other religions, especially of Christianity and Judaism, which also claimed a cultural hero in

Abraham. This tolerance may have been influenced by a custom of excusing Muslims from taxes. Under this policy, the more converts to Islam, the fewer remaining taxpayers. Thus, in some Islamic regimes, conversion was not very vigorously pursued. In Eastern Europe there were times when the population preferred Turkish rulers because they were less intrusive in matters of religion than were their Frankish competition.

Christian authorities, still attempting to solidify Church authority, continued to be preoccupied with heresies, which they viewed as a threat not only to the spiritual life of the culture but to the unity and therefore military strength of Christendom as a whole. Given the spiritual and military competition posed by Islam, the threat was not to be taken lightly.

Sensitive to any hint of heresy, Church authorities continued to suppress the skeptical questioning that characterized ancient Greek philosophical thought. The Islamic world, however, was neither indifferent nor hostile to the great books of the ancient world, including those of the Greek philosophers. Their scholars enthusiastically translated the works of Plato, Aristotle, and other Greek thinkers into Arabic and made them available in their libraries. Eventually Jewish scholars translated some of Aristotle into Hebrew; these works were in time rendered in Latin.

Beginning around 750, Viking raiders appeared along the European coasts and river systems, attacking and looting throughout the Frankish Empire, especially in the territories that are now part of France, Germany, and Italy. The Vikings used boats much like those that had traversed the Mediterranean in the classical Greek period, and they were ferocious warriors. Their attacks stimulated defensive measures, including the construction of forts, castles, and moats. In France those who could afford horses mobilized them for warfare. The Vikings arrived by water but fought on land, and soon adapted horses to their own uses as their raids transformed into campaigns of conquest. A system of local self-defense was created. Castles were fortified and moats built so that a vassal and his family and servants could hide their valuables and themselves in the castle until the attackers withdrew. The military self-sufficiency of each vassal created the conditions for the atomization of power that characterized the age.

The introduction of stirrups, probably in the eighth century, welded man to horse in a revolutionary way. Prior to this invention, a man on a horse could easily be dismounted by a blow from either side. Stirrups made it possible for heavy cavalry to employ both hands wielding lance and shield and to be stabilized on the horse at the same time. For the hapless foot soldier, this new weapon system was terrifying and lethal.

The mounted armored knights evolved into a class of warrior aristocrats who could afford horses and armor and had leisure time to practice the arts of war. The wealth produced around the castle and its surrounding lands was dedicated to the support of the knight, who provided the people of his fiefdom with protection from predators. War and fighting became the exclusive domain of this class, whose time was devoted to achieving the skills needed for individual combat and whose interests were not connected to those of a state. The knights honed their skills for both battle and the competitive jousting tournaments.

Feudalism had evolved as the Roman state collapsed and the Western Empire's wealth and power was gradually splintered among the great estates of Italy and the rest of the western Europe. The feudal system was characterized by local self-sufficiency and a military hierarchy. The primary form of government within the various fiefdoms could best be described as military dictatorship.

The gulf between the lives of the knightly class and those of the common people, both peasants and townspeople, was immense. For the average person, life in these and subsequent centuries was mean and mean-spirited. The castles were fortresses managed by the warrior class. Warfare among kings and vassals was incessant, and resources—including food—were often looted to supply armies. Hunger was ever-present.

> In the Middle Ages . . . hunger appeared everywhere and
> as a permanent phenomenon. It showed its fleshless mask
> now in England, now in Germany and France. Eastern

Europe was almost always hungry. As soon as famine seemed to have left one place, it arose in a neighboring region, fed for a while like an eternal fire, and returned once more to the land it had left. (Jacob 1944, 141)

The towns were walled and their inhabitants lived in prisonlike conditions. A gatekeeper recorded every person who left its walls and guarded against strangers entering unbidden. Each town minted its own money, which was useless in neighboring towns. Trade was seriously stifled. There was a real key to the city because at night the gate was locked. Highwaymen lurked along the roads and were known to kill strangers, butcher them, and sell them as meat in the markets. Every arrangement reflected the need for defense:

> No architecture was uglier than the town architecture of the Middle Ages. It was based upon the animality of man's nature. Its fundamental conception sprang from fear, the common creeping fear of attack from one's neighbor. . . . Everything served the end of defense. . . . A history of terror compelled them to do so. The security of the Roman peace had long since vanished. (Jacob 1944, 133)

Charlemagne (Charles the Great), a Frankish emperor, conquered and united most of the Christian nations of western Europe. The grandson of Charles Martel and son of Pepin the Short, he was the greatest of the Carolingian rulers. On Christmas Day in the year 800, he was crowned in Rome as the first emperor of the Holy Roman Empire by Pope Leo III. The pope thus legitimized a powerful alliance with the Roman Church.

Between 772 and 804 Charlemagne waged war almost constantly against the heathen Saxons, finally subduing and forcibly converting them to Christianity. In 774 he led an army to Italy and defeated the Lombards. He conquered Avars and Slavs, and by his death in 1814 had extended his domain from northeastern Spain to eastern Germany and south to Rome.

Charlemagne did more to establish Medieval Christendom than anyone else during the Middle Ages. As an active attempt to revive the perceived glories of Christian Rome, his conquests exhibited some of the zeal of a revitalization movement. At the same time, he was engaged in the utopian project of attempting to Christianize all of Europe—often by military conquest and forced conversions.

Charlemagne established the largest European empire since the days of Rome's power, but his interests were not limited to conquest. Wishing to revive all forms of learning that had existed in the Roman era, he assigned the task to the Church, which had preserved writing in its monasteries. Charlemagne led a movement to revive the Latin language, even bringing teachers and churchmen to Europe from Ireland and England. He established the Church as the intellectual and cultural center of western Europe, and his work energized the Church's role in preserving ecclesiastical history and Christian texts useful to the education of priests. After his death, Charlemagne's descendants fell into arguing over division of the empire, and three grandsons fought one another to exhaustion.

During the tenth century the horse harness and horseshoes were invented. The horse harness, unlike previous harnesses that encircled a horse's neck, was located over the breastbone and permitted a horse to pull much more weight than before. The horse's increased productivity launched a revolution in agriculture (Lucas 1943, 375). Draft horses made it possible to produce more food, and more food resulted in population increases. The clearing of more arable land and the decline of forests inevitably followed. Despite the expansion of food production, the population outstripped the supply of food, and famine continued to haunt Europe.

One of the most important events of the eleventh century was the appearance on the Islamic scene of the Turks, a people from the interior of Asia. They brought a new military vigor to the region, conquering Baghdad in 1055. The Turks were relatively recent and zealous converts to Islam, and they exhibited an intolerance toward Christianity that other Muslims had rarely displayed. Islamic governments had allowed Christian pilgrimages to Jerusalem since the days of Muhammad, but the Turks were less accommodating and sometimes blocked Christian pilgrimages to the Holy City. Turkish conquests advanced steadily into Asia Minor, threatening the Byzantine Empire and even Constantinople itself.

Until late in the eleventh century, western Europe remained politically fragmented. Small empires arose in the north as Viking ships explored the North Atlantic and established colonies in Iceland—the first European colonies outside Europe. The Scandinavians had been proselytized into the Christian orbit, and by the eleventh century it was Canute, a Catholic king from Denmark, whose empire included England, Denmark, and Norway. Descendants of the Vikings ("Norsemen") who had colonized Normandy invaded England in 1066.

The Eastern Christian Church was more and more dominated by Constantinople, which had assumed an increasingly independent attitude toward Rome. In 1054 a schism resulted when Byzantium's Michael Cerularius was excommunicated by Roman papal ambassadors after he closed the Latin churches in Constantinople and ordered the sacraments torn from the churches and trampled underfoot in the streets. These events precipitated the final division of the Church into the Eastern Orthodox and Roman Catholic Churches, which retain their separate identities to this day. In 1060, Pope Nicholas II secured a treaty that created what amounted to a feudal relationship with the Normans of southern Italy, subjecting them as vassals to the Vatican. For the next thirty years the Normans fought to conquer southern Italy and expel the Byzantines there, and to expel Muslims from Sicily. Both objectives were accomplished by 1091.

A struggle had arisen over the leadership of the papacy in Rome. Henry III, the German king and emperor of the Holy Roman Empire, had gained considerable control of the papacy, even at one stage appointing a pope. After Henry's death in 1056, the Vatican instituted a revitalization project aimed at creating institutions that would be free from secular interference. In 1075 Pope Gregory VII issued a decree demanding that secular princes not appoint church officers, upon penalty of excommunication.

The new emperor, Henry IV, was unwilling to surrender the powers of his predecessor and ignored this decree. He promptly appointed five bishops in Germany and Italy. When he ignored warnings and convened a council of German bishops that "deposed" the pope, Gregory VII not only excommunicated him but declared him deposed from his throne. The strategy worked. Henry found himself forced to prostrate himself before the pope, spending three days in the cold of winter begging forgiveness at the pope's window.

In 1080, Henry was once again defiant, and once again Pope Gregory VII excommunicated him. This time, however, Henry was prepared, having convinced supporters in Germany that he had been abused by Gregory. In 1084 Henry led an army into Italy and seized Rome. Although the emperor soon retreated, Gregory was forced into exile in southern Italy and he died a short time later. In 1088 Pope Urban II was elected. Urban II proved to be an activist, traveling throughout Italy, convening councils of bishops, working to oppose clerical marriages and appointments of priests to office by secular princes, both of which were seen to be serious evils by his movement.

Despite the split between Rome and Constantinople, Byzantine Emperor Alexis Comnenus issued a plea to the West for military aid to help stop the Turks from overrunning Eastern Christendom. What he was hoping for was a few companies of mercenary knights to reinforce his own troops. Pope Urban II gave this request a great deal of thought. He convened a large congregation of churchmen and nobles at Clermont in southern France and on November 27, 1095, delivered a speech that would change the course of world history. He called on the Catholics of Europe to join together to attack the Turks and to drive them from the holy places of Asia Minor. "An accursed race," he said, "has invaded the lands of these Christians." Europe was experiencing a serious economic depression and, in some regions, near-famine conditions prevailed. To motivate his troops, the pope portrayed Europe as an impoverished region that was rapidly becoming overcrowded and faced with famine:

> Our land is shut in on all sides by the sea and mountains
> and is too quickly populated. There is not much wealth
> here and the soil scarcely yields enough to support you.
> On this account you kill and devour each other.

The pope went on to describe the torture and slaughter of Eastern
Christians by "the infidel" and again appealed to the Europeans'
self-interest. There was plenty of land under the Turks, he said, that
could be divided up into fiefdoms for European nobility and
homesteads for the adventurous peasantry:

> [T]ake the land from the wicked people, and make it your
> own. That land which, as the Scripture says, is flowing
> with milk and honey, God gave to the children of Israel.
> Jerusalem is the best of all lands, more fruitful than all
> others, as it were a second Paradise of delights. (Lucas
> 1943, 359; Thatcher and McNeal 1905, 518–521.)

The pope promised a ready-made utopia and his call to arms was
met with enthusiastic fervor. One of the primary purposes from
the standpoint of potential crusaders was plunder—seizing property from a people in a foreign land. He also promised salvation
to those who expired en route or in battle against Christendom's
enemies. Echoing the traditional story of Constantine's battle at
Rome, the pope instructed the crusaders to go into battle display-
ing the cross.

Few in the pope's audience at Clermont—indeed only a small
percentage of all Christians—could read, and the Church therefore
provided all they knew about the teachings of Christ. Although the
Church had previously held that Christ was the Prince of Peace,
when the pope offered that it was their durty to go to war in the
name of God, few questioned the contradiction.

Some modern scholars dislike the emphasis on imperialism
and plunder that other historians associate with the Crusades; and
they question the accuracy of reporting by people who either were
not present at the event or wrote an account of it at a later time. It

is impossible, however, to ignore the air of excitement the pope's pronouncements stirred, or to account for the enthusiasm that would eventually send peasants into battle against warriors and children into the field during the Children's Crusade—unless it is explained as the kind of religious exhilaration we find in revitalization movements. Fulcher of Chartres, a crusader whose chronicle is one of the important surviving accounts from the period, confirmed the enthusiasm for the pope's mission:

> For [the pope] restored peace and re-established the rights of the Church in their former condition. He also made a vigorous effort to drive out the pagans from the lands of the Christians. And since he endeavored in every way to glorify everthing which was of God, nearly everyone freely submitted in obedience to his paternal authority. (Fulcher of Chartres, in Fink 1969, Book I, 68–69)

The pope's speech, which can be considered one of the most important events in Western history, was generally underreported in subsequent accounts of the origins of the Crusades. The imperial pope at the head of the western European states—that is, Christendom—urged that God demanded its warriors undertake a conquest of a foreign land. It was a dramatic step in what would become a European quest for world domination.

One of the first consequences of the pope's call to violence on non-Christians was a massacre of 800 Jews in Worms in May 1096 and more Jews in other cities in Germany (Billings 1987, 15). The long history of the robbery and murder of Europe's Jews had begun. Each subsequent crusade would be prefaced with a pogrom, or massacre, of Jews. Pogroms occurred at Berlitz near Berlin in 1253, in Paris in 1290, and in many other towns over the following two centuries (Tannahill 1975, 61).

The word "crusade" is derived from the Latin word for "cross" and signified the cross going to war. The First Crusade was marketed as a holy war and filled Catholic Europe with the spirit of unity, piety, and invincibility, while diverting attention from the countless petty struggles that plagued Christendom. It was a project designed to forge a Christian European identity under Church leadership.

Pope Urban II personally appointed a French bishop to lead the First Crusade, but the clamor for new land and loot and the honor of serving as God's own army was so great among the crusaders that many packed their carts and began the long trek to Jerusalem without benefit of either organization or planning. Emperor Comnenus got much more "help" than he had asked for. The first response to the pope's call to make war on an Eastern civilization was a kind of disorganized land rush in the form of a peasant crusade. Foraging off the land, a mob of some sixty thousand made its way to Constantinople, a city larger than all those of western Europe combined. When Emperor Alexis Comnenus observed this rabble approaching, he quickly closed the gates of the city and kept them at bay.

Commenus urged the leaders to wait until the army of knights arrived, but the mob insisted on going forward and were ferried the eight hundred yards across the Bosporus to Asia. The crusaders immediately attacked and slaughtered people of some nearby villages who, it turned out, were Christians and not Muslims after all. The sword of God, it would prove, was blind as well as heartless. Poorly armed and untrained, this first wave of fanatic Christian invaders was quickly decimated by the Turks a few miles into Anatolia before Urban's official First Crusade was underway. Anna Comnena, daughter of Alexis and historian of his reign, reported that the bones of the crusaders were left in a huge pile, an image that could serve as a monument to religious fanaticism for the ages.

In 1097 about one hundred thousand crusaders in four armies passed through Constantinople and crossed the Bosporus. Some sixty thousand knights, the largest assembly of medieval heavy cavalry in the history of the world, began their trek across the hills of Anatolia toward Jerusalem, a thousand miles away. The first phase turned into a death march. The searing desert provided little water at some times and drenching torrential rains at others. The crusaders had only the money they could assemble for the adventure to sustain them, and many were cast into a condition of extreme poverty and hunger.

Of the original horde, possibly two out of three died along the way. As few as twenty thousand knights eventually arrived at Jerusalem, but on the way there they won two important battles against the Turks. In 1098, after the crusaders captured the city of Maarat an-Numan, reports confirm the first of many episodes of barbarism. Anna Comnena reported that the crusaders massacred those they captured and lapsed into an orgy of cannibalism: "In Maarat our troops boiled pagan adults in cooking pots. They impaled children on spits and devoured them grilled" (Foss 1997, 98–99).

The exploits of the French knight Bohemond during the First Crusade were chronicled by an anonymous knight of his army in a book called *Gesta Francorum* (Deeds of the Franks). The chronicler confirms this story:

> Then for one month and four days we stayed in Maarat an-Numan. While we were there some of our men were still desperate for both food and plunder, since there was nothing to be had outside the city. So they ripped up the bodies of the dead, hoping to find bezants [gold coins] hidden in the entrails, and others cut the dead flesh into slices and cooked and ate them. (Foss 1997, 156)

At the siege at Nicaea, Anna Comnena reported that the crusaders "ravaged the outskirts of Nicaea, acting with horrible cruelty to the whole population. They cut some of the babies to pieces. They impaled others on wooden spits and roasted them over a fire" (Foss 1997, 98–99). Stories survive of a group, the Thafurs, who were said to feed on the dead bodies of the enemy. (Tannahil 1975, 37). The crusaders captured Antioch on the Syrian coast in June 1099 and slaughtered its inhabitants. They stormed Jerusalem and raised the cross over the city. They killed every Muslim they could find and burned the Jews in their own synagogue. The massacre at Jerusalem was not merely a sponta- neous act of violence but planned and deliberate, the result of settled policy. It had been determined that Jerusalem was to become a Christian city. Infidels of whatever stripe were to be cleansed (Payes 1985, 102–103). The papal revolution that had sought to unify Europe under the direction of the Church had reached its logical conclusion:

> This was holy slaughter. This was what the Crusade was about. They had become in their own eyes the instruments of the Last Judgment, and if they killed Christians as well as Jews, so be it. (BBC, *The Crusades* 1995)

The invasion was successful partly because the crusaders had arrived at a moment of disunity in the Islamic world, which had a tradition of strong monarchies. The crusaders set up four Christian principalities in Asia Minor. The pope who had set the European invasion in motion died before learning that the city of Jerusalem was in Christian hands. Christian possession of Jerusalem lasted until 1187, when the Muslim leader Saladin recaptured the city. Two subsequent crusades made little headway against united Muslim forces, but the lust for conquest continued unabated.

In 1202 Pope Innocent III launched the Fourth Crusade. Instead of going to the Levant as the pope ordered, his army sailed to Constantinople to assist deposed emperor Isaac Angelus in regaining his throne. The emperor had promised to supply gold and soldiers for the Crusade. The crusaders restored him to his throne, but the citizens of Constantinople soon revolted under his rule. When Isaac Angelus died soon afterward, the crusaders proceeded to seize Constantinople for themselves. They sacked the city, installed their own emperor, and went on to conquer Greece and Thrace. The quantity of booty carried off from Constantinople was among the greatest seized by a conquering army from one place up to that time. As far as the record shows, not a single Muslim was killed during the Fourth Crusade.

After conquest by the crusaders, the Byzantine Empire, which the original crusaders had pledged to rescue, virtually ceased to exist. In 1261, however, the remnants of the Eastern Empire under

Michael Palaeologus drove the Latin Christians from Constantinople. The Byzantine Empire was reestablished but was seriously weakened and never recovered its former strength.

It is difficult to give a date for the end of the Crusades. Battles continued between Islamic and Christian forces. It took some two centuries for the Islamic world to produce a warrior culture and a religious fanaticism as fierce and as cruel as the armies of the pope. Although Western historians remember Saladin as the hero of the forces of Islam, many Arabs remember King Baybers, who led Egyptian fighters in massacres of Christians at Acre and other places and drove the Europeans out of their country.

The wars for the Holy Land brought many unanticipated and unwanted changes. The style of warfare, for example, changed. Responding to the Arab style of fighting, the crusaders reintroduced the crossbow. The Arab fighters preferred composite bows fired from fast horses in skirmishes to pitched battles and hand-to-hand combat, and in that kind of warfare the crossbow was a useful weapon. Soon armor-piercing crossbow arrows were developed that could unhorse a man at a hundred yards, a development that boded ill for the future of the European knight.

For more than a century prior to the First Crusade, commerce had been gaining momentum in western Europe, from Scandinavia to Italy. Venice, a north Italian city on the Adriatic Sea, was a leader in this movement. Originally founded by Italians fleeing the invasion of the Huns, Venice had for centuries been a western outpost of the Byzantine Empire. In the eighth century it had become increasingly independent, while remaining a strong trading partner with Constantinople. Venice and the other commercial cities of Italy profited greatly from the Crusades and by the twelfth century dominated the economy of the Byzantine Empire. They shipped foodstuffs and materials to the crusader states, ferried pilgrims and munitions to the east, and returned carrying eastern products. Other western European cities, especially Marseilles and Barcelona, joined in the prosperity.

The Crusades accelerated the desire for more products from the east. Silks, porcelain, and other manufactures were sought from the Far East, and spices from the islands of the Indian Ocean were in demand. Europeans acquired a practically insatiable desire for sugar and even established plantations on islands in the southern Mediterranean, a development that would later provide a model for colonial expansion. European cities that bordered the Adriatic or Mediterranean Seas joined in this commerce and grew wealthy. This growing trade had a revolutionary impact on the West.

The twelfth century saw a social revolution that was an indirect result of the increase in commerce stimulated in part by the Crusades. The rise of trade brought a shift in population from medieval fiefdoms to towns and cities. Peasants left the feudal manors to become laborers and artisans in the cities and towns where a new middle class grew in wealth and influence. Newly arrived townsmen resisted the imposition of laws and customs requiring payment in labor and exacting the services required under the ancient laws of the manorial system. They demanded and received charters that included a list of rights. The rise of towns and classes of people not part of the manorial system signaled a decline in the power of feudalism. When the lords of the manor began accepting money in lieu of services, customs and relationships that had been in place for centuries began to give way.

The Crusades also stimulated renewed and intensified interest in Greek and Roman philosophy. The works of Aristotle became more available to Church scholars in the twelfth century. Thomas Aquinas and other churchmen worked to create a synthesis of Aristotelian logic and Christian dogma in the works of St. Thomas Aquinas in the thirteenth century. The philosophers who tried to combine Christian thought with ancient Greek philosophy were called the "schoolmen" and the tradition they created "scholasticism." Aquinas' work was eventually approved by the Church and "scholastic" thinking remains a foundation of Roman Catholic doctrine to this day.

At about this time another chapter was being played out in the history of Europe and the Roman Catholic Church. Although the Church had long fought the twin threats of heresy and magic (witchcraft or sorcery), between 1450 and 1750 the campaign intensified. During this period a court of Inquisition was set up to prosecute people who uttered unorthodox beliefs or were believed to practice witchcraft. Books were carefully scrutinized for any hint of heresy, and both authors and publishers could be imprisoned and subjected to unspeakable tortures. The theory of witchcraft derived from Christian doctrine. Since God had departed from the earth, God's powers were presumed to have departed, except for those specifically designated to representatives of the Church through various rites. People who appealed to any power except through the Church were thought to be appealing to the forces of darkness.

Thus were faith healers and herbal medicine healers thought to be in league with evil spirits and even the Devil, and accusations against these people became more and more frequent. Following the great plague of the sixth century, the Church assumed authority over all healing practices, including the procedure known as bleeding. Ordinary people—usually women—who had practiced traditional methods of healing using herbs, powders, or potions were accused of practicing magic. Since they had not gone to the Church for the power to heal, it was clear to the authorities that they were going somewhere else.

The fear of magic extended beyond the healing arts to everyday relationships in the community. If, for example, a person experienced some misfortune after refusing to give alms to a beggar, the beggar could be blamed and accused of using witchcraft to exact revenge. A person with whom one had quarreled could be blamed for an illness in the family, a crop failure, or the death of livestock. Accusations could be built around a limitless set of possibilities. The accused would be arrested, examined before the Inquisition, and tortured to extract a confession. Confessions were extracted in a very high percentage of these interrogations as peoples' limbs were literally torn from their sockets. In certain European castles the instruments of interrogation have been preserved and include many of the most ingenious inventions of the age. These instruments, some of which are still in use by governments around the world today, were capable of inflicting excruciating pain while keeping the victim alive and, for the most part, conscious. The accused were expected to admit to specific actions such as applying a powder or ointment to their brooms or chairs to enable them to fly in the middle of the night to a secret meeting in the forest with other witches. These covens required their adherents to forsake Christ and to engage in a variety of carnal acts with animals and other people. The accused were required under torture to name other witches, who were then arrested and subjected to the same interrogation to discover more witches. In the end, many were burned at the stake or executed in other ways, and their property was often forfeited to the Church or the state..

No one knows how many people were killed in the witch hunts in Europe, but some writers have suggested that the numbers could have been in the millions. There is no question that the numbers were high. Unmarried or widowed older women, especially if they owned property, were especially victimized. For three hundred years, beginning in the mid-fifteenth century, witch hunts and the torture and murder of large numbers of people who were perceived as undesirables was a characteristic feature of European life.

Bibliography

BBC documentary. "Crusades: Pilgrims in Arms," 1995.

Billings, Malcolm. *The Cross and the Crescent: A History of the Crusades.* New York: Sterling, 1987.

Boussard, Jacques. *The Civilization of Charlemagne.* New York: McGraw-Hill, 1968.

Comnena, Anna. *Anne Comnene Aleiade: Regne de lempereur Alexis I Comnene (1081-1181).* Ed. and trans. Bernard Leib, 3 vols. Paris: Societé d'edition les belles lettres, 1937–1945.

Foss, Michael. *People of the First Crusade.* New York: Ancade, 1977.

"Fulcher of Chartes" (trans. Frances Rita Ryan). In Harold S. Fink, ed., *A History of the Expedition to Jerusalem, 1095–1127,* Book I. Knoxville: University of Tennessee Press, 1969.

Hoffman, Valerie. *Sufism, Mystics, and Saints in Modern Egypt.* Columbia, S.C.: University of South Carolina Press, 1995.

Jacob, H. E. *Six Thousand Years of Bread: Its Holy and Unholy History.* New York: Doubleday, Doran & Co., 1944.

Lucas, Henry S. *A Short History of Civilization.* New York: McGraw-Hill Book Co., 1943.

Payes, Robert. *The Dream and the Tomb: A History of the Crusades.* New York: Stein & Day, 1985.

Tannahill, Reay. *Flesh and Blood: A History of the Cannibal Complex.* New York: Stein & Day, 1975.

Thatcher, O. J., and E. H. McNeal. *A Source Book for Mediaeval History.* New York: Charles Scribner's Sons, 1905.

SIX
Behind the Veil
of Discovery

Was all the bloodshed and deceit—from Columbus to
Cortes, Pizarro, the Puritans—a necessity for the human
race to progress from savagery to civilization? Was Morrison* right in burying the story of genocide inside a more
important argument of human progress? Perhaps a more
persuasive argument can be made—as it was made by
Stalin when he killed peasants for industrial progress in
the Soviet Union, as it was made by Churchill explaining
the bombings of Dresden and Hamburg, and Truman
explaining Hiroshima.

Howard Zinn, *A Peoples' History of the United States*

Historians have called the three-century period beginning about
1300 the "Renaissance," a term that means "renewal" and refers
to the revitalization of Western culture with conscious reference
to the classical civilizations of the Mediterranean. The changes
that first supplied the momentum for this movement, however,
came in the form of economic developments that had begun
prior to the Crusades. Spurred by the need to transport and
supply crusaders, Italian cities expanded trade dramatically and

---

*Samuel Elliot Morrison was a renowned historian who wrote *Admiral of the
Ocean Seas: A Life of Christopher Columbus* (1942), a book until recently considered by many to be the definitive biography of Christopher Columbus. As Zinn
points out, Morrison's account ignores historical documentation of the savage
treatment of the Indians.

began the process that was to create a new economic, political, and social order and transform European culture. Increased trade created a climate in which visible wealth and the introduction of exotic goods and "foreign" ideas led to dissatisfaction and mounting pressures for change.

New technologies provided the means to implement it. Silver miners introduced new techniques for extracting ore from rock formations; these innovations were soon applied to other metals, including copper. Around 1300 A.D. gunpowder was invented, and within a generation came the introduction of cannon. Europe was fortunately positioned for this event. Casting large bronze bells for churches was a highly developed art, and the technology proved applicable to the development and production of cannon just as more metal was becoming available for such purposes. Bronze, which had forged a military age in the ancient world, was about to make a second significant appearance in Euope's military history.

Developments in both the architecture of defenses and the technology of cannon manufacture marked the beginning of a pattern of warfare that produced an unending arms race. The first cannon made a lot of noise but did minimal damage. As the art of both making and using cannon developed, the technology progressed from boulders to cast-iron cannonballs, which were much more dense and did more damage. Earthen walls proved an effective defense against cannonballs, and in response weapons manufacturers built bigger and better cannon, which were in turn countered by stronger defensive walls. When cannon were improved enough to breach walls that had made the world reasonably safe for centuries, a new strategy developed: defenders acquired cannon of their own and fired back at the attackers.

By the mid-fourteenth century the modern era was fast approaching, spurred to a significant degree by a radical new development in maritime technology. The design of ships had remained relatively unchanged from the time of the Phoenicians. Although sails had been invented, the boats that carried the goods of commerce in the fourteenth century were still propelled primarily by oars, just as they had been a thousand years earlier. These boats were seaworthy, could travel long distances, and were adequate to handle the increased commerce—except for one thing. Increased commerce created an irresistible urge for socially unacceptable forms of plunder, especially piracy.

Italian merchants seized the opportunity to expand the commercial shipping that had been a traditional source of wealth, but piracy posed a grave threat to their unarmed vessels of commerce. Cannon offered a hope of defending their ships, but only if a major technological problem could be solved. Cannon could not be placed near the water because to do so would displace too many oarsmen. Nor could the big guns be placed on the upper deck above the oarsmen because the cannon would make the vessel top heavy and create the danger of capsizing. The answer was to replace the oarsmen with gunners, but how would the ship be propelled?

Of course the answer to that problem—sails—had already been invented. By mid-century maritime laboratories in Italy's Po Valley were feverishly working on the problem of creating fast, effective sail-powered vessels. We do not see true sailing vessels capable of crossing the great seas until the development of commerce necessitated the invention of armed vessels capable of defending their cargo. At around this time the compass, an invention of the East, arrived in Europe, and in time other instruments would be developed that would give ships' captains a fix on their position and make navigation more reliable. In developing a maritime technology that could move cargo quickly and efficiently, Italian merchants grasped the opportunity to create unprecedented wealth.

Needing to recruit people who were skilled in the use of the cannon, merchants made arrangements with local princes to use military men for this purpose. Thus very early in this period, commerce was militarized, and the entity that was to become the state became the equivalent of a business partner with the merchants. The marriage of commerce and the military generated money to pay for guns, which cleared the path to a lucrative trade. The profits from trade supplied money for more guns, which could be used to strengthen the then-embryonic nation-states.

These conditions gradually brought the demise of most of the remaining tiny independent principalities that had developed under feudalism. To survive in this new environment, a prince needed successful merchant partners and agreements that would bring wealth to buy defensive and offensive weaponry. As governments invested more to expand world trade and then to protect their goods and their access to resources, the arms race accelerated and the level of violence in Europe increased, with stronger powers dominating and incorporating the weaker. Commerce and warfare, or the threat of armed violence, would become the founding partnership in the production of modernity, a collaboration that continues, in one guise or another, to the present.

Because of increased contact with the Near East during the Crusades, the classic works of Greek and Roman secular philosophy once again became available in Italy. The Italian Francesco Petrarca (1304–1374), known as Petrarch, became an avid scholar of classic philosophy and endeavored to reconcile it with his Christian beliefs. He and other scholars formulated a philosophy that became instrumental in breaking the binding power of medieval theology on European thought, together with the dominance of the philosophy, art, and letters of the Middle Ages. An influential scholar and poet, Petrarch rejected the Church-dominated otherworldliness of the Middle Ages, while retaining his Christian faith. He supported classical secularism, especially Cicero's insistence that individuals have an obligation to cultivate their human faculties through exposure to literature, music, and other secular arts.

Cicero had observed that Socrates had brought philosophy down from the heavens to earth. The spirit of Socrates had been absent for about one thousand years in the Latin West. Its new incarnation, which would eventually be termed secular humanism, restored the ancient Greek pursuit of the ideal to Western culture. It was the first step toward the Enlightenment of the eighteenth century and a systematic challenge to orthodox Christian dogma. Humanism promoted belief in the individual as a being endowed with reason and personal responsibility. It endorsed a confidence in the individual and urged people to think for themselves and depend on themselves. The human being, not the Church, began to be the measure of human life.

Humanists such as Petrarch looked back on classical Greece as a time when the great ideas about virtue and truth flourished. Petrarch believed that people living in those ancient cultures enjoyed privileges and the stability of a rational existence and that the best way to recapture their wisdom was to read their works in the original language. Following the teachings of classical philosophy could bring about a transformation in ethics and morals that offered hope for a more perfect world.

Initially only Latin versions of the classics were available. Works in the original Greek found their way to scholars in Italy with the arrival of Manual Chrysoloras, a Byzantine Greek who possessed a thorough knowledge of both the language and its classic works. He taught Greek at the University at Florence, and thereafter knowledge of Greek and ancient Greek thought spread rapidly among the educated classes in western Europe. Scholars scoured Europe's cathedral and monastic libraries, where they found rare copies of classic works that, although largely ignored, had survived the centuries since the collapse of the Roman Empire.

The humanistic movement brought the writings and ideas of the ancient Greeks and Romans to western European culture and stimulated one of the great cultural movements in Western history. With this movement came the idea that education was an essential part of what formed the cultured individual's personality. An Italian gentleman was valued not only for his skill in the use of arms for but courteousness, grace, and the ability to converse about learned topics.

Conflicts between the Church and secular authorities continued in the fourteenth century. Following an attempt to assassinate Pope Boniface VIII in a dispute over whether princes could levy taxes on Church property, Boniface's successor, Clement V, a Frenchman, moved the papacy to Avignon for his personal safety. Removal to France brought a decline in the prestige of the papacy. It was considered, first of all, to have become a tool of the French king. Second, the French popes were preoccupied with expanding the Church's wealth through numerous schemes to bring in revenue. As historian Barbara Tuchman observed, "Everything the Church had or was . . . was for sale" (1978, 26).

The moral corruption of the Church so disgusted scholars like Petrarch that it speeded the process of breaking the Church's stranglehold on intellectual life. Petrarch described the bishops at Avignon as "rich, insolent, and rapacious." The earthy tales in Giovanni Bocaccio's *Decameron* depict clerical celibacy as a joke because many priests and friars were known seducers of women. While the Church devoted itself to accumulating wealth, it opposed many forms of economic activity carried on outside the Church, pronouncing them worldly and not conducive to salvation. The Church's wishes were incorporated into secular law throughout Italy. To ensure that no one gained an advantage over anyone else, commercial law prohibited innovation in tools or techniques, underselling below a fixed price, working late by artificial light, employing extra apprentices or wives and underage children, and advertising wares or praising them to the detriment of others (Tuchman 1978, 37).

The proscribed activities were, of course, exactly those that were fueling the growing wealth in Italy that was needed to support the developing Renaissance and cultural revolution. The activities necessary to function in the rising capitalist culture of the time rendered people sinners in their business life and helped increase cynicism about the theories and practices of the Church, which seemed to take every opportunity to absolve the individual of sin for a fee—by selling papal indulgences.

Despite corruption, however, obedience to the Church was still enforced, as persecutions increased and relations between Church and state remained complex. The Knights Templar were a quasi-religious order of knights who had served directly under the authority of the pope during the Crusades. They were a powerful force and, because of their great wealth, became bankers to the papacy. They remained powerful even after the Crusades. In 1307, King Philip the Fair of France denounced the Templars, accusing them of crimes such as sorcery. Philip was in need of money and may also have been genuinely afraid of their power throughout Europe. Coercing Pope Clement V, who was French, into going along with his plan, Philip arrested all the Templars in France, seized their properties, and caused them to be tortured into making confessions. Many were burned at the stake. Philip prevailed on the pope to suppress the order throughout Europe. These events would become a precedent for the witchcraft trials a century later. In 1313, the Grand Master of the Templars, Jacques de Molay, uttered a prophecy of doom on those responsible for the persecutions, as the flames engulfed him at the stake. Whether by coincidence or divine retribution, within less than a year both Clement V and Philip the Fair were dead. Philip's three sons died without supplying a male heir to the throne, leaving a power vacuum that triggered a war with the English (the Hundred Years' War, 1337–1455) that would last for several generations.

Petrarch, like his contemporary Bocaccio, lived during the time of the great plague (1347–1350). In 1347, a Genoese ship sailing from the Crimea arrived in Sicily with dead and dying men aboard. The bubonic plague, later known as the Black Death, swept through Europe with devastating force. It is estimated to have killed a third of the whole population. In some places, entire populations vanished, either destroyed by the plague or left with too few people to carry on. Settlements were abandoned. Terror was universal; many believed that the Black Death was sent by God as a punishment for humanity's sins.

In 1429, as the war between the English and French continued, a young peasant girl who came to be called Joan of Arc (circa 1412–1431) inspired French troops to attack and drive away the English during a siege of Orleans. She was later captured, tried by a court of Inquisition as a witch and heretic, and burned at the stake in 1431. In the Middle Ages, people gave loyalty to individuals, not to nations. Joan of Arc gave inspiration to nationalism in France. The Hundred Years' War, which had begun as a feudal war over succession to the throne of France, ended up a national war that fueled patriotism in both England and France.

This long war also resulted in the French monarch obtaining the power to levy taxes, which greatly enhanced the power of the throne. French monarchs set out to subdue the feudal lords and to unify the country, and though France was not yet an absolute monarchy, by the end of the fifteenth century, it was on the road to becoming a true nation-state.

The city of Constantinople had withstood all assaults—except that of the Fourth Crusade—for over a millennium, but the Turks finally breached its walls with cannon in 1453. The fall of Constantinople signaled the end of access to direct overland trade routes to Asia, giving middlemen a virtual monopoly on access to the lucrative trade in spices, silks, china, and other goods. This situation added urgency to the European search for a water route to Asia.

In the fourteenth century, Italian merchants and their Byzantine partners had dominated trade, but other members of Europe's Mediterranean community were anxious to become players in these developments. By the fifteenth century, the elements necessary to trade with the east were present in Europe: a lucrative market environment that provided wealth for capital ventures; a level of technology that could support exploration; governments ready to mobilize the resources of the state—both military and commercial—on behalf of commerce. The Turkish capture of Constantinople added the necessary incentive.

Portugal launched the earliest and most ambitious effort to find a route to the Orient by sea. It began with explorations along the coast of Africa and in 1415 conquered Muslims at Ceuta in Morocco. A Portuguese ship, under the command of Captain Lanzarote, was exploring the African coast when a storm caught his ship and drove it into the Atlantic. He found himself off the coast of the island in the Canary Islands that now bears his name. These islands had been settled many centuries earlier by a North African people known as the Gaunche. At that time there was an estimated population of 80,000 people on the islands.

Spain had acquired rights to these islands under laws meant to govern the crusaders. With some help from France, Spain began a military invasion in 1492; it met with heavy resistance that lasted until around 1496. The first black African slaves were delivered by Lanzarote to Lisbon in 1441, and shortly thereafter the pope issued a statement offering his blessings to the project of kidnapping, murder, and various other activities undertaken to obtain more captives. The Portuguese colonized other Atlantic islands, such as Porto Santo and Madeira, beginning in 1418. The colonizers caused severe environmental damage by introducing nonnative species and destroying forest cover, and Porto Santo became a veritable desert. Portugal would claim a considerable overseas empire, eventually including lands along the African coast, in Asia, and other islands in the Atlantic.

European colonization of the Atlantic islands would serve as a kind of practice run for other colonization, especially in the Caribbean. The Gaunches were invaded and the Canary Islands conquered because, by the rules of the day, nations and the boundaries of nations were determined primarily by military force and economic power. A people who did not possess the economic resources, technology, and fighting skills to protect themselves from attack were considered fair game, especially if they were not Christian (Davis 1966, 100.) A papal brief issued to Portugal by Nicholas V permitted and justified the enslavement of non-Christians:

> [W]e grant to you by these present documents, with our
> Apostolic Authority, full and free permission to invade,
> search out, capture and subjugate the Saracens and pagans
> and any other unbelievers and enemies of Christ wherever
> they may be, as well as their kingdoms, duchies, counties,
> principalities, and other property . . . and to reduce their
> persons into perpetual slavery . . . (Brief Dom Diversas,
> 16 June 1452, quoted in Maxwell 1975, 53.)

A similar grant was directed to the kings of Spain in 1493 (Maxwell 1975, 55). This grant of license to confiscate lands and people coincided with the influx of black captives from Africa, some of whom were Muslim, and nearly all of whom were non-Christian when captured. It became customary that slaves or their descendants who converted to Christianity were not freed. The deprivation of rights would be extended to indigenous peoples across the globe and across the centuries.

The indigenous Gaunches had no rights under any rules known to the Europeans. They could be killed or captured, their lands seized, and their bodies forced into slavery without any justification being required. The colonization of the Canaries, including the destruction of the Gaunche society and its peoples, was carried out by European military forces and not as a process of settlement. The Gaunches fought back bravely, retreating to mountainous ground and dropping heavy rocks on their tormentors. They gained the respect of the aggressors, especially the Spanish. Final conquest required almost the whole century and ended when an epidemic wiped out most of the remaining defenders—a hint of what was in store for the indigenous peoples of the Western Hemisphere.

Guanche slaves were transported to Madeira, where they were used to create infrastructure for the development of the island by digging irrigation ditches. Sugar had become popular during the Crusades, and before long there appeared on Madeira sugar plantations, mills, slave trading, and a cane-processing system. All the trappings of the modern world were being produced before Columbus set sail, including a good sampling of its future horrors. Slavery as invented here was distinct from the way it had been practiced in Europe in the past. For the first time, the purpose of slavery was to generate a product (or products) for an emerging market economy, and it was more tightly woven into the fabric of the commercial interests of the state. Henceforth slaves would raise export crops, and slavery thus became one of the midwives at the birth of the modern world economy.

The Gaunche died in great numbers from the combination of plagues and the very harsh conditions imposed by the Portuguese and were in fact driven to extinction as a distinct people. They were soon replaced by slaves from the African coast. By 1455 Madeira was exporting sugar in such quantities that the island became the most economically successful European colony and made a major contribution to financing Portuguese explorations. All of this was in place at mid-century when Constantinople, weakened more than two centuries earlier when it was sacked by Christian crusaders, finally fell to the Turks.

Christopher Columbus was born in the Italian city-state of Genoa around 1451, the son of a middle-class wool weaver. During the summer of 1476 he went to sea in one of a fleet of five ships bound for England to buy wool and sell wine and other goods. Somewhere off the coast of Portugal this little group of ships was attacked by privateers from France. Rather than surrender their cargo to the enemy, the Genoans set it ablaze, and Columbus swam to shore, where he joined a colony of Genoan immigrants in Lisbon. Here he met and married a woman of noble but modest estate, Felipa Perestrella Moniz. Columbus was soon immersed in the Portuguese sailing culture, associating with Europe's most experienced and daring explorers.

He visited many places in the Atlantic aboard Portuguese ships, including Africa, the British Isles, and, he claimed, Iceland, and hundreds of miles beyond that, out into the Atlantic. He made a living, apparently a comfortable one, as a sugar merchant and map maker, but he had dreams and a driving ambition that would cost him his little fortune, drive him heavily into debt, and carve his name in the annals of history.

Columbus floated his initial proposals to sail west to Asia to King John II of Portugal, probably in 1483 or 1484. The Portuguese king was intrigued, but his court persuaded him to launch in secret the expedition Columbus had proposed and to leave the Genoan out of it. This expedition sailed into the deep Atlantic but found nothing. When Columbus heard about this betrayal, he took his proposal to other courts. He had a problem finding a Crown whose advisers would agree with his calculations about the distance to Asia from Europe sailing west. Ancient Greek mathematicians had predicted the world was about 25,000 miles in circumference, and they were about right. Columbus calculated it at around 3,000 to 4,000 miles less. If the earth were 25,000 miles in circumference, the distance to Asia would be some 7,000 miles. The ships of this time could not cross an ocean 7,000 miles wide because without fresh food and water, the crews would perish. The wooden barrels used to store water could not keep it potable long enough. From this history we can deduce that unbending determination and good fortune—up to a point—were guiding his destiny.

Columbus was granted an audience before the Spanish Crown on January 28, 1486, and his proposal was handed over to Father Hernándo de Talavera for further study and recommendations. The following spring he was informed that Spain was completely preoccupied with war against the Muslims and had no time for such a venture at that time. The Spanish did, however, grant him money to stay in Spain until their attention could turn to such matters. While he was waiting, he met Beatruz Enriquez de Arana and had a son by her in 1488. In late 1491, in a report that incorporated the wisdom of the day, Talavera wrote a strongly worded rejection of Columbus' proposal and the idea behind it. King Ferdinand and Queen Isabella acknowledged the report but stated that they would make a decision at the end of the war.

Granada fell to the Spanish in January 1492, and Columbus was called before the court and informed that his project had definitely been rejected. He made preparations to approach the French Crown, but before he could reach France, King Ferdinand's treasurer, one Luis de Santangel, pleaded with the queen on behalf of Columbus' proposal, offering to fund it himself if they refused to do so. Queen Isabella relented and Columbus got the money.

In European history 1492 was a watershed year. The Moors were expelled from Spain and, as always happened during a crusade, the Jews had their property confiscated. They were forced to embrace Christianity or be expelled from the country. The Spanish Inquisition was gaining momentum. Columbus sailed for the Atlantic Islands and beyond to the Caribbean. Of course, he did not know he had arrived in a land unknown to his forefathers, and his early impressions carry an appropriate account of astonishment at the unknown and unexpected. Columbus' arrival at the Leeward Islands of the Caribbean can properly be called an encounter, but the observation by Columbus that the natives knew nothing of European arms and that a few Spaniards could conquer them and make them do as they wished was, of course, prophetic. The subsequent voyages of Columbus produced a story that was little short of horrific.

The Spanish embodied the full development of European military power in 1492. They had at their disposal the product of three thousand years of military development: standing armies, armor, armored cavalry, pikesmen, cannon, dogs, swords, crossbows, shields, firearms. The Spanish were well organized for conquest and plunder. Europe's population had rebounded from the plague of the fourteenth century and the Continent was full of men apparently eager to try their hand at war. As Columbus' ships sailed westward, clouds of war were gathering over the Continent that would rage for more than one hundred fifty years. By the time these wars ended, the hegemony of the Catholic Church would be severely diminished and the modern nation-state would be emerging.

In 1492, after more than a month at sea, Columbus' crew spotted land at what turned out to be one of the Leeward Islands in the West Indies. He immediately set about naming every geological point of interest—islands, rivers, mountains—after Spanish people, places, and mythology. He then took "possession" of the land in the name of the Crown of Spain, an act that carried with it both elements of a claim to sovereignty and an allegation of a property right. With the papal bull of 1493, Pope Alexander VI granted Spain sovereignty over all such lands.

Native people came out to greet the ships, and Columbus described them as generally young, well built, and handsome, without clothing, without iron, and with no knowledge of religion, as far as he could determine. In short, most of his description was about how they were not like Europeans. He would spend a little more than three months among the Indians on this first journey, and his log records show that he thought they were a gentle and innocent people who did not murder or steal (again, apparently denoting how they were unlike Europeans).

Columbus' log is filled with references to the expectation of finding gold, and he soon did find some Natives who had small quantities of it used as jewelry. He started rounding people up to be sent as slaves to Spain, the first order of booty from the islands, and in time he captured thousands more to work the mines and fields the Spaniards set up. He demanded that every Indian provide "a hawk's bill" of gold every month. Those who complied were given a token that they would be required to present upon demand. Failure to possess a token resulted in punishment, the most infamous of which was to have a hand or other body part chopped off by Spanish steel. There are old woodcuts showing this being done.

Indians were rounded up and forced into what can only be called slavery. They were worked to exhaustion. The men were separated from the women, and husbands and wives were allowed to see each other only rarely. Women were routinely raped and taken as concubines by the Spanish. Indians were punished with impromptu amputations of hands or feet at the slightest provocation. Dogs were used to tear Indians apart, sometimes for amusement, and to hunt down the large numbers who ran away to the mountains, where they were hunted and where they starved.

The cruelty of the Spanish was boundless. Their literature includes graphic pictures, apparently intended to be used to instruct others how to inflict the most horrible pain and to cause it to last as long as possible. Mass public executions were the order of the day. A priest, Bartolomé de las Casas, exclaimed that when he arrived, of the eight million Indians originally estimated to inhabit the island of Hispaniola, only 60,000 remained. The numbers may be exaggerated (there were almost certainly far fewer Indians on Hispaniola to begin with), and other estimates range between 100,000 and 1,000,000. If the numbers are exaggerated, the horrors are not.

Many deaths can be attributed to the conditions imposed by the Spanish, not simply to executions. It is estimated that some 200,000 indigenous people died in the four large Caribbean islands in a quarter of a century "from overwork, fear, and loss of faith in the future, not from Spanish steel" (Thomas 1993, 69). Indians died in great numbers, exhausted from the labors demanded by the Spanish. Because most of the Indians who had raised food were forced to produce gold, near-famine conditions prevailed. Women could not provide milk for their babies, and few babies survived. The islands dominated by the Spanish became huge death camps where unarmed Indians were subjected to extreme cruelties, humiliation, and inhumane death. The extent of this holocaust can hardly be imagined, but it was well documented and has been commented upon repeatedly to this day. On island after island, within a generation, the Indian populations were driven to extinction, or near extinction, under the Spanish yoke. Most of this happened prior to the arrival of viral disease in the second decade of the sixteenth century. There is little disagreement about the motive for all this. "Let us be truthful," wrote Peter Martyr to the pope, "and add that the craze for gold was the cause of their destruction" (Thomas 1993, 68).

There were rebellions. An Indian group in Hispaniola held out against the Spanish until the latter granted them a peace treaty. Most Indians were not so successful. There was no successful Indian resistance in Puerto Rico or Cuba, and a Spanish expedition wiped out a whole Indian nation in Florida.

A system of great estates was set up under Spanish noblemen in order to grow export crops, similar to the systems used on the Atlantic islands. The preferred crop was, once again, sugar. As the Indians died off, slaves were imported in increasingly large numbers from Africa. African slaves proved more durable than the Indians, but no one should underestimate the horror of that slave trade. Since that time, no book of fiction or movie depiction of horror has ever been produced that matched the reality of the historical record.

When the Spanish entered an Indian village, they carried before them a document called *El Requerimiento*, originally written by the Jesuit priest Dr. Palacios Rubios. A priest read the *Requerimiento* to the Indians, in a language few or none of them could understand:

> On the part of the King, Don Fernando, and of Dona Juana, his daughter, Queen of Castile and Leon, subduers of the barbarous nations, we their servants notify and

make known to you, as best we can, that the Lord our God, living and eternal, created the heaven and the earth, and one man and one woman, of whom you and we, and all the men of the world, were and are descendants, and all those who come after us. But, on account of the multitude which has sprung from this man and woman in the five thousand years since the world was created, it was necessary that some men should go one way and some another, and that they should be divided into many kingdoms and provinces, for in one alone they could not be sustained.

Of all these nations God our Lord gave charge to one man, called St. Peter, that he should be Lord and Superior of all the men in the world, that all should obey him, and that he should be the head of the whole human race, wherever men should live, and under whatever law, sect, or belief they should be; and he gave him the world for his kingdom and jurisdiction.

And he commanded him to place his seat in Rome, as the spot most fitting to rule the world from; but also he permitted him to have his seat in any other part of the world, and to judge and govern all Christians, Moors, Jews, Gentiles, and all other sects. This man was called Pope, as if to say, Admirable Great Father and Governor of men. The men who lived in that time obeyed that St. Peter, and took him for Lord, King, and Superior of the universe . . . so also have they regarded the others who after him have been elected to the pontificate, and so it has been continued even until now, and will continue till the end of the world.

One of these Pontiffs, who succeeded in the room of that St. Peter in that dignity and seat which I have mentioned as Lord of the world, made donation of these isles and Terra Firma to the aforesaid King and Queen and to their successors, our lords, with all that there are in these territories, as is contained in certain writings which passed upon the subject as aforesaid, which you can see if you wish.

So their Highnesses are kings and lords of these islands and land of Terra Firma by virtue of this donation; and some islands, and indeed almost all those to whom this has been notified, have received and served their Highnesses, as lords and kings, in the way that subjects ought to do, with good will, without any resistance, immediately, without delay, when they were informed of the aforesaid facts. And also they received and obeyed the priests whom their Highnesses sent to preach to them and to teach them our sacred faith; and all these, of their own free will, without any reward or condition, have become Christians, and are so, and their Highnesses have joyfully and benignantly received them, and also have commanded them to be treated as their subjects and vassals; and you too are held and obliged to do the same. Wherefore, as best we can, we ask and require you that you consider what we have said to you, and that you take the time that shall be necessary to understand and deliberate upon it, and that you acknowledge the Church for Lady and Superior of the whole world and the high priest called Pope, and in his name the King and Queen Dona Juana our lords, in his places, as superiors and lords and kings of these islands and this Terra Firma by virtue of the said donation, and that you consent and give place that these religious fathers should declare and preach to you the aforesaid.

If you do so, you will do well, and that which you are obliged to do to their Highnesses, and we in their name, shall receive you in all love and charity, and shall leave you your wives, and your children, and your hands free without servitude, that you may do with them and with yourselves freely that which you like and think best, and they shall not compel you to turn Christian, unless you yourselves, when informed of the truth, should wish to be converted to our sacred Catholic faith, as almost all the inhabitants of the rest of the islands have done. And, besides this, their Highnesses award you many privileges and exemptions and will grant you many benefits.

But, if you do not do this, and maliciously make delay in it, I certify to you that, with the help of God, we shall powerfully enter into your country, and shall make war against you in all ways and manners that we can, and shall subject you to the yoke and obedience of the Church and of their Highnesses; we shall take you and your wives and your children, and shall make slaves of them, and as such shall sell and dispose of them as their Highnesses may command; and we shall take away your goods, and shall do you all the mischief and damage that we can, as to vassals who do not obey and refuse to receive their lord, and resist and contradict him; and we protest that the deaths and losses which shall accrue from this are your fault, and not that of their Highnesses, or ours, nor of these cavaliers who come with us. And that we have said this to you and made this Requisition, we request the notary here present to give us his testimony in writing, and we ask to rest who are present that they should be witnesses of this Requisition. (*Conquerors* 1852, 116ff)

Of all the promises made to the Indians in the course of the conquest, history affirms that the conquerors kept this one. When the Indians failed to comply, the Spanish methodically put them to the sword. Some Indians were exempted from the formality of the reading of the document because of the suspicion of cannibalism and were simply attacked.

There are few documents of conquest that express more clearly the ideology and intentions of the conquerors. Although there is language that suggests the positive intentions of the Spanish (such as the suggestion that Christianity will be voluntary), there were so many exceptions in practice that positive intentions are rendered historically meaningless. The document is a study of the mentality of the Crusades. Sometimes the proclamation was read quietly at night outside the Indian village to be attacked the following day. The exercise of bringing a priest to initiate the process is an example of following the letter but not the spirit of the law, for there is some evidence the "Highnesses" were trying to find a path toward peaceful conversion of the Indians.

Africans suffered a similar fate in their own lands. Raiding parties entered agricultural villages early in the morning and rounded up the people. Babies were typically heaped in a pile, men and women divided up, old people put to one side. Then the babies, small children, and old people were killed. The others were marched to the coast, where they were held in stockades like cattle until the slave ship arrived. This pattern was typical. Anyone who caused any trouble was whipped, beaten, or killed. The women were raped. Once aboard ship, conditions were little better. Cramped into a space the size of a coffin, slaves were forced to cross the oceans chained together in a hold, where they were subjected to unimaginable odors of urine, feces, and vomit. It is said that on the high seas one could smell a slave ship before one could see it. Every day during the crossing the crew went below to gather the dead slaves and throw the bodies overboard. Some slaves committed suicide.

Those who survived were subjected to a regular regimen of torture and coercion. The women were commonly subjected to continuous threat or experience of rape and a variety of tortures intended to produce submission and obedience. No horror movie ever made comes even close to depicting conditions as terrifying as these. The slaves who survived were usually assigned to plantations. The average life span of people who made it to the plantation experience was seven years because of the extremely difficult conditions. In the course of human history there were many periods when people demonstrated what can best be called a depraved indifference to human suffering, but the Spanish treatment of the Indians and the subsequent Spanish, English, and

Dutch treatment of African slaves is surely a textbook example of what that phrase can mean.

The Romans, centuries earlier, were extremely cruel and had done many of the same things—enslaved foreigners and forced them to labor on great estates—but not even the Romans, heartless conquerors of the ancient Mediterranean, had committed crimes against people on this scale.

The first stage of the Conquest was an orgy of kidnapping, torture, rape, coercion, and murder. It would not end there.

Bibliography

Anderson, S. E. *The Black Holocaust for Beginners.* New York: Writers & Readers, 1995.

The Conquerors of the New World and Their Bondsmen: Being a Narrative of the Principle Events Which Led to Negro Slavery in the West Indies and America, N.A. London: William Pickering, 1852. Reprint, Miami: Mnemosyne, 1969.

Crosby, Alfred W. *Ecological Imperialism: the Biological Expansion of Europe, 900–1900.* New York: Cambridge University Press, 1986.

Davidson, Basil. *The African Slave Trade: Precolonial History 1430–1850.* Boston: Little, Brown, 1961.

Davis, David Brian. *The Problem of Slavery in Western Culture.* Ithaca, N.Y.: Cornell University Press, 1966.

Duncan, T. Bentley. *The Atlantic Islands: Madeira, the Azores, and the Cape Verdes in Seventeenth-Century Commerce and Navigation.* Chicago: University of Chicago Press, 1972.

Hayes, Carlton J. H., and Marshall Whithed Baldwin. "History of Europe," vol. 1, to 1648. New York: MacMillan, 1949, 1957.

July, Robert, W. *A History of the African People.* New York: Charles Scribner's Sons, 1970.

Lucas, Henry S. *A Short History of Civilization.* New York: McGraw-Hill Book Co., 1943.

Maxwell, John Francis. *Slavery and the Catholic Church: The History of the Catholic Teaching Concerning the Moral Legitimacy of the Institution of Slavery.* London: Barry Rose, 1975.

Miller, Joseph Calder. *Way of Death: Merchant Capitalism and the Angolan Slave Trade.* Madison: University of Wisconsin Press, 1988.

Thomas, Hugh. *Conquest: Montezuma, Cortez and the Fall of Old Mexico.* New York: Simon & Schuster, 1993.

Todorov, Tzevetan. *The Conquest of America: The Question of the Other.* New York: Harper & Row, 1984.

Tuchman, Barbara W. *A Distant Mirror: The Calamitous 14th Century.* New York: Ballantine Books, 1978.

Zinn, Howard. *A Peoples' History of the United States.* New York: Harper & Row, 1990.

SEVEN
New World Silver and the Origins of the World's Money Supply

> Civil government, so far as it is instituted for the security of property, is in reality instituted for the defense of the rich against the poor, or of those who have some property against those who have none at all.
>
> Adam Smith, *The Wealth of Nations*, 1776

> In *The Wealth of Nations*, Adam Smith discusses at great length the import of American silver in causing worldwide inflation. . . . The new wealth in the hands of Europeans eroded the wealth of all other countries in the world and allowed Europe to expand into an international market system.
>
> Jack Weatherford , *Indian Givers*

European thought in the sixteenth century concerned itself with two types of aspirations: the secular pursuit of the ideal and the religious pursuit of salvation and the Kingdom of God, and within those two streams there were great and devastating disagreements. Both excluded the value of non-European thought. There was little awareness of the contributions of the indigenous peoples of the Americas. If these cultures contributed to the story of humankind, it was in the way trees or whales had done, as resources to be exploited. Even the supporters and sympathizers of the Indians rarely contradicted this sensibility. But in fact indigenous cultures of the Americas played a pivotal role in the evolution of the contemporary world in two obvious ways: through the technology that enabled the extraction of gold and silver, and centuries of agricultural development that provided important foodstuffs and fibers.

Although the conquest of the Caribbean was dramatic and devastating to the Indians, it did not immediately change life in Spain or enrich the Spanish Crown. Spain suffered an economic downturn between 1502 and 1508, and starvation stalked the population. Because it shared in the high profits of the wool trade, the Crown supported the Mesta, the powerful sheep-owners guild, against the peasant farmers, allowing the guild to graze its flocks across their lands. This practice spoiled many cultivated areas that had produced food and reduced the food producers to poverty. The lure of cash crops caused similar dislocations throughout Europe for the next five centuries, especially in England in the sixteenth and eighteenth centuries. Even today the process is continuing, in one guise or another, as peasants or small farmers are driven from the land by a cash crop economy. The resulting widespread hunger, which is not produced by natural calamities such as drought but is socially manufactured, remains the dominant form of hunger in the world.

Years of warfare, an expanding population, and land lost to food production caused widespread poverty in Spain. These conditions spurred ambitious young noblemen, *hidalgos,* with minor titles and little fortune, to consider trying their luck in the newly discovered islands of the Caribbean. Some two hundred ships left Spain between 1506 and 1518. Some of the hidalgos were blessed with an *encomienda,* a grant by the Crown to a conquistador, soldier, or official of a specified number of Indians living in a particular area. The *encomendero* could demand tribute in labor, gold, food, or anything else he desired; in return he was obligated to protect the Indians and instruct them in the Christian faith. In practice, the Indians often starved or died from the harsh conditions of slave labor while the encomendero gained control of their lives, their lands, and their resources for his own enrichment.

Some hidalgos prospered. One man became wealthy in Cuba when one of his Indian slaves found a thirty-five-pound gold nugget, but there was in fact little gold on these islands and few fortunes of note were made. A quarter century after Columbus' initial voyage, the Spanish soldier-colonists had become restless.

In 1517 Francisco Hernández de Córdoba, at the urging of Diego Velázquez, the governor of Cuba, led an expedition to Yucatán. It would be the first contact between Spaniards and Maya since a possible sighting on the water by Columbus, and would prove to be an interesting adventure. Córdoba and his men initiated their exploration of Yucatán with a short skirmish with some Maya, people who had a long history of contact with the Indians of the Caribbean islands and who may have heard about the demonic strangers and their treatment of the islanders. Not every Indian group attacked the Spaniards, however. Córdoba and his men generally tried to treat Indians with a measure of respect and soon found themselves feasting at a village near present-day Provenia. Here the Spanish came into possession of a few samples of Mayan gold, silver, and copper art, all of which would soon serve to stir the imagination of their comrades in arms. The expedition next stopped near Champotón, where they were attacked and driven back. Córdoba would later die of his wounds.

The following April, Juan de Grijalva led four ships from Cuba under orders from Governor Velázquez. Planning to explore the Mexican coast, the expedition reached Yucatán in June. They came upon an island not far from Veracruz, where they found a temple bearing the signs of recent human sacrifice. The Spanish had not known such practices occurred in Mexico, and the discovery sent shivers of fear through the explorers. Shortly after this discovery they met Indians from the mainland bearing gifts of feathered cloaks. The Spanish asked them if they had any gold.

This was the Totonac Nation, a people who chafed under the tribute imposed by the Mexica, although scholars have since determined that the Mexica taxes were not as oppressive as the Totonac presented them. These people provided the Spanish with excellent hospitality, and when the latter said they needed gold, the Totonac brought them some. It was here, among the Totonac, that Grijalva first heard of the Mexica (later Aztec) Empire. Grijalva's expedition returned to Cuba, having established two things: a great monarchy existed on the mainland, and there was gold in Mexico. Governor Velázquez made plans for a further exploratory expedition to Yucatán and Mexico, planning a larger armada, headed by himself, for a later date. For now, he wanted a foray, a kind of scouting party, to provide intelligence for what he hoped would be a subsequent and more glorious enterprise. For this expedition he chose Hernán Cortés, a nobleman who had served as mayor of Santiago, Cuba, and was with Velázquez during the conquest of the island.

About three weeks after Grijalva's return, Cortés and Governor Velázquez signed an agreement that designated Cortés as the leader of the expedition but left at least somewhat vague the scope of the mission. Cortés interpreted the mission as a license to pursue an empire, an objective Velázquez clearly did not approve. Cortés proceeded to make elaborate plans. In mobilizing the expedition, he went about with his followers carrying banners that proclaimed, "Let us follow the sign of the Holy Cross in true faith, for under this sign we will conquer"—a gesture in keeping with the spirit of the Crusades.

Within a month Cortés had six ships and three hundred men mobilized for the effort. Velázquez, realizing Cortés was planning to go far beyond his orders, canceled Cortés' commission and ordered him to stand down. The messenger bringing this news was murdered and Cortés prepared to set sail knowing he was doing so against the wishes of the governor. Velázquez received word of Cortés' imminent departure and arrived in time to confront him from a rowboat in Santiago harbor, but Cortés would not be turned back. He left Cuba in November of 1518 in command of six ships and cruised the Spanish Caribbean recruiting more men and ships until he finally assembled eleven ships and 530 European adventurers.

Cortés was a singularly ambitious man. He began his grand adventure, arguably one of the most remarkable adventures in human history, in Yucatán with a series of skirmishes with Maya

Indians. It is said that this was the first time horses were used in battle in the Americas, and that the Indians at first thought man and beast were a single animal (Thomas 1993, 169). Following a battle at Potonchán in Yucatán, a chief gave the Spanish twenty women. One of these women, La Malinche, renamed "Marina," spoke two languages: Chantal Maya and Nahuatl. She was destined to become Cortés' consort and translator and the most famous woman in Mexican history. Cortés and his army moved on toward Mexico, arriving near present-day Veracruz on Good Friday, 1519. Cortés set out at once to contact local Indians and to make preparations to visit Tenochtitlán, the capital of the Mexica Empire.

The people of the empire Cortés approached had arrived in the central valley of Mexico several generations earlier from the north. Although they are known to history as the Aztec, they knew themselves as the Mexica, and their capital city, Tenochtitlán, is now known as Mexico City. On the day of Cortés' arrival on the coast, Tenochtitlán boasted a population four times that of Seville, the largest city in Spain. The Mexica excelled at warfare, and their warriors had conquered almost all of their world. In light of its technology, the Aztec Empire had reached, or almost reached, its geographic limits.

The Mexica have been compared to the classical Greeks, and there are, to be sure, similarities. Their culture was a splendid classical civilization with highly developed mathematics and astronomy; architecture, including great pyramids; large planned urban centers; agriculture; gold, silver, and copper smithing; and a venerable military tradition. The peoples of a vast part of the Americas based their agriculture on corn, and the Mexica were no different. Indians of Meso-America had domesticated turkeys, which were the primary domestic animal used for meat. No one has successfully domesticated wild turkeys since. In Central America food production was so successful that hunger was probably rare (Jacob 1944, 195). The agricultural history of Central America provides compelling evidence that whatever cannibalism was present, it was not practiced to provide a protein supplement.

Their religion obligated Central American Indians to practice human sacrifice. Most of those sacrificed were combatants captured in battle, and the need for sacrificial victims made warfare something akin to a religious obligation for Tenochtitlán's fighting men. It was not only a great disgrace to survive a battle when one's comrades were defeated; it also meant near-certain death as a prisoner of war. Fiercely hierarchical societies provide their rulers with the power of life and death over the citizenry and captured enemies, and the empire was as hierarchical as any of the classical civilizations of the ancient Middle East. As is the case with such empires, the emperor demanded to be treated as a demigod. His subjects dared not gaze upon his face as one dares not gaze upon the face of the sun. The current emperor was Moctezuma, who reigned from 1502 to 1520. His tyranny and willingness to murder his subjects on a whim were legendary in all Mexico.

Like other rulers of the ancient world, Moctezuma used the services of astrologers, mediums, and fortune tellers to interpret portents and omens (Collis 1963, 53). There were probably few among the ruling class more attuned to prophesy than the emperor. Ancient prophesies allegedly foretold the coming of a man-god who was expected to return from the east to reclaim his empire. Prior to Cortés' arrival, Moctezuma had received several ominous signs: a comet unexpectedly streaked across the sky; a fire mysteriously burned down a sacred temple. And now, word from the coast described the approach of bearded men dressed in metal.

Moctezuma was, by some accounts, terrified and, by other accounts, confused. He sent messages to Cortés saying that he could not meet with him and that he should turn back. Cortés meanwhile was discovering that the Indians who had been conquered by the Mexica were hoping the Spanish would deliver them from their oppressors. Cortés saw it differently, expressing delight that the Indians were divided and could thus be more easily conquered. Greatly helped by La Malinche, who in a short time became one of history's most accomplished translators, Cortés pressed on toward Tenochtitlán.

Very early in the expedition, at Villa de la Cruz, Cortés' authorization for an expedition into the interior was questioned by some of his own men. Upon reading the contract made with Velázquez, they concluded that the mission the governor had stipulated was already accomplished. Cortés had apparently foreseen this possibility and had made preparations for it with his most faithful followers. He resigned his commission and, upon previous arrangement, was promptly nominated as chief justice and captain of the army of the instantly created town of Villa Rica de la Cruz. To justify this action, he called upon an obscure, rarely used provision of Spanish law that allowed a Spanish settlement a degree of autonomy. For these actions he would later be accused of treason, but at the moment, the possibility of such accusations must have seemed remote.

At Cempoallan, the Spanish approached the Totonac Indians, whose chief told Cortés that his nation and many others hated the Mexica and, united with the Spaniards, could defeat Tenochtitlán. This information, which sounded like an offer to organize a rebellion against Mexico, was probably the spark that inspired Cortés to try to conquer the Mexica. He originally intended to build a colony on the coast, but the possibility of an assault on Tenochtitlán was not in his plans until this meeting.

Cortés inspired what can best be described as a tax rebellion among the Totonacs, offering that as allies of Spain they no longer were required to pay tribute to Tenochtitlán. When the Mexica mobilized a military garrison to put down the rebellion, Cortés and his men easily routed them and seized the garrison. This first action against the Mexica military convinced Cortés that the Indians had few military skills, and his confidence in the success of his plans soared. The rout of the garrison also convinced the allied Totonacs that the rebellion could succeed.

Cortés left the coast for Tenochtitlán on August 16 with about 300 conquistadors and 800 Totonacs. There were also some 150 Cuban Indian slaves in the entourage. While Cortés and his expedition slowly negotiated the 250 miles from Cempoallan to Tenochtitlán, things were not going well for the Mexica emperor.

Moctezuma was undecided and unable to formulate a strategy to deal with the intruders. He fell into a kind of anxiety-induced depression and, according to later accounts, abused members of his court. He ordered his magicians to cast spells to stop the Spaniards, but the magicians were not successful.

Mexica laws and customs, similar to Greek laws and customs two thousand years earlier, required that all sides play by the same rules of war and peace. Warfare, the so-called "flower wars" engaged in to produce captives for sacrifice and tribute to support the empire, were to be carried on under certain circumstances and at certain times of the year. Combat was designed not to kill the enemy but to provide captives. There was no provision for dealing with an enemy who did not play by the rules, and Moctezuma could not find a clear course of action to follow. According to Mexica custom, he was not at war with the Spaniards, and since the latter were sending diplomatic messages, he appears to have felt obligated to receive Cortés as an ambassador. He was also terrified that some kind of supernatural force was approaching with the power to destroy him and his empire.

Cortés' early conversations had led him to believe that all the Indian nations subjected to the Mexica so hated their conquerors that they would be friendly to the Spanish and would join them in the march on Tenochtitlán. He was astonished and angered when his contingent was attacked by an army of Indians from Tlaxcala. In the fighting two horses were killed—an indication to the Indians that the horses, at least, were mortal—but Cortés' men were able to kill several dozen Indians with no Spanish fatalities. Spanish arms, especially the swords made of Toledo steel, were vastly superior to Indian obsidian swords, and horses both terrified and overwhelmed the Indians on open ground. Indeed, the Spanish advantage in hand-to-hand combat was so great that on some days the Spanish soldiers complained that their arms grew tired from killing Indians. Indian tactics, which required soldiers to fight one rank at a time instead of en masse, also worked to Spanish advantage.

The Spanish were the military elite of Europe. Spain had been at war in one theater or another for generations, and many families had generations-long military traditions. They especially prided themselves on their swordsmanship, and there is no doubt their armies were the equal, man for man, of any in the world. One result of protracted warfare, however, was that Spanish society suffered not only from the violence of warfare but also from that of its soldiers off the battlefield.

The Tlaxcala, although they had been attacked by the Mexica, had not been conquered by them and were considered autonomous. The Otomi Indians, vassals to the Tlaxcala, led the fighting in this first encounter and attacked a second time. They captured a horse, which they later sacrificed to their gods, and mortally wounded at least one of Cortés' men. Cortés responded with ferocity, attacking the civilian population, pillaging and destroying towns, and perpetuating unnecessary cruelties such as cutting off noses, hands, feet, and testicles of prisoners in a display of terror arguably worse than the acts suffered at the hands of the Mexica.

The next day the Tlaxcalans sent the Spaniards a peace offering of three hundred turkeys and a hundred baskets of maize cakes, apparently to gain time. They were meanwhile assembling their army for what would be the fiercest battle between Spaniards and Indian since Columbus' first journey. The Indians attacked with stones from slings, arrows, and spears launched from atl-atls, and the Spaniards returned fire with crossbows, cannon, and harquebuses, but in the end the Spanish sword was the most effective. Only one or two Spaniards were killed, but all the horses and sixty men were wounded. The next day, Cortés raided ten towns, burning and pillaging in an effort to terrorize the Indians into submission. As he returned to camp, the Indians attacked again and the results were again indecisive.

Following this battle, the Tlaxcalas sent emissaries, ostensibly to talk about negotiations but in fact to spy on Cortés' camp in preparation for another attack. One of the spies was caught and confessed. Cortés had the hands of some and the thumbs or ears of others cut off and tied around their necks. They were sent back to the Tlaxcala with a warning and a challenge.

The fighting continued relentlessly. The Indians attacked repeatedly. Although few Spaniards fell in battle, some were dying of their wounds and from fevers: fifty-five had died since leaving Cuba, and all knew that ahead were the Mexica, who could assemble much larger armies than they had seen thus far. While this fighting raged, Moctezuma sent Cortés a message, offering that he would gladly be a vassal to the king of Spain and would yearly offer tribute but that Cortés should not come to Tenochtitlán because of bad roads, no food, and other hardships. Some of the men wanted to turn back, but Cortés' eloquence held them to the expedition for the moment.

Cortés' good fortune held when the Tlaxcalan ambassadors arrived with presents, sued for peace, and offered themselves as vassals to Spain. In a letter to Charles V, Cortés later wrote:

> [T]hese natives have been and still are faithful vassals of Your Majesty, for they were subjects of Mutezuma [sic] . . . When they heard through me of Your Highness and of Your very great Royal power, they said wished to become vassals of Your Majesty and my allies, and asked me to protect them from that great lord who held them by tyranny and by force, and took their children to sacrifice to his idols . . . (Pagden 1986, 51)

Cortés and his little army entered Tlaxcala on September 18. Totonac help was crucial to the expedition's survival in this series of battles, and later the Tlaxcalans proved equally essential. When dealing with his enemies, Cortés adopted a strategy similar to that of Alexander the Great. He showed unbridled brutality at times, and at other times could be generous to those he had recently defeated. He understood that his objective was to find allies, and his own troops would sometimes complain that he treated recent enemies better than his loyal troops. Fairness was not an issue for Cortés, who operated out of an instinctive and ruthless pragmatism, like that which Machiavelli raised to a fine "art" in *The Prince*, in 1513.

At Tlaxcala, Cortés' men were offered a number of Indian girls as gifts. The girls became consorts to the Spanish, and the births of the first Mestizos of Mexico soon followed. The Tlaxcala were traditional enemies of the Mexica, and Moctezuma's anxiety mounted when he heard that Cortés' party was staying with them. He sent a message to Cortés, inviting him to Tenochtitlán in order to lure the Spanish away from Tlaxcala as quickly as possible.

Cortés sent two of his men ahead to Tenochtitlán as scouts, and on October 12, with his new Tlaxcala allies, he marched the twenty-five miles to the Chululo Nation. In Chululo stood the largest pyramid in the world—120 steps to the top and enclosing 500,000 square feet. Whether too poor or simply unwilling, by the third day of their visit the Chululo failed to provide food for Cortés' party, an assemblage that now included several thousand Tlaxcalans. Word was brought to Cortés that the Mexica planned to ambush and kill the Spanish. Cortés ordered the lords of Chululo—over a hundred people—into the temple courtyard, where they assembled, unarmed. Cortés' men then fell on them with swords, slaughtering them to the last man. Cortés and his Indian allies spent the next few days sacking the city, burning, raping, torturing, and looting.

Mexica ambassadors were present during this massacre and were told to go to Moctezuma with the message that the Spanish, who originally intended to enter Tenochtitlán as friends, were now to be considered enemies. Cortés left Chululo on November 1, 1519, and made his way across mountain paths toward the capital of the Mexica, accompanied by perhaps one thousand Tlaxcalan warriors.

The massacre at Chululo was later seized upon by historian Bartolomé de las Casas, who described it as an act of terror similar to other such acts committed by Spaniards at Hispaniola and Cuba. Most of Cortés' men subsequently failed to mention this deliberate slaughter of unarmed nobility, or the role of the Indian allies in exacting revenge for past injuries.

The heavy hand of past conquests was visible in Old Mexico. The Tlaxcalans, for example, employed a custom of addressing the Otomi, a people they had conquered, with a term equivalent to "idiots." The Mexica had conquered the Coyoacan people in the 1420s, and most of the original population had been enslaved. There were many similar examples throughout Mexico. It is difficult to find a great civilization that does not have a history of conquests and the scornful or brutal treatment of conquered peoples. Cortés' invasion and subsequent conquests by the Spanish must have seemed simply another chapter of Mexican history to the Tlaxcalan and other Indians.

Cortés' small army approached Tenochtitlán in grand array: four armored horsemen at the lead, the standard bearer, followed by rows of infantry with swords drawn, then more horsemen, then soldiers with crossbows. These were followed by more horsemen, soldiers armed with guns—the heavy harquebus, and Cortés with a small group of horsemen. Behind them followed the Indian allies. The Spanish arrived on a portentous day of the Aztec calendar: One Wind, the day of the Robber, when opportunists were expected to hypnotize their hosts, violate their women, and steal everything of value. It was November 8, 1519.

It is said that Moctezuma, carried on a litter, met Cortés at the edge of the city, exchanged greetings, and escorted Cortés and his entourage to lodgings in a palace once owned by his grandfather. Moctezuma gave a speech at some point in which he expressed something the Spanish interpreted as voluntary submission to Spanish authority, although subsequent events suggested that Moctezuma may have been giving a customary welcome or greeting in ritual diplomatic language, rather than offering submission.

Moctezuma gave Cortés a tour of the city. Atop the main pyramid, Cortés delivered a speech—one of many during his career—strongly urging Moctezuma to abandon his gods and embrace Christianity exclusively. The Spanish were more self-righteous than usual about the superiority of Christianity because they were repulsed by the idea of human sacrifice and disgusted by the evidence of cannibalism that sometimes accompanied the sacrifices. They could disembowel a person without flinching, slaughter a village, or burn a person to death slowly over fires for days but could not stomach cannibalism in any form. (The acts of cannibalism by crusaders at Maarat an-Numan and Niceae during the First Crusade were unlikely to have been preserved in popular memory.) Moctezuma politely declined Christianization, but did cause construction of a space for Christians to conduct mass. During this construction, one of Cortés' men discovered a recently sealed doorway, and found, on opening it, that it led to a room that held a considerable store of gold and featherwork. When Cortés informed Moctezuma of this find, Moctezuma told him to keep the gold but to leave the featherwork for the gods.

Fighting broke out at Cempoallan when Moctezuma's tax collectors clashed with Totonacs and Castilians, and Castilians were among those killed. When he learned of this incident, Cortés confronted Moctezuma and took him hostage. Cortés had probably been planning to seize Moctezuma all along, and the latter unwittingly exposed himself to captivity. Moctezuma became a puppet of Cortés, and soon all Tenochtitlán became aware that their emperor was a prisoner of the foreigners.

Qualpopoch, a trusted lieutenant of Moctezuma, and his sons were arrested for the violence at Cempoallan and brought to Tenochtitlán, where Cortés had him tortured until he confessed his responsibility for the fighting. He and his sons were then burned to death in public at Cortés' orders. After that incident, life in Tenochtitlán settled into its old routines for a while, with Moctezuma acting as emperor at Cortés' pleasure. The great weakness of the Mexica political structure was exposed during this episode. Moctezuma was absolute ruler, and there was no process to replace him should he become senile, mad, or the prisoner of deceitful enemies. Cortés took advantage of this weakness. He seized and imprisoned other key nobility of the Aztec Empire and forced them, by some accounts, to give oaths of loyalty to the Crown of Spain, a strategy that enabled him to treat any subsequent resistance to Spanish authority as an act of rebellion.

Cortés and his men looted whatever gold they could find or extort from the nobility. Early in 1520, Cortés ordered Moctezuma to provide wood and carpenters to build ships to carry all the gold back to the Spanish colonies. The ship-building gave Moctezuma hope the Spanish were departing, a hope Cortés cultivated. Just as the last ship was being finished, news arrived of more Spanish ships off the coast. Cortés was alarmed because of the possibility that he had been denounced in the Spanish courts and an expedition had been sent to arrest him.

Cortés had earlier sent a ship laden with gold out to sea with orders to bypass Cuba and go directly to Spain. He was hoping King Charles V would reward him before Diego Velásquez could rein him in. Unbeknownst to Cortés, the ship made a stop in Cuba, and Velásquez heard the story of Cortés' good fortune and the gold. He initiated an inquiry, accusing Cortés of rebellion and his lieutenants of a variety of misdeeds. At about this time the first smallpox epidemic reached Cuba. The epidemic appears to have arisen in Spain and migrated to Hispaniola, where it had a devastating effect on the few remaining Indians, virtually wiping them out by the end of 1519.

Cortés' own people had some success defending his interests in Spain, but his enemies succeeded in launching an expedition under Panfilo Narvaez to arrest him. Narvaez landed in Mexico and communicated with men in Cortés' party, calling on them to abandon their leader. He even communicated with Moctezuma, then held prisoner by Cortés. Narvaez maneuvered unsuccessfully to capture Cortés, but Cortés had bribed members of Narvaez' force so lavishly that it was later said the expedition against Cortés was awash in Aztec gold. Cortés was not one to panic in such circumstances. Although facing a superior force, Cortés mounted a nighttime attack on May 29 that completely surprised Narvaez' forces. Narvaez lost an eye in the fighting and was captured by Cortés, who imprisoned but later released him. Narvaez's army was almost completely absorbed by his enemy. Before Cortés could savor his victory, however, word arrived of trouble in Tenochtitlán.

The trouble erupted at a Mexica ceremony. The Spanish, reacting to rumors of a rebellion, attacked the unsuspecting and unarmed Mexica and massacred more than one thousand noblemen. It is thought that the rumors were spread by enemies of the

Mexica. Cortés' men slaughtered most of the remaining hostages, sparing Moctezuma, but placing him in chains.

The Mexica now determined to resist the Spanish. Mobs of Indians gathered and began throwing rocks and spears at the Spanish. Alvarado, the Spanish commander left in charge by Cortés, ordered Moctezuma to the palace roof to call off the attack. Moctezuma complied, calling on his people to halt the attack, probably saving the Spaniards, but the fight was far from over. When Cortés returned, he was angry with Alvarado but even angrier with Moctezuma because he had corresponded with Narvaez. Cortés refused to speak to him. Moctezuma's authority evaporated rapidly after the massacre; his plea to the people to stop the attack was the final order they would obey.

In resisting the Spanish, the Mexica faced a huge problem. Many who might have provided leadership had been killed in the massacres or were among the few hostages who remained alive. The Mexica resisted by refusing to provide the Spanish or their allies any food and by closing the markets, but there seemed no way for the Mexica to raise new leadership.

Cortés demanded the markets be reopened, and Moctezuma suggested his brother, Cuitlahuac, could accomplish this. Cuitlahuac was set free. He had originally opposed allowing the Spanish into the city and, once free, he set about the task of organizing the resistance. Almost immediately the Mexica attacked Cortés' forces in relentless street fighting that injured many Spaniards and killed a few. The Spanish countered by pressuring Moctezuma to go to the palace roof and plead for peace. It didn't work. The Mexica showered Moctezuma with missiles and stones and he was hit at least three times. Whether he died of these wounds or was killed by the Spanish is unclear, but he seems to have died the next morning, on June 30. The Indians who found his body after the Spanish left would claim he had suffered stab wounds. Following his death, the Spanish slaughtered the remaining captive aristocrats.

Cortés and his men tried to fight their way out of the city, but on the first attempt were driven back when the Indians pounded them from the roofs with heavy stones. Cortés distributed some of the gold among his troops and at midnight on July 1, 1520, the retreat began. They were discovered almost immediately and the Mexica gave chase in the dark. In the battle the Indians fought to kill. In the confusion many Spaniards drowned. Some of them died because they refused to drop the heavy gold as they attempted to escape. Much of the gold was lost, including a mare loaded with what was designated the "king's gold." Some six hundred Spaniards died that night, the worst defeat of Europeans at the hands of Indians thus far. Although they continued to harass the Spanish, Mexica leaders seem to have assumed that this retreat meant a final victory over their tormentors.

Cortés, roundly defeated, was determined to return and crush the Mexica. Later he explained in a letter to Charles V that he had hoped to conquer the Mexica peacefully through diplomacy and persuasion, but that was no longer possible. Cortés' little army was attacked and harassed as they retreated, but the Indian allies offered critical help when he reached them, especially the Tlaxcalans, who some Spaniards credited with saving their lives. These Indians extracted promises from Cortés that, in exchange for their help, they would be rewarded with booty and political power and would not pay tribute. Cortés agreed.

Cortés soon returned. His strategy was to cut off the Mexica from their allies and send terror into the hearts of the whole Indian population. The Castilians and Tlaxcalans first attacked and defeated the Topeaca Indians. They murdered many of the men and branded and sent the women and children into Spanish slavery. At Quechula Cortés used deception and a truce to disarm the warriors, and had all the men slaughtered and the women and children enslaved. With minimal losses to his troops and those of his allies, Cortés destroyed a number of Indian nations in a reign of butchery and terror.

Another terror was stalking Old Mexico. Epidemics arose, probably brought by Narvaez' men. It is usually assumed to have been smallpox, but the symptoms were different—a cough, nose-bleed, and bladder infection, followed almost always by death. The scourge moved across Yucatán and into the Central Valley in

September 1520 and spread like a prairie fire among the Indians, killing great numbers. This plague was as devastating as the great plagues in Europe in the middle of the fourteenth century, but now plague was an ally to a conqueror.

The Tlaxcalan Nation was decimated, as were the Mexica. Cuitlahuac, the new emperor, succumbed. The epidemic killed as much as half the population of infected settlements. The Spaniards, who had mostly escaped the disease, were barely aware of the devastation around them. It has long been believed that the viral infections were of a type to which most Europeans had some immunitiy. For the Indians, the epidemics marked the end of their world. Famine followed because, as happened during previous plagues, most of those who grew and prepared the food had died.

The Spanish and their Indian allies occupied themselves fighting skirmishes and sacking the small cities in the area. Many more towns sued for peace in exchange for homage to Spain. Prepared for a long siege, Cortés reappeared within sight of Tenochtitlán in January 1521. Cortés had earlier described Tenochtitlán as one of the most beautiful cities in the world, and his and other descriptions of it leave little doubt that it was an elegant, well-planned city. He had hoped to capture this prize without a battle, In a letter to Charles V, following the destruction of the city, he wrote:

> Seeing that the enemy was determined to resist to the death, I came to the conclusion that they would force us to destroy them totally. This last caused me the greater sorrow, for it weighed on my soul. (Blacker and Rosen 1962, 125)

The Mexica were unprepared for the siege Cortés would launch, since warfare among the Indians usually lasted only a few days and was expected to conclude with defeat, but not annihilation, of one side or the other. The Mexica, however, put up a fierce fight. Cortés had brigantines built and stationed them in the lakes around Tenochtitlán. His plan was to starve the city by cutting off the canoes that supplied it with food. He set about organizing an army of Indian allies and Spanish soldiers. The Mexica broke the causeways to the city almost every night to slow the Spanish invasion, and almost every day Cortés' Indian allies filled them in. When the invading army entered the city, the Mexica attacked them with rocks from the tops of the buildings that lined the streets. The invaders methodically burned and leveled the buildings; the Indian allies used the rubble to refill the causeways. The Mexica resisted fiercely, fighting from barricade to barricade, street to street. Against superior numbers and weapons they held out through almost three months of constant fighting.

When the city was finally captured, Cortés demanded to be given gold, which was, after all, the primary object of the conquest. He did receive a quantity of gold, but the Mexica did not cooperate with him to the extent he would have liked. The Mexica survivors, sick and starving, were either slaughtered (mostly by the allies) or taken into slavery. Casualties were estimated at 120,000 to 240,000 (O'Connell 1989, 129). Their aristocracy had been rendered virtually extinct in the massacres and subsequent fighting. The libraries of the Mexica were burned, and Tenochtitlán had been reduced to a pile of rubble. As a nation, the Mexica were annihilated. Their darkest prophesies of the end of the world had come to pass.

A year earlier, in 1520, rebellion had broken out in Spain, Martin Luther was excommunicated, and the Protestant Reformation was launched. Charles V, emperor of the Holy Roman Empire and king of Spain, was forced to take measures to secure his authority. Intrigues and corruption were rife in the Spanish court. Events raging in Europe preoccupied Charles V and would put developments in the Americas near the bottom of a long list of concerns.

After reigning for seven years as absolute ruler of a huge Mexican empire extending from the Caribbean to the Pacific, Cortés was ordered to Spain in 1528 to face charges ranging from insubordination to treason. He brought a wealth of treasure to the emperor, who allowed him to return to New Spain in a minor position. The remainder of his life was spent in litigation, as he struggled to clear himself of various charges—including murder—made by his enemies.

The events that led the Spanish to Peru can be traced to 1508, when an expedition landed in Panama and established a base there. Vasco Núñez de Balboa (1475–1519) crossed the isthmus and "discovered" the Pacific Ocean. Panama became the base of further operations southward because the local Indians told of a fabled kingdom in the mountains in that direction. Pedrarias Dávila, the governor of Panama, appointed Francisco Pizarro (1476–1541) to lead the explorations. Preliminary forays in 1524 and 1526 produced evidence of gold and silver and confirmed the existence of a kingdom in the mountains to the south. Before going to Peru, Pizarro made a trip to Spain during which he secured vast powers for himself and subsequently outraged a rival conquistador, Diego de Almagro. This rivalry would eventually cost Pizarro his life.

As the Spanish were approaching, the Inca were involved in a very serious civil war. Atahualpa, leader of one faction, won the contest (if only barely) over his half-brother, Huascar. Atahualpa captured his opponent and destroyed not only his power but killed his wives and consorts and favorite children. Pizarro left Panama early in 1531 and, with some horses and 180 men, made the long tortuous trip from the sea up the Andes toward the land of the Inca. Atahualpa was camped, along with his army of 30,000 warriors, near the town of Cajamarca. The tiny band of Spaniards allowed Atahualpa to think his own forces were vastly superior and, when Pizarro invited him to meet in the town of Cajamarca, Atahualpa accepted. It was a fatal mistake.

Spanish eyewitnesses described the spectacle as Atahualpa and his noblemen formed an impressive procession into the town. Attendants swept the road ahead of the royal litter, assuring that no pebbles or other debris would impede the progress of the emperor. When the Inca party was inside the square, a Spanish priest came forward and read a version of the now-infamous *Requerimiento*, demanding that Atahualpa swear allegiance to the king of Spain and commit all his worldly possessions and the bodies of his people to the service of that Crown. Atahualpa replied something to the effect that if the king of Spain believed that people would agree to such a demand, he must be intoxicated. The priest then ran for cover, and the Spanish soldiers did their work.

Surrounding Atahualpa was a huge cadre of noblemen, all unarmed. The army of warriors remained outside of town. According to the rules of Andean warfare, the Inca party was under what amounted to a flag of truce. Under Spanish practice, they had foolishly allowed themselves to fall into a trap. The Spanish slaughtered the Inca noblemen, killing a number that may have exceeded seven thousand. Not a single Spanish soldier was killed or seriously wounded. Pizarro remembered well the tactics of Cortés: shock the enemy with massacres and seize the emperor as a prisoner. Atahualpa remained a prisoner, and like Moctezuma, he was allowed for a time to continue to give orders and act as emperor.

Atahualpa offered to ransom himself from captivity. Asked how much gold he could offer as a ransom, he said he could fill a room with gold to a height of nine feet. Pizarro accepted and the Inca complied, bringing their artwork of gold, which the Inca goldsmiths were then obliged to melt into gold bars for the Spanish. Gold had been a medium of exchange since ancient times in Europe, Africa, and Asia, and people in those regions accepted it in payment for everything from services to property. It is a socially created representation of wealth, however, only as valuable as the people who trade in it make it to be. Gold had more significance to the Europeans than mere wealth, because gold was the foundation of currencies, and currency was what paid the armies. Armies and currency were (and are) what created the political power known as sovereignty in Europe.

The Andean people attached no such value to gold. They used it to create important artifacts and artwork, but they must have been puzzled by the Spaniards' demands. It has been said that the Spanish demand for gold would have fallen on Andean ears with the same impact as if invaders from outer space came to earth and demanded all the world's butterfly wings.

It was the most expensive kidnapping and ransom in history, and an item for the record book in many ways, for never had so few men accomplished the conquest of so much gold since the beginning of human memory. Even that much gold did not help Atahualpa. Pizarro decided it was too dangerous to allow him to go free and that, in any case, he had served his purpose. Atahualpa was accused of treason and, after a sham trial, was sentenced to death. The typical gesture of conquistador kindness was to offer him the less painful death by garrote instead of burning if he would accept conversion to Christianity. He did, and was strangled in August 1533.

Pizarro and Cortés—but especially Pizarro—accomplished the largest transfers of wealth from the hands of one set of peoples to another ever attempted. The precious metals obtained by each conquistador dwarfed the booty looted at Constantinople during the Fourth Crusade. Columbus had dreamed of finding gold, which he hoped could be used to continue the Crusades. His successors found at least 180 to 200 tons of gold between 1500 and 1650. The Indian cultures of Mexico and the Andes had achieved success mining in high elevations, and their skills in gold and silver smithing cannot easily be exaggerated. Prior to these conquests, Europe had been dependent on the African Gold Coast for its gold. As a region emerging from a feudal culture and economy, Europe had a very limited money supply. This was to change. Between 1492 and 1542 the amount of gold in the European market economy increased threefold. In Spain gold began to appear in art museums and cathedrals as never before. These artifacts can be seen today, evidence of huge amounts of gold from the Americas fashioned into Christian symbols and an enormous legacy of conquest.

It was not the only such legacy. Although gold created the possibility of an ostentatious display of wealth, it was silver that did the most to change the world. Silver was the medium of exchange for small transactions all over Europe, and without it the money supply for everyday life was lacking. When silver became available in sufficient quantities, it became the foundation for a money supply for an emerging world economy.

In a single year during this period, sixteen tons of silver entered Seville from the Americas. It has been estimated that silver production in the Americas was ten times that of the rest of the world combined. The Spanish rounded up Indians to work the mines of Mexico as virtual slaves, under conditions that killed thousands of them. Their labor supplied the greatest silver minting town of all time, Potosí in Bolivia (Davies 1996, 187). This infusion of precious metal had such an impact on Europe that land and commodity ownership ceased to be the primary evidence of individual wealth. The money supply multiplied an estimated fifteen-fold in a century, bringing a period of prosperity and inflation.

Money is not wealth, but rather a claim on wealth, and unless that claim is exercised in some sustainable way, the wealth can evaporate. All the wealth—the gold and silver—initially went to Spain, but did not stay there long. With little manufacturing and the absence of a drive to invest in means of production, Spain simply bought what it needed from other countries. Its capital went quickly from Spain to Holland or Italy for most manufactured goods. Silver and gold went to China for porcelain and to the Ottomans for spices. Gold and silver made a world economy possible and fanned its flames. With few exports besides gold and silver, Spain experienced severe payment deficits. While Spain's economy floundered, most of Europe's economy boomed, as did the demand for tea, coffee, silk, and cotton.

As the principal European state combatting Islam and defending Catholicism against the Protestant Reformation launched by Martin Luther, Spain was involved in wars throughout this period, in Holland and against the Turks in Eastern Europe and around the Mediterranean. By 1557 the Spanish state, which had long tottered on the edge, was bankrupt. It had taken on too much, and not even the gold and silver from its American colonies could pay all the bills.

This newly found wealth had a negative effect on Africa, too. Africa had been Europe's primary source of gold, but with the ready availability of gold from other sources, some African trade routes were abandoned and some trading cities stagnated. For a time the Gold Coast was severely depressed. With gold supplied more cheaply by Spain, Africa had only one commodity the emerging Euro-American economy wanted: slaves.

Meanwhile, the Bolivian city of Potosí became the world capital of silver production, spurring the development of capitalism by supplying an essential ingredient to capital formation—money. When Indians died from the very difficult conditions in the mines, they were replaced by African slaves who, in the high regions of the Andes, also died. African slavery did not replace Indian slavery in wide areas of the Andes, and Indians worked these mines for the next three centuries in truly appalling conditions, under a system virtually equivalent to slavery.

Although Bolivia, Peru, and Mexico were central to creating the money that formed the foundation for the modern world's capitalist system, their stories are not of prosperity. The precious metal resources were not used to develop those countries but were instead appropriated for the development of European nations. Today the Andean and Mexican towns that produced gold and silver are backwaters in the world economy. The case of Spain is similar. It went through a long decline following the period when it controlled the largest empire in the world.

Early in the sixteenth century, even before Pizarro went to Peru, the cruelty the Spanish visited upon the Indians had begun to spark increasingly strong opposition among some of the clergy and even some people at the court of Charles V. Bartolomé de las Casas (1474–1566), a Spanish colonist who took vows as a Dominican in the New World, had himself once possessed an encomienda. His was a strong voice in the opposition to Indian slavery. He championed the idea that the Spanish had no right to subject the Indians to military force, take their property, and enslave them. He argued that the Indians could become good subjects of the Crown and good converts to the Holy Catholic Church, and around 1513 he began a long career of writing and advocating reform in the treatment of Indians. Las Casas' arguments grew long and intricate, but his basic ideas were that Indians had rights that the conquistadors had illegally and immorally swept aside. These rights included a right to their property, a right against being enslaved, and a right to their lives. He and some other members of the clergy sought to deny communion and other rights to conquistadors who abused Indians.

The king, on the other hand, was opposed to allowing the development of an unchecked oligarchy with enough power to challenge Spanish authority in the colonies, and he understood the estate system with its feudal lords and the encomienda system to be that kind of threat. In the years following 1492 many expeditions were financed not by the Crown but by individual entrepreneurs whose interests were sometimes in conflict with those of the Crown. The emperor therefore listened closely to Las Casas and in 1542 put forth what were called the New Laws, which would have ended further enslavement of the Indians, ordered release of illegally enslaved Indians, and terminated the encomienda with the death of the holder. This caused a conquistador rebellion. When Viceroy Blanco Núñez Vela, newly appointed by the king, arrived in Peru in 1544, Gonzalo Pizarro had him executed. The conquistador revolt lasted almost ten years.

Eventually Charles V called for an investigation into whether the conquest was just, and in 1550, at a moment when the Spanish empire was at its height, the Council of the Indies met in Valladolid Spain to consider the question. The lawyer for the conquistadors would be Juan Ginés de Sepúlveda, an admirer of Hernán Cortés and the historian of the conquest of Mexico and Charles V's reign. The lawyer for the Indians was Bartolomé de las Casas. Through the long hot summer, the two sides presented their evidence and made their arguments. It was a landmark event in Western history.

The task of the propagandist/historian, from the point of view of the conqueror, is to explain the conquest, plunder, and other behavior in a fashion acceptable to their own culture. Sepúlveda based his arguments on the writings of Aristotle. The conquered peoples Aristotle had found to be mentally deficient and incapable of engaging in high culture—and therefore fit only for perpetual servitude and manual labor—were rediscovered in the form of the Indians of the Americas. Sepúlveda mustered a series of arguments justifying racism—indeed he is identified as the "father" of racism in the modern world. His arguments included the assertion that the inferiority of the Indian was biological in nature, and that therefore Indians' lives should be dedicated to the service of their natural superiors, the Spanish. The Indian had no right to worldly goods. The culture of the Indian should be eradicated, and he should be grateful to be conquered by such benevolent and sophisticated people as the Spanish.

> How can we doubt that these people—so uncivilized, so barbaric, contaminated with so many impieties and obcenities—have been justly conquered by such an excellent, pious, and most just king as was Ferdinand the Catholic and as is now Emperor Charles, and by such a most humane nation and excellent in every kind of virtue. (Hanke 1965, 123)

The perfect world that Plato thought human intelligence had the capacity to create found its most political expression in the mid-sixteenth century as an argument to justify the horrors of rape, murder, torture, robbery, and genocide, which were, for the Indians, the lived experience of the conquest. The revitalization movement that occurred when ancient Greek texts and the philosophical tradition of the pursuit of the ideal were embraced by Western Europe came to justify the .most horrible abuses. One side argued that Indians were noble savages, the other that they were simply savages. When Cortés had urged Moctezuma to embrace Christianity and abandon indigenous practices, the emperor replied that the religion of the Spaniards would not be appropriate to his people. It would not have occurred to the Christian West to discuss such an idea, since the Christian utopian enterprise was founded on the belief that there could be only one Truth, one right way.

Although the encomienda system as such would eventually disappear, the discussion about the rights of the Indians has not been resolved in Latin America. The conquest placed Indians in the position of a lower caste, a condition that still exists. Indian rights to property, especially communal rights to aboriginal property, have never been recognized in most places, and only in the late twentieth century has it been truly illegal for a white man to murder an Indian. The legacy of the Spanish conquest has been a continuing disregard for the rights of the Indians, in many ways similar to that described by Las Casas.

Bibliography

Blacker, Irwin R., and Harry M. Rosen, eds. *Conquest: Dispatches of Cortés from the New World.* New York: Grosset & Dunlap, 1962.

Collis, Maurice. *Cortés and Moctezuma.* London: Faber & Faber, 1963.

Davies, Glyn. *A History of Money from Ancient Times to the Present Day.* Cardiff: University of Wales Press, 1994, rev. 1996.

Diaz del Castillo, Bernal. *The Discovery and Conquest of Mexico, 1517–1521.* New York: Da Capo Press, 1996.

Hanke, Lewis. *The Spanish Struggle for Justice in the Conquest of America.* Boston: Little, Brown & Co., 1949, 1965.

Howard, Cecil. *Pizarro and the Conquest of Peru.* New York: American Heritage Publishing Co., 1968.

Jacob, Heinrich Eduard. *Six Thousand Years of Bread: Its Holy and Unholy History.* Garden City, N.Y.: Doubleday, Doran & Co., 1944.

Lockhart, James, ed. *We People: Nahuatl Accounts of the Conquest of Mexico.* Berkeley: University of California Press, 1993.

O'Connell, Robert L. *Of Arms and Men: A History of War, Weapons, and Aggression.* New York: Oxford University Press, 1989.

Pagden, Anthon, ed. *Hernan Cortés: Letters from Mexico.* New Haven and London: Yale University Press, 1986.

Prescott, William. *History of the Conquest of Peru.* New York: Dutton, 1968.

Smith, Adam. *An Inquiry into the Nature and Causes of the Wealth of Nations.* books i–iii: Penguin Books, 1997.

Thomas, Hugh. *Conquest: Moctezuma, Cortés, and the Fall of Old Mexico.* New York: Simon & Schuster, 1993.

Todoroy, Tzvetan. *The Conquest of America: The Question of the Other.* New York: Harper & Row, 1984.

Wachtel, Nathan. *The Vision of the Vanquished: The Spanish Conquest of Peru Through Indian Eyes, 1530–1570.* New York: Barnes & Noble, 1977.

Weatherford, Jack. *Indian Givers: How the Indians of the Americas Transformed the World.* New York: Crown Publishers, 1988.

EIGHT
Nationalism and the Rise of Representative Government

Machiavelli . . . suggested doubts about whether it was possible, even in principle, to combine a Christian view of life involving self-sacrifice and humility with the possibility of building and maintaining a powerful and glorious republic, which required not humility or self-sacrifice on the part of its rulers and citizens, but the pagan virtues of courage, vitality, self-assertion and, in the case of rulers, a capacity for ruthless, unscrupulous and cruel action where it was called for by the needs of the state.

Isaiah Berlin, *The Crooked Timber of Humanity*

Two of the most powerful ideologies of the West are the idea of progress and the idea that liberal representative democracies represent the ideal path toward the improvement and prosperity of humankind. Both ideas have roots in the struggle between important men of commerce and the ancient system of aristocracy over whose interests would govern England. A similar struggle in France resulted in the emergence of an absolute monarchy accompanied by a movement among intellectuals we know as the Enlightenment, which provided advice to despots about how to rule in the best interests of the state and its people. In England this struggle was played out in civil war and the eventual ascendancy to power of a class whose primary ambitions centered around the production and accumulation of wealth. These ambitions came to be identified, at least among British economic philosophers, as synonymous with the pursuit of the ideal.

The sixteenth century proved a time of great change in European culture. Machiavelli's *The Prince* is more than a treatise recommending a path of pragmatism to rulers; it also contains ideas that support the development of strong state power. His book would eventually establish Machiavelli as a conservative political thinker who influenced statesmen of the modern era. In 1517 Martin Luther posted his ninety-five theses on a door of a Wittenberg church, thus launching what would become the Protestant Reformation. Luther's movement involved many theological differences with the Catholic Church, and key among these was his assertion that an individual could achieve salvation without intervention of that ancient institution. Sometime in the 1440s someone (it is generally believed to be Gutenberg) invented the European version of movable type. The resulting explosion of printed material led to a rapid increase in literacy in Europe. Since relatively few people were able to read Latin, the printed material was largely in the vernacular languages, giving them a legitimacy they had never had and stimulating the consciousness of the relationship between language and identity.

That consciousness led in time to the ideology that a people are identified by a language and should be unified and recognized under a single state. People wanted to read the Bible in their own language, and in those countries where this idea became popular, the grip of the Church was significantly loosened. Luther's translation of the Bible into German is still considered a seminal piece of German literature. Loyalties began to shift from individual rulers to the idea of a people or nation. The Protestant Reformation, seized upon at first by local rulers who coveted Church property as much as by religious inclination, unwittingly promoted nationalism, a key element in the development of modernity.

The European country that most successfully challenged Spain for world domination was England. For at least a century prior to Columbus' voyages (and probably earlier), feudalism had been declining in England. The great landed estates, which had defined an economy based on peasant duties performed in exchange for use of land, were gradually being transformed as demand for wool rose and as ancient obligations were increasingly settled with cash payments instead of labor. Although this trend was already evident and growing, it accelerated following the flood of gold and silver that found its way from the Americas on Spanish ships during the early decades of the sixteenth century.

With the expanded money supply, prices rose, creating a dilemma for many landowners. The English squires, or landed gentry, were restricted by ancient customs and traditions that included fixed rents and other cash obligations of their tenants. At the time when the trappings of manorial life were becoming increasingly expensive for the landed gentry and aristocracy (who by mid-sixteenth century owned about 80 percent of the land in England), they could not raise rents. Wool merchants and other newly rich entrepreneurs, flush with cash, sought secondary investments for their wealth, and an obvious choice was land. Many estates were sold, and the new landowners, who were often absentee owners, discarded the old customs and ordered the estates transformed into profitable investments.

The medieval villages that dotted the English countryside were peopled with highly skilled and relatively prosperous laborers as well as small landholders. The old landowners had relationships with the people of these villages, but the new landowners had no established relationships with them and wanted none. At the beginning of the sixteenth century, rural England, like much of Europe, included a large population of rural tenants and small landholders who, by custom and/or deeds, held rights to land that was part of a great estate in a complex system of land usage. Disasters such as the Black Plague and crop failures had reduced the number of small landholders, and the change in land ownership now brought about their virtual disappearance. The new landowners imposed new rules that forced the small rural landholder off the land, piece by piece, by a process called "enclosure." Under enclosure, lands formerly used for the production of food and fiber were fenced off to be used to raise sheep The peasants produced wealth in the form of food and fibers, but being self-sufficient, they consumed much of what they produced. They had enjoyed the products of the land to a much greater degree than did, for example, the Indians on an encomienda in Mexico.

As enclosure drove both tenants and small landholders from the land, wool production concentrated the wealth in the hands of far fewer people. If wealth were measured in terms of the value of the things produced from the land, the system of small landholders probably produced more; but if wealth were calculated in terms of the amount of money flowing through the marketplace, the enclosure system would produce better numbers.

Most historians who reported on this period did so from the point of view that enclosure served a purpose in the developing economy as England lurched toward the future—but as yet unanticipated—Industrial Revolution. The fact remains, however, that the earliest indicators of economic growth in England were linked to an increase in homelessness and hunger. Some modern scholars argue that by the seventeenth century the most brutal impacts of enclosure had passed and that enclosure involved much less land and had a lesser impact than has been reported (Heaton 1948, 312). Others find that small farmers and small farming were marginalized and that rural England came to be dominated by large estates (Moore 1966, 512–517). In *The Making of the English Working Class,* E. P. Thompson summarized the impact of enclosure over the long term.

> In village after village, enclosure destroyed the scratch-as-scratch-can subsistence economy of the poor—the cow or geese, fuel from the common, gleanings, and all the rest. The cottager without legal proof of rights was rarely compensated. The cottager who was able to establish his claim was left with a parcel of land inadequate for subsistence and a disproportionate share of the very high enclosure costs. (Thompson 1963, 217)

Enclosure not only enabled the wealthy to take over the common lands that served as pasturage for the peasants' animals, it began a process that severely reduced the population of the countryside.

The new landowners used sheriffs and courts to evict families and then had their houses pulled down. Without land to grow their food or money to buy it, large numbers of peasants were banished to the roads and hunger became widespread. By the middle of the sixteenth century, the enclosures had created widespread agrarian crisis and a small peasant revolt. Poverty came to be defined by whether the average annual income was equal to the daily cost of bread. Often it was not, and many starved. These homeless poor would one day provide the pools of human recruits available for other uses: colonization of foreign lands, impressment into the Royal Navy or other armed forces, and a labor force for mines, factories, or domestic service.

In 1600 it is estimated that about half the manors in England had at least part of their holdings from enclosure. The rich were waging a kind of war against the poor, and the poor had few defenders. There are no biographies of England's displaced poor from the sixteenth century, no novels, no illuminating public records describing their lives. Their names appear, when they appear, on birth, death, marriage, and arrest records. Otherwise, although they made up the majority of people living in England at the time, they remain silent and invisible in the historical record. Their contributions, however critical, are passive and are considered to add little to the story.

For the next century the roads of England were filled with beggars. When commenting on this production of misery, historians point to the similarity of conditions in the Third World today. The modern Third World poor are also displaced peoples who have been historically forced or coerced from the land in modern processes similar to enclosure. It is argued, even by some of the more enlightened scholars, that enclosure, however horrible, was essential to the production of the technological and economic conditions of industrial England in the twentieth century.

Conditions of desperation and oppression tend to produce visions of utopia. Sir Thomas More's famous work *Utopia*, completed in 1516, was translated into English in 1556. A reaction to the wretched conditions of poverty and injustice being produced in England, it provided a vision of a world where economic justice could only be realized through a form of communism.

Other examples of exploitation and oppression can be found in the history of the sixteenth century. Around 1565 English capitalists invited investors to participate in what they called the "Ulster enterprise," a plan to expand English holdings in Ireland in order to exploit the forests. When the Irish resisted, propagandists denounced them as pagans, although Ireland had been Catholic for more than seven centuries and Irish monks had played a crucial role in a Christian revitalization movement at the time of Charlemagne. The Irish were depicted as a subhuman race not protected under Christian law. Armies were sent, land was seized, populations were massacred, and the defeated people were subjected to insult, scorn, and other treatment reserved for the conquered. Although the Irish were not yet fully conquered, this era is called the Elizabethan Conquest of Ireland.

An example of how white-on-white racism was manufactured and sustained, the conquest of Ireland was to prove a practice run for colonization and conquest in the Americas, New Zealand, Australia, and elsewhere In 1562 France attempted to build a colony in Florida; and the English captain John Hawkins initiated the slave trade between Africa and the West Indies. In 1563 the Spanish invaded the islands they dubbed the Philippines and founded Manila. At that time the *Black Ship* (the first regularly scheduled trans-Pacific vessel) began to make annual trips from Manila to Acapulco on Mexico's Pacific coast. From there, overland caravans to Veracruz carried goods that then were shipped across the Atlantic to Spain, completing a second European trade route across the globe. The first was established when the Portuguese sailed around the southern tip of Africa and established lucrative trade and colonies in India and the faraway Spice Islands. Beginning in 1571, English law forbade export of wool, with the aim of supporting the manufacture and export of more expensive finished woolen goods. In 1579 the first English colonists settled in Newfoundland, the same year a colony was established in India. Three years later Sir Walter Raleigh made an attempt to establish a colony in Virginia.

From the earliest voyages, the Spanish had dominated cross-Atlantic travel, making colonization in America difficult and dangerous for other Europeans and heightening tensions, especially with England. After England separated from the Catholic Church when the pope refused to give King Henry VIII an annulment of his marriage to Catherine of Aragon, the English and Spanish became enemies. In 1572 Francis Drake led a daring raid on Panama and returned to London in 1580 with loot valued at over 163,000 pounds sterling, whereupon Queen Elizabeth I knighted him on the deck of the government-sanctioned pirate ship the *Golden Hind.*

Spain's King Philip II still hoped that Mary, Queen of Scots, a Catholic, would ascend to the English throne, but after a Catholic assassination plot directed at Elizabeth I was uncovered, Mary was executed as a national security risk. Spain reacted by building what was, up to then, the largest maritime armada ever seen in European waters and in 1588 launched an attempted invasion of England. The Armada was destroyed by storms and the very able English Navy. The casks of corned beef washed ashore from the Spanish shipwrecks are said to have given birth to the Irish taste for corned beef and cabbage. A second Spanish Armada met a similar fate in 1597, and a few years later Spain was decisively defeated. A Spanish army surrendered to the English in Ireland in 1602, the same year Shakespeare introduced *Macbeth.*

The seventeenth century saw the expansion of European colonization in the Americas. With the Spanish menace out of the way, the English made haste to realize their cross-Atlantic colonial ambitions. In 1606 the Virginia Company of London was granted a royal charter, and the following year Jamestown, Virginia, was founded. Despite all the wealth looted in the Americas during the previous century, Spain was forced to declare bankruptcy. Samuel de Champlain, a French colonist, founded Quebec in 1608; and a rebellion in Ireland collapsed. A year later, Henry Hudson sailed up the river that bears his name; and the Dutch East India Company made its first shipment of tea to Europe. The next year Henry Hudson fell victim to mutiny while searching for a water route to Asia, and he and his small son were set adrift to perish in the frigid waters of Hudson's Bay.

In 1612 Manhattan was founded by the Dutch; and John Rolfe became the first European to plant tobacco successfully. The following year England minted its first copper coins; and the year after that Rolfe married the Powhatan Indian woman, Pocahontas. Rolfe went on to found Virginia's tobacco industry, which dominated southern agriculture until early in the nineteenth century. Rolfe and Pocahontas had a son, Thomas Rolfe, who was among the founding members of the Virginia elite. Pocahontas was urged to go to England, where she was well received and apparently well liked. Before embarking for home, however, she became ill, possibly with tuberculosis, and died at around twenty-three years of age. She was the first American Indian woman to marry an Englishman, among the first to visit England, and the first to be buried there.

In 1619 the first African slaves arrived in Virginia and were put to work on the tobacco plantations. The following year, Pilgrims founded a colony at Plymouth. In 1621 the Dutch West India Company was chartered. In that year potatoes were planted in Germany for the first time. Potatoes, which were among the astonishing varieties of cultivars originally produced by the Indians of the Andes, were to play a major role in European economic history. Because this crop produces a great amount of food on a small area with much less labor than traditional European crops such as wheat, the number of unemployed increased and their labor could be diverted to other tasks during the Industrial Age.

Peter Minuit "bought" Manhattan Island from the Indians in 1626, and the Massachusetts Colony was founded in 1630. In 1633 the Dutch settled in Connecticut, followed by English colonists two years later. In 1638 torture was officially abolished in England. Montreal was founded in 1642. In 1641 Catholics massacred Protestants in Ulster, Ireland; and cotton was first manufactured in Manchester, England.

Elizabeth I—"Good Queen Bess"—had died in March 1603 and was succeeded by James I of Scotland. Henry VII, Henry VIII, and Elizabeth I had ruled England with a strong hand, but since the defeat of the Spanish Armada, English sentiments had shifted away from favoring a strong monarchy. Parliament, which had been in existence for some three centuries, initiated a struggle for power after James ascended the throne. The struggle lasted throughout most of the seventeenth century. The Upper House, or House of Lords, played a minor role in this contest, while the House of Commons, made up primarily of landed gentry and particularly of Puritans, led the struggle. In France an absolute monarchy had prevailed because the Crown had been able to secure the power to levy taxes. In England the House of Commons demanded the right to decide disputed elections of its members and objected strenuously but unsuccessfully when the king unilaterally placed import duties on a shipment of currants. James then tried to rule by royal proclamation without the benefit of Parliament, and in 1614 he dissolved it for seven years. Other Parliaments met and squabbled with the king until his death in 1625. His successor, Charles I, had stormy relationships with Parliament from the beginning. When Parliament refused to appropriate money he demanded, he dismissed that body and tried to collect it without their authority. To do so he imprisoned wealthy businessmen and impressed many poorer people into the army. Disputes between king and Parliament continued until the latter was dismissed in 1629. It did not meet again for eleven years.

During the interim, King Charles ordered severe repression of his Puritan enemies, including mutilations and branding of those he accused of sedition. The royal persecutions prompted accelerated migration of Puritans to New England. In 1633 William Laud became Archbishop of Canterbury and chief adviser to the king. The archbishop's authoritarian attempts to enforce the use of Church of England ritual throughout the country proved extremely unpopular among Puritans and other "dissenters." When Laud's prayer book outlining official changes reached Scotland, the people responded with riots and a document called the "National Covenant," which opposed Laud's changes and was signed by many people throughout the whole of England. Charles' reaction was to raise an army to invade Scotland to humble the opposition, but the Scots met him with an even larger army, and he was forced to back down without a fight in what came to be called the First Bishops' War.

King Charles returned to England determined to finish the work he started in Scotland. When the king reconvened Parliament to raise money for the war, that body refused to provide it until he agreed to share power with them, and that he refused to do. He dismissed Parliament after only three weeks, but a Scottish invasion of England (the Second Bishops' War) forced him to reconvene it to seek funds. The Parliament, composed mostly of landed gentry and wealthy merchants, supported the rights and privileges of the wealthy elite. The members moved to attack the king's most trusted advisers and ordered the deaths of Archbishop Laud and Sir Thomas Wentworth, Earl of Strafford, then chief adviser to the king. After Strafford was executed, Parliament demolished the courts the king had set up as instruments of repression and enacted laws forbidding dissolution of Parliament. On the subject of transferring power from king to Parliament there was considerable unity, but when leaders addressed religious issues and the question of who was to control the army, they split into various factions. Tensions were exacerbated when word arrived from Ireland of the massacre of Protestants.

The Parliament passed, by the narrow margin of eleven votes, the "Great Remonstrance," a lengthy recounting of the sins and errors of the Crown. King Charles reacted by charging leaders with sedition and leading a party of supporters to arrest them, but they had been forewarned and escaped down the Thames. The English Civil War was now inevitable. Charles assembled his forces in the north and war was declared on August 22, 1642. The Civil War pitted the Royalists against the Roundheads (supporters of Parliament) and Scots and brought to prominence Oliver Cromwell, the Puritan landowner and military leader who was destined to become dictator of England. In June 1645 the two sides met in a decisive battle at Naseby, and the forces of Parliament were victorious. King Charles was imprisoned.

The winning side, which had united against the abuses of King Charles, was deeply divided on issues ranging from leadership to religion, and Charles did what he could to take advantage of these divisions. Parliament moved to tax the Royalists to pay for the war, a move that was intended to cause many to lose their estates, and embarked on a period of religious persecution directed against Roman and Anglican Catholics, Unitarians, Congregationalists, Baptists, and other non-Puritans.

The army included a faction known as Levelers, who proposed radical democratic reforms far beyond those advocated by Parliament. All these forces contended for power until Cromwell and Parliament charged Charles with treason, a result of his constant intrigues, and executed him in January, 1649. Although perhaps more brutal and oppressive than some other English monarchs, Charles had not broken any actual laws of the realm; he was executed purely as a matter of political expediency. With his death, Cromwell became virtual dictator and created his own government—the Commonwealth, which has been described by some as an experiment in democracy. Dominated by Puritan extremists, the new government enacted "blue laws," which were a constant irritation to non-Puritans and created such unpopularity and dissension that in 1653 Cromwell dissolved Parliament and England fell under a military dictatorship. The Puritans abolished many popular forms of English entertainment, including theater, cock fights, and even church festivals. Puritanism from Elizabethan times tended to be particularly intolerant of other beliefs. Puritan rule was so glum and unappealing that people began to call for a restoration of the monarchy. When Cromwell died in 1658, Parliament soon recalled Charles II, son of Charles I, whose coronation signaled the end of the Puritan phase of the revolution.

Before he returned from Holland, Charles II was required to recognize Parliament's authority over a number of issues. The Restoration Parliament abolished vestiges of the feudal laws that recognized the king's ownership in theory of all the lands of England. Henceforth the gentry and aristocracy could claim to be landowners and not merely landholders. The country was deeply in debt as a result of the Civil War. Charles II appointed Lord Clarendon as chief adviser and head of the Privy Council, and Clarendon essentially ruled England for the next seven years. Eventually he became very unpopular and ended his days in exile on the Continent.

A complex struggle for power characterized this period. Modern scholars argue whether it was dominated by religious competition or class interests, or by the struggle between monarchy and Parliament. In fact, all these elements were involved, but overall the conflict between the interests of the monarchy and those of Parliament had left the government firmly in the hands of the landed and mercantile class. The monarchy, however, continued to rule in ways that worked to the advantage of the Crown. The king's practice of granting charters and monopolies, seeking to control trade, and managing foreign and domestic affairs for the Crown's benefit at times worked to the disadvantage of the business community. Attempting to strengthen the position of the mercantile class, Parliament extended the navigation acts that protected English trade in 1660. Goods entering England were required to be carried on English ships or ships from the country of origin. The colonies were to provide raw materials that could not be produced at home and they could only import English goods or goods that had passed through England. The navigation acts lengthened the list of colonial exports that could be shipped only to England. This would eventually mean, for example, that molasses produced in Jamaica could not be shipped to Boston but had to be first shipped to England and could be unloaded in Boston only after Englishmen had enjoyed a profit handling it. This action was aimed directly at England's chief maritime rival, Holland, whose ships carried goods to and from the English colonies, but it also reflected a desire to exploit the colonies. It precipitated the Second Dutch War (1665–1667). The previous year, English squadrons had seized Dutch posts on the African coast and the Dutch colony of New Amsterdam, which included Manhattan and what would come to be called New Jersey. For a time the region was under the direct proprietorship of the Duke of York, and part of it eventually consituted New York State.

Charles II made some serious mistakes in the ensuing years, entering into intrigues with France against Holland that included a secret promise to reintroduce Catholicism to England. Parliament reacted by rejecting these goals and passed laws that made

Catholics ineligible for some high public offices. Fears of popish plots dominated public life until Charles finally dissolved Parliament in 1678. During this time (possibly in 1675), England's first true political parties were born: reactionaries, conservatives, liberals, and radicals. The two emerging mainstream parties were the Whigs, representing the liberal middle-class Protestant factions who wanted Parliamentary supremacy, and the Tories (conservatives) who supported the powers of the Crown and the supremacy of the Church of England.

Whig majorities dominated subsequent Parliaments, and Charles dissolved each of them. In 1681, when an election produced another Whig majority, Charles dissolved Parliament and ruled for four years in its absence. He died in 1685 and was succeeded by his younger brother, the fifty-three-year-old Catholic, James II. James II ruled only three years. His maneuvers and appointments of Catholics to coveted offices were very unpopular and led to what has been called the Glorious, or Bloodless, Revolution, which forced his abdication and exile to France and brought Protestant William of Orange to the throne of England. It marked the end of real royal power and the beginning of limited or constitutional monarchy. The struggle for power between the Crown and Parliaments dominated by wealthy merchants and landed gentry, which had occupied most of the seventeenth century, concluded with the latter in power and England poised at the frontier of another and different kind of revolution.

Thomas Hobbes, who some think the most important of the political philosophers of this era, published *The Leviathan* in 1651. He argued that a stable government that applied the law consistently would minimize the dangers of tyrannical rule, while ancient systems of privilege that excused some from living under those rules because of divine right or custom were a formula for anarchy. His was a powerful argument for the promotion of a nation-state. Another voice, that of John Locke, stands out. Locke returned from exile when William of Orange arrived in England at the time of the Glorious Revolution and proceeded to become one of the most influential philosophers of his time. His writings compliment the revolution, supporting the rule of Parliament and offering arguments for a balance of power among the branches of government. He is credited with being a major inspiration for the American founders of the U.S. government almost a century later, but his influence hardly ends there. In his *Second Treatise on Government*, Locke argued that Englishmen in the Americas, ostensibly because they are engaged in pursuing society's ideal of a prosperous future, were justified in driving Indians from their lands because the former made rational use of it and the latter did not. Echoing arguments made by Sepúlveda more than a century earlier, Locke's work promoted the idea that there is but one correct way to use the land, that Europeans have that correct way, and that the use of force to seize the land is therefore justifiable.

In other writings, Locke reinforced the political theory of "possessive individualism," which rationalized practices, long in place, that defined early capitalism. He said that money had replaced nature as a more perfect medium for the concentration and accumulation of wealth and had provided an incentive for rational behavior. Under this prescription, "rational" behavior was rewarded with profits, and an individual was, with the invention of money, motivated to accumulate wealth, through which all good things could be accomplished. This argument supported the proposition that human agency could solve the world's problems, and it placed both acquisition of money and the interest of the individual at the center of this problem-solving equation. Capitalism—the acquisition of money for the purpose of investing in activities to make more money—was believed to be the engine of this process.

Bibliography

Beer, G. L. *The Origins of the British Colonial System, 1578–1660.* New York: The MacMillan Co., 1908.

Berlin, Isaiah. *The Crooked Timber of Humanity: Chapters in the History of Ideas.* Princeton, N.J.: Princeton University Press, 1998, 31.

Cocker, Mark. *Rivers of Blood, Rivers of Gold: Europe's Conflict with Tribal Peoples.* London: J. Cape, 1998.

Copland, Ian. *The Burden of Empire: Perspectives on Imperialism and Colonialism.* Melbourne: Oxford University Press, 1990.

Crosby, Alfred W. *Ecological Imperialism: The Biological Expansion of Europe, 900–1900.* New York: Cambridge University Press, 1986.

Hammon, J. L., and Barbara Hammond. *The Village Laborer, 1760–1832: A Study in the Government of England Before the Reform Bill.* New York and London: Longmans, Green & Co., 1920.

Heaton, Herbert. *Economic History of Europe.* New York: Harper & Row, 1936, 1948.

Johnson, A. H. *The Disappearance of the Small Landowner.* London: Oxford University Press, 1909, 1963.

Moore, Barrington, Jr. *Social Origins of Dictatorship and Democracy: Lord and Peasant in the Making of the Modern World.* Boston: Beacon Press, 1966.

Roberts, J. M. *The Penguin History of the World.* New York: Penguin Books, 1976, 1997.

Said, Edward W. *Culture and Imperialism.* New York: Knopf, 1993.

____. *Orientalism.* New York: Vintage Books, 1978, 1979.

Smith, Woodruff D. *European Imperialism in the Nineteenth and Twentieth Centuries.* Chicago: Nelson-Hall, 1982.

Tawney, R. H. *The Agrarian Problem in the Sixteenth Century.* New York: Burt Franklin, 1912.

Thompson, E. P. *The Making of the English Working Class.* New York: Vintage Books, 1963.

NINE
Revolutions and Conquests

Take up the White Man's burden—
Ye dare not stoop to less—
Nor call too loud on Freedom
To cloak your weariness;
By all ye cry or whisper,
By all ye leave or do,
The silent, sullen peoples
Shall weigh your Gods and you.

Rudyard Kipling, 1899

A number of significant movements in the history of Western Civilization embraced ideas and ideals that were highly speculative and ultimately unrealistic. It was more assertion than fact, for example, that intense interrogation of ideas would produce morally improved individuals, as Socrates had insisted. There was no concrete evidence, and history would not confirm, that a Kingdom of God was or is about to arrive on earth as Jesus and his disciples thought. The project to unite Europe and to expand Christianity through military force proposed by Pope Urban II as the wars of the cross, although it produced changes, did not produce the changes initially sought. The idea, promoted by such Renaissance thinkers as Petrarch, that secrets that could improve humanity were to be found through the study of the ancient Greek and Roman texts did not produce a kinder, gentler European in history. These were ideas—images in men's minds—that produced imaginary/visionary ideals that were adopted by idealists, people obsessed with the version of invented reality they found most pleasing to their purposes.

True idealists face an insurmountable dilemma. They may not compromise their ideals or they will betray the very concept that frames their identity. They may not negotiate their articles of belief with nonbelievers, because the beliefs of idealists are absolute and not negotiable. Since the beliefs represent perfection, agreeing to something else (by definition not perfect) betrays the ideal itself. When idealists are faced with antagonists who are nonbelievers, they feel they have no choice but to overcome or conquer or, in the face of overwhelming power, be conquered themselves. The religious wars that followed the Reformation were fought by men unwilling to compromise on ideals, particularly on the issue of how to achieve salvation. Revitalization movements have been known to give rise to forms of idealism that produce intense intolerance that could be resolved, in the view of the participants, only through repression, conquest, or violence.

The advance into modernity did not prove to be an antidote to this ancient tradition. Revitalization movements continued to support rationalizations for war, internecine violence, repression, appropriation, wholesale expulsions or removals of peoples from their homelands, and genocide. Each was rationalized by a form of idealism such as defense of the faith, progressivism, nationalism, or racism.

The Enlightenment—the European intellectual movement associated with the eighteenth century to 1789—set the stage for the popular optimism that accompanied the period known as the Age of Revolution (1789–1848). The body of thought that characterized the Enlightenment embraced the idea that humanity was experiencing an ascent, that scientific knowledge was expanding almost daily, and that humankind was on the verge of having enough information to solve all physical problems through science and could solve all social problems by applying the "scientifc" method (logic and reason) of the classical Greek philosophers. All this could be accomplished, it was thought, without the intervention of Divine Providence. These beliefs would evolve into a challenge to the Church and to monarchy, the institution founded on a theory of Divine Right.

The Enlightenment was a revitalization of European culture that was broad in nature and did not require a charismatic leader or visionary, or even an authoritative vision that excluded competing views. Philosophers of the Enlightenment advanced and popularized the idea of progress, a powerful idea in Western culture that has utopian roots. The eighteenth century embraced the idea with characteristic enthusiasm and established it firmly in European thought. This optimistic view of the future helped create the confidence to sweep away old orders and institutions and to move toward a new and expectantly better world. Progressive thinkers and later, revolutionaries, were united in the expectation that scientific and technological knowledge together with correct social theory would inevitably lead to the perfectibility of human society. Enlightenment thinking laid the foundation for an ideology of progress that would come to dominate Western thought. Renaissance intellectuals had worshipped the accomplishments of the ancient Greeks and Romans and had inhabited a world whose mood acknowledged decline from a glorious past and the imminent end of the world, but had not fundamentally challenged the Christian traditions of medieval society. English writers such as Hobbes, Locke, and Berkeley had challenged the idea of the supremacy of the monarchy but not the existence of God. Some Enlightenment writers would do so. The Enlightenment set a truly new direction.

Some trace the origins of the Enlightenment to Giordano Bruno, a former monk who was arrested, tried for heresy, and burned to death by the Inquisition at Rome. His execution became a symbol of the struggle for free thought and free speech. The French philosopher René Descartes, an early enthusiast of scientific knowledge, had tried to rationalize the skepticism of his pursuits with Christian dogma. He and his followers attracted the enmity of the Church because the latter required faith in authority, which it saw undermined by following the individual dictates of reason. It was a French Protestant clergyman, Peter Bayle, who urged that the Church's claim to authority could not be substantiated through natural reason and therefore could claim only the status of opinion as opposed to fact. Signaling a clear break with the old order, these ideas would set the stage for both political and cultural revolutions by promoting reason as a vehicle for challenging tradition and authority.

Enlightenment philosophers could disagree on major issues. David Hume, a Scot, doubted that the existence of spiritual substance could be proven and voiced doubts about the existence of an afterlife. The French philosopher Voltaire, one of the giants of the Enlightenment, did not doubt the existence of God but attacked the authority of the Church and clergy. A German, Paul Henri d'Holback, advanced materialist ideas and doubted the existence of the human soul. Jean Jacques Rousseau wrote passionately about the damage done to humanity by the creation of the idea of property. He idealized "natural man" and "natural law," believing that man had once existed in a state of harmony without government. In *The Social Contract*, he denies the validity of any "contract" between rulers and subjects that does not recognize the people as sovereign and operates without the consent of the majority. He insisted that where logic failed, feeling would yield the truth. His emphasis on intuition and feeling would be a foundation for Romanticism, a new movement in European intellectual thought.

The German philosopher Immanuel Kant urged that it was the human mind (and not the material world) that gave the impression of order, raising individual human consciousness—as distinct from divine revelation or the dictates of authority—to a position of importance. Johann Gottlieb Fichte carried the importance of consciousness even further, exalting the creative process of the mind more than any significant writer had done before. Philosopher Isaiah Berlin credits Fichte with the invention of Romanticism, which he defines as an important chapter in the pursuit of the ideal. Idealism was and is a strong component in the construction of nationalism because an idealist must be true to his/her beliefs despite the costs, and those beliefs arise legitimately from emotions or feelings with little regard for a fact pattern or a context of history that might argue against them. It is summarized, somewhat crudely, in the expression "my country, right or wrong." Fichte argued that the consciousness of freedom could obligate one to make sacrifices for the good of others. A duty to make sacrifices for the common national good was a departure from the ruling tradition that duty was owed to God (through the Church) and king.

The Italian nationalist Joseph Mazzini, who wrote passionately about feelings toward one's country and one's people, emerged as the great nineteenth-century proponent of the ideas that comprise nationalism. Carried to their extremes, these ideas would rationalize actions inspired by idealistic assumptions based on emotions that would lead to extraordinary sacrifice, violence, and destruction. Nationalism became the most powerful ideology ever to appear on the world stage, more powerful even than the idea of progress, and although it arises from European experiences, it is found to some degree in virtually every society in the world.

The Glorious Revolution had equipped England with a government that was willing to undertake conquest on behalf of profits through trade. When Scotland and Wales united with England in 1707, creating the United Kingdom of Great Britain, England became the largest free-trade market among Western nations. The next step, industrialization, required that six economic supporters be in place: capital, labor, technology, natural resources, transportation, and markets. England had access to capital. It was blessed with iron ore and abundant coal, and these would prove to be crucial.

One of the products of the England's Glorious Revolution was a 1688 law that designated the rights to underground minerals, previously reserved to the Crown, to the individual landowner. Early in the eighteenth century primitive steam engines (the Newcomen) were used to pump water out of coal mines, enabling increased coal production. In the first half of the eighteenth century, a process to use coal to make coke and to use coke in iron production was invented by the Darbys at Coalbrookdale, just as the forests that had previously provided charcoal were beginning to become exhausted in some iron-producing areas. Other important inventions followed: Smeaton's air pump (1760), the flying shuttle (1733), the spinning jenny (1767), and James Watt's steam engine (1776). Beginning in the early decades of this century, England's population began to grow, and migration to the colonies and beyond increased. As had happened in ancient Greece, mining and metallurgy gave rise to a period of expansion. Much of the eighteenth century was fairly peaceful and prosperous, but new trends in power, driven by the now-established oligarchy, began to emerge. Of the five wars Britain would fight, four would be for territory and markets at the behest of its lords of commerce.

Inventions, along with developments in the political, scientific, and philosophic arenas, helped fuel the ideology that categorized changes in material conditions over time as "progress." A significant advance in this idea occurred around 1776, and is especially evident in Adam Smith's famous work, *An Inquiry into the Nature and Causes of the Wealth of Nations*. Offering the metaphor of an "invisible hand" that naturally regulates the free market, Smith expands on ideas previously articulated by John Locke on the benefits derived from individual self-interest in a free market economy. Some of these ideas can be seen as evolving directly from the struggle for hegemony between the monarchy and the bourgeoisie. The monarchy in this paradigm represented state control, monopoly, and a self-interested government. The oligarchy, on the other hand, supported free markets, the absence of regulation of any kind, and the assertion, expressed by Smith, that the free market would bring more benefits to society than a regulated economy could ever provide.

The ideology of progress guided by an invisible hand is more clearly an extension of the pursuit of the ideal than has been generally acknowledged. Progress is a road to a golden future made possible by human agency acting within the framework of the belief in societal perfectibility. Although the idea that things are destined to get better over time can be found in other sources, no single source so articulates the ideology of progress, which was destined to become a dogma and one of the most powerful movements in the West. The idea of an invisible hand, especially in the minds of Smith's successors, has metaphysical overtones that are typical of a revitalization movement.

The "Industrial Revolution" is the term used to describe England's economic development from about 1780 to 1870 (though historians differ on the exact dates). England became its birthplace because the necessary social, political, economic, and geological conditions first converged there. England was also blessed with adequate ports and some navigable rivers, enough to give commerce a start. London became the largest city in Europe and provided a reliable market for a number of industries. One necessary ingredient for this revolution was a supply of cotton, which England's climate could not produce. When one thinks of the Industrial Revolution, one must think of cotton, and when one thinks of cotton, one must think of the cotton gin, the American South, Egypt, colonies, textile mills, slavery, imperialism, and world markets.

While all of these elements were necessary, many were the result of what can only be described as good fortune. No amount of planning would have substituted for the existence of abundant coal or iron, ore both of which were gifts of nature. The availability of labor, likewise, was not planned. When the peasants were driven from the land, their homes destroyed, and their families subjected to beggary, none of the burghers was able to say, "You'll be all right. In a couple of centuries, you'll be able to get factory work."

Of all of the requirements, markets and sources of cheap raw materials not available in the motherland are most often acquired through politics and warfare. England pursued both courses vigorously. Although domestic markets were a necessary condition for the rise of industry, domestic markets expand slowly while external markets can multiply and provide rapid expansion. England, whose oligarchy was strengthened by royal mismanagement of the American Revolution and subsequent mental illness of King George III, sought to invade as many of these foreign markets as possible and to cripple foreign lands' abilities to be self-sufficient.

Local self-sufficiency is the bane of global markets and was, in this case, an obstacle to British colonialism. One of the results of the Industrial Revolution was the rebirth of colonialism and the second wave of European overseas imperial expansion, which was to extend into most of the remaining populated world.

In 1785 the world was a predominantly rural place. In most European countries, 90 percent or more of the population lived in the countryside and engaged in some form of agricultural production. The second wave of great enclosures that occurred in eighteenth-century England assured there would be plenty of available labor, and extra labor could always be recruited from immigrant groups. The work demanded by the technology that was developed in the eighteenth century was relatively easy to master, and English rural folk had worked long and hard for centuries and hard work was no stranger to them.

Outside Europe, most production was on plantations, except in the northern United States and Canada. In English, French, and other colonies, labor was provided by black slaves, and in Spanish America it was also provided by Indians who lived very much like slaves. In much of Europe serfs and peasants provided labor under the ancient system, living in conditions not much removed from slavery.

France had extracted some measure of revenge against England by assisting the American colonies during the American Revolution, but as a result was bankrupt. An estimated 50 percent of the tax revenues of the kingdom were required to service the debt, most of which was incurred during the war, and this factor contributed to the idea that the American Revolution laid the foundation for the French Revolution. In order to raise money, King Louis XVI faced a formidable dilemma. He needed to dismantle the fabric of privileges enjoyed by the aristocracy and the clergy; and while these privileges enabled them to escape taxation, the system of privilege was the foundation of the absolute monarchy.

In 1787 Louis turned to an "assembly of notables" to begin this process, and this led to a meeting of the Estates-General, a feudal assembly that had not met since 1614. The French Revolution, one of the most important and influential events in European history, began with an attempt by the aristocracy to recapture the state. The nobility and clergy reasserted ancient privileges to command access to official posts. At the same time they used their ownership of estates to squeeze even more from the peasants, thus rendering themselves unpopular with both the small property owners and the poor, who—combined—made up the vast majority of the population of France.

It has been said that philosophers have acted as agents of social change and revolution. While this was a factor in the French Revolution, there were other important factors as well. Crop failures had brought near-famine conditions in 1788 and 1789, and in the latter year a particularly bad winter was experienced. Food prices soared at a moment when the economy stagnated, leaving poor people, both urban and rural, in desperate straits.

The Estates-General met on May 5, 1789, and within six weeks had reconstituted itself as the National Assembly. It set out to write a new constitution, with a claim that it spoke for all of France. In 1789 the National Assembly issued the famous Declaration of the Rights of Man and Citizens, a statement by the bourgeoisie attacking hierarchical privileges, but not an assertion of democratic or egalitarian principles. The American Revolution had put forward a solution for the problem of how to conceptualize sovereignty in the absence of the institution of the Crown. Sovereignty was to reside in the "people," or the "nation," and the Declaration so provided. Placing the principle of sovereignty as belonging to the "French nation" raised important new questions: What was a nation? How did it relate to other nations with competing national interests that were likely be settled by war? This idea of nationalism had two goals: to free people from feudal institutions and the prospect of tyranny under the rule of men; and to establish a rule of law to be applied, in principle, to all.

The National Assembly operated at a moment of turmoil in France's history. A Parisian riot and rural revolts occurred. The king distanced himself from the privileged aristocracy and made many concessions to the Assembly. The Assembly did what it could to dismantle the feudal order by seizing lands of the Church. There was growing resentment and reaction to these changes, and significant numbers of the aristocracy fled France. The king was viewed with growing suspicion as a reactionary. By 1792 France was at war with Austria and Prussia; a Parisian insurrection overthrew the monarchy; and a new assembly, the Convention, moved to the center of political power. The Convention voted to execute the king in January 1793 and launched the Terror, a period during which the Convention exercised intolerance and intimidation toward many of those dubbed its enemies. The French Revolution, however, did not result in wholesale executions, and fewer people fled France during and following the Revolution than fled the United States during and following the American Revolution.

By 1797 the Revolution had evolved into a constitutional government whose radical pedigree was quite modest. Although it was overthrown in a coup d'etat in 1799, the first ten years of the Revolution had left indelible marks on France and, by extension, on the rest of Europe. The terms "right" and "left," designating political tendencies, arose during the early stages of the Revolution from the custom whereby the radicals sat on the left side of the Assembly and the conservatives on the right side. On the side of the Left were support for and emphasis on free speech and press, expanded suffrage, and individual rights, and on the Right support for the practical usefulness of hierarchy, discipline, and attention to duties as opposed to the rights of the individual. These ideas and tendencies were exported from France to the rest of Europe and, ultimately, to the rest of the world.

The coup of 1799 brought a military man, Napoleon Bonaparte, to power. Bonaparte sought to legitimize his ambitions to build an empire by designating himself emperor through a plebiscite. He could thus claim a mandate to rule from the people of France. Under Napoleon, France raised armies and carried on conquests from Portugal to Moscow, but the Napoleonic Wars served to unify a coalition of European powers against him, led by

England. British naval power defeated Napoleon at Aboukir in 1798 and Trafalgar in 1805. The beginning of the end arguably came in 1812, when France invaded Russia and Napoleon's great army withered away before the Russian winter. By 1814, when France was threatened in the southwest by an English army and on the east by Austrian and Prussian armies, French military and political leaders at last put Bonaparte aside and sued for peace.

Although peace brought a restoration of the Bourbons, Bonaparte's regime had cemented permanently in place many of the reforms of the French Revolution that characterize it as a movement toward modernization. Bonaparte was remembered fondly by his countrymen for success on the battlefield, but with his rule something appeared that had rarely been seen in Europe since the time of the Romans. Bonaparte was a modern (post-feudal) leader, a popular military dictator as opposed to a hereditary monarch. His popularity was intensified by the new nationalistic mood. Many of those who served in his armies did so with an intense enthusiasm and loyalty because they were, in principle, fighting for France and the French and for everything they stood for, including French charisma and the supposed superiority of French culture. Napolean's armies, and indeed the French people, were willing to identify with and make sacrifices for the enterprises their emperor represented in ways the world had not seen before. The idea emerged that the nation represented a public interest greater than that of rulers and that competition among nations to settle national interests was legitimate. In this context war among nations could be seen as somehow logical.

This new and intense variety of nationalism carried the potential to set whole peoples against one another. The underlying principle—that there was a national public interest and that everyone had a compelling stake in that interest—was vague and often not well understood, while at the same time emotionally appealing. When conditions made it possible for this kind of nationalism to be energized by some form of utopian enterprise, the potential was formed for acting on the basis of popular sovereignty to pursue goals that were at best marginally realistic.

Some of the shaping events that would determine how nationalist agendas would be played out happened even before the Vienna settlement of 1815. In 1804 a Serbian pork dealer led a revolt that culminated in the creation of an autonomous Serbian principality in 1817, an early sign that the Ottoman Empire was crumbling and an early step in the violence that would characterize the breakup of the empire in eastern Europe. Another example was the revolt of the "Greeks" in 1821 and the subsequent emergence of the kingdom of Greece in 1832.

The 1840s were a time of economic hardship that included the potato famine in Ireland in 1846 and other crop failures in Europe in 1847. A subsequent round of revolutionary activity came in 1848. An uprising in Paris was crushed and revolutions in Germany also failed. Steps were taken to create a more unified Germany.

Almost certainly the most significant event of the year was the appearance of a pamphlet by Karl Marx that would come to be known as *The Communist Manifesto*. Marx was appalled by the cruel conditions visited on the workers by the Industrial Revolution. While attacking utopian socialism, he offered the theory that history was on the side of those who, as revolutionaries, championed the interests of the proletariat. This theory was to beget one of the most powerful revitalization movements of Western civilization and would usher in profound changes over vast parts of the globe. It began with an interpretation of history as a story of class struggle:

> [T]he whole history of mankind . . . has been a history of class struggles, contests between exploiting and exploited, ruling and oppressed classes; . . . a stage has been reached where the exploited and oppressed class—the proletariat — cannot attain its emancipation from the sway of the exploiting and ruling class—"the bourgeoisie"—without at the same time, and once and for all, emancipating society at large from all exploitation, oppression, class distinction, and class struggles. (Lucas 1943, 804, from *Manifesto of the Communist Party* by Karl Marx and Frederich Engels)

A revitalization movement, we have seen, is a conscious effort to undertake changes to create a more satisfactory culture. While Marxism quickly became a formula to overturn the abuses of industrial civilization, it remained, for the most part, faithful to the ideas that formed much of the optimism of the Enlightenment. At its heart it prescribed one and only one remedy for bourgeois hegemony—proletarian revolution. The economic interpretation of history rejected the idea that moral arguments about injustice could succeed and urged that the rise of a proletariat signaled the evolution of a period of inevitable revolution that would lead to the emergence of a more just society. As Marxism evolved and grew, it took the rhetoric of revolution from the liberals and transformed it into its own vision. As during the Enlightenment, the utopian vision was fueled by optimism about the absence of limitations on progress. Science and technology would inevitably reduce the toil of the workers by increasing the amount of wealth and reducing the amount of labor necessary to create wealth. The result would be an utopian society that came to be called the Workers' Paradise.

At the time Marxism was first proposed, only England possessed in significant numbers workers who fit this definition of the proletariat. Marxism, however, spread to many lands, some of which had barely experienced the Industrial Revolution. The spread of Marxism to societies with little industrialization and no real industrial working class to form the foundation of revolution illustrates the degree to which Marxism became a kind of religion that called upon people to have faith in a process of history believed to be inevitable.

Marxism generated enormous enthusiasm as well as revulsion. Like many revitalization movements, enthusiasm often carried it to extremes—to ideas and practices its detractors described as unrealistic. Its history is a curiosity because the revolutions of which it speaks did not arise from the workers in the industrialized countries of England, the United States, Canada, Germany, France, Holland, Italy, or any other industrialized or industrializing country. It arose instead by political coup d'etat in Russia and peasant revolution in China and was spread, in many cases, through force of arms. Although its primary argument involved the inevitable forces of history, it failed to predict the reforms that would be won by workers, ranging from issues of safety in the work place and a demand for an eight-hour day to child labor and minimum wage laws, retirement benefits, and more. Marxism influenced these and other developments but predicted none of them. Nor could it predict that capitalist culture would also evolve and, in many cases, reform. In many of the countries in which Marxism later came to power, these issues were not of primary importance because there was little capitalist culture to reform. Marxist regimes are a phenomenon of the twentieth century, an aftermath of the Russian Revolution of 1917, and to understand why an ideology of resistance to Western economic and political expansion could gain such acceptance around the world, we need to know about another great historic movement of the nineteenth century.

For a while, colonialism had experienced a period of unpopularity among European powers. The colonies of the first wave of conquests, including most of England's North American colonies and most of Spain's possessions in the New World were, one by one, achieving independence—falling away from the colonial powers, as someone put it, like "ripe fruits falling from the tree." The Industrial Revolution changed the situation because it created a need for markets. Technology made it possible for fewer workers to produce more, and markets were needed to sell the products of this rapidly expanding industrial capacity. In addition, it generated a need for new sources of cheap raw materials. Shortly after this phase of industrialization was underway, European nations embarked on a second period of overseas colonization. The need for markets together with rising nationalism were the main reasons for colonial expansion, but it should also be mentioned that advances in military technology had made colonial conquest far easier. European inventions in military technology during this period progressed from the breech-loading cartridge to the machine gun, and non-European peoples were virtually defenseless against the new generations of weaponry that Western powers, particularly Britain, could bring to bear.

[C]onquering markets by war and colonization required not merely an economy capable of exploiting those markets, but also a government willing to wage war and colonize for the benefit of British manufacturers. . . . Here the advantage of Britain over her potential competitors is quite evident. Unlike some of them (such as France) she was prepared to subordinate *all* foreign policy to economic ends. Her war aims were commercial and . . . naval. (Hobsbawm 1968, 49)

No European army ever lost a war against a people not similarly armed, except for one singularly memorable encounter with the Zulu nation in South Africa. England's armies were practically invincible and enabled it to seize New Zealand in 1840, Hong Kong in 1842, Natal in South Africa in 1843, the Malay States in 1874, and the Fiji Islands in 1874. In 1882, in an effort to control the Suez Canal and the shortest sea route between England and India, British forces bombarded Alexandria, Egypt, and in 1899 they seized the Egyptian Sudan.

This renewed interest in colonies was also due in part to increased tariffs around Europe and the growing industrial capacity and productivity of the United States, Germany, Italy, and other countries. Nationalist sentiment was also influential. When other European countries saw England's expansion, they followed suit, but one cannot underestimate the power of ideology in this quest. There arose a belief that European nations, because of their claim to the benefits of superior civilization, "owed" it to the rest of the world to spread those benefits. The obligation to engage in armed aggression was termed the "white man's burden." It was a burden that would prove quite profitable for a great number of Europeans. This argument, which by this time also included the rising ideology of progress, was nurtured in the context of scientific observations made by Charles Darwin, which many interpreted as the idea of the "survival of the fittest."

In the "white man's burden" we find echoes of the arguments of Sepulveda at Valladolid in 1550 about the superiority of Spanish culture and the rights of the Spanish to take the property and freedom of the Indians. It became a code or shorthand incorporating European thinking that defined utopianism in the age of conquests we call the modern world, from the appropriation of Aristotle to John Locke's *Second Treatise on Government* and beyond. Europeans were inventing Aryanism at the same time, and the "white man's burden," in three words, articulated all the ideas of the rights of European ruling classes over everyone else in the world. In short, the white man had rights to all the wealth of the world because he carried the burden of a superior civilization on the road to solving all the problems of mankind. Whatever was necessary to exercise this right—murder, rape, kidnaping, torture, genocide—could be rationalized under this self-imposed mandate. This wave of European imperialism, which was also a new wave of cultural revitalization, found its roots in a combination of an ethnocentric intellectual tradition, a newly energized "scientific racism," and the perceived demands of world trade. Interestingly, an important intellectual origin of the emerging racism arose in class antagonisms.

> The dreams of racism actually have their origin in ideologies of *class* . . . in claims to divinity among rulers . . . No surprise then that . . . on the whole, racism and anti-semitism manifest themselves, not across national boundaries, but within them. In other words, they justify not so much foreign wars as domestic repression and domination. Where racism developed outside Europe in the nineteenth century, it was always associated with European domination. (Anderson 1986, 136-37)

In 1870 Africa, except for a few coastal areas, was largely unknown to Europeans. Although France had long held Algeria and England held Egypt and a colony at the southern end of the continent, the vast central area of the continent was largely blank on European maps. Around 1840 a Scottish physician/missionary named David Livingston ventured into the "dark continent" and was rumored to have become lost. A New York journalist, Henry Stanley, searched for and found him, giving rise to the legendary line: "Dr. Livingston, I presume." Stanley did some exploring of his own, wrote a book enthusiastically describing the potentials for wealth he had seen, and returned to Europe seeking investors for the exploitation of the Congo. He found a warm reception with Belgium's King Leopold II. The king invested heavily and soon had what amounted to slave plantations of African natives, harvesting rubber in a country eighty times the size of Belgium and wholly owned by the king. In time, treatment of the natives became so horrific that it became a scandal even among Europeans of the day, a pattern we have seen repeated in the history of such exploitations. Thus did tiny Belgium lead the European conquest of Africa, a conquest that consumed about fifty years. France, England, Holland, Spain, and Germany vied for territory across vast expanses where no European had previously gone.

Beginning in the sixteenth century, Europe had exported devastating diseases to the peoples of the islands and the Americas. During the nineteenth century Europeans exported "race science"—a pseudoscientific ideology that in some ways would prove just as deadly. Race science was all the rage in Europe in those days, and for students of central Africa the key doctrine was the so-called Hamitic hypothesis, propounded in 1863 by John Hanning Speke. Speke's basic anthropological theory, which he made up out of whole cloth, was that all culture and civilization in central Africa had been introduced by the taller, sharper-featured people, whom he considered to be a Caucasoid tribe of Ethiopian origin, descended from the biblical King David, and therefore a superior race to the native Negroids (Gourevitch 1998, 50–51). This theory represented the genesis of the racial antagonisms that would play out in genocide in Rwanda between the Hutu and Tutsi peoples more than a century later. Rwanda experienced Christianization, colonization, and the importation of a remarkable combination of race science and Old Testament mythology that rendered the repeated episodes of genocide there ultimately of Western origin.

In 1886 European nations drew maps establishing the boundaries of the various colonies. Agreements were also made, for the most part among European nations, allocating parts of Asia as "spheres of influence." Only one non-European empire—Japan—emerged to challenge European hegemony and to seek colonies of its own. Japan also fought and won a war against Russia (which ended in 1905) to secure territory for itself. As the century neared its end, the United States exercised its own territorial ambitions in a war with Spain that extended U.S. holdings to include Puerto Rico and a number of territories in the Pacific, including the Philippines, and continued to declare Latin America as its sphere of influence. By 1910 Europe had about 85 percent of the globe under either a European flag or under a settler regime dominated by descendants of European colonists. Most of the new colonies were in regions with climates unsuited to Europeans and populated by peoples hostile to them and therefore did not attract massive immigration from Europe. In addition, they proved not to be very profitable, either for outright plunder or for restricted trade, while at the same time they could be quite expensive in terms of long-distance administration. Colonialism as a form of exploitation again began to lose popularity among the European ruling class between wars as the twentieth century wore on, although it was far from dead as World War II approached.

In the decade prior to World War I, there were a number of conflicts in Eastern Europe, some of which involved Serbia and Herzegovina, but there were no overwhelming economic competitions that should have led to war. Indeed, during much of this time people were optimistic that wars among European states might be a thing of the past because these nations' economies were increasingly interconnected in ways that should have produced motivations for peace. Although economic competition was not the primary factor in the outbreak of war, Germany's rise as a significant industrial power produced fears in a number of countries, and especially in England, that Germany was a significant rival.

World War I was not the first war fought by numerous European nations across many continents and seas, but it was, until that time, the largest of these conflicts. In many ways it was a kind of European civil war, ignited ultimately by what can best be described as a crisis in diplomacy fueled by modern nationalism. Narrowly defined national interests had led to a series of treaties of mutual defense that called upon countries to assist each other in case of attack. For a while, the complex set of alliances—designed to create a balance of power such that no nation emerged dominant—seemed to be working. However, the treaties were structured so that when trouble came, the machinery to mobilize military defense was not effectively countered by similar machinery to access peacekeeping.

When Archduke Ferdinand of Austria-Hungary was assassinated by Serbian nationalists on June 28, 1914, and Austria-Hungary shortly thereafter declared war on Serbia, the system of military alliances that came into play plunged all Europe into war. No one could have known how this series of events was destined to change the course of history.

In the early stages of the war, German armies achieved stunning successes, crossing Belgium and coming close to Paris, but at the Battle of the Marne their advance was halted. The two sides then settled into trench warfare, neither able to gain an advantage over the other. As 1914 dragged on, the war ground to a standstill. New engines of war came into prominence: British tanks, aircraft (on both sides), the machine gun, poison gas (by Germany), and submarines. Germany was especially successful with a blockade of England using submarines. At the beginning of the war, the United States was strongly in favor of neutrality, but German submarines began to sink U.S. shipping, on the grounds that it supported England's war effort. President Wilson warned that Germany must stop sinking neutral ships, but Germany continued, and U.S. public and government opinion went against Germany. The United States entered the war on the side of Britain and the Allies in 1917.

The British blockade of Germany produced serious shortages of essential materials and food. Germany challenged the blockade only once, in a battle on the North Sea. Although the German Fleet inflicted heavy losses on the British blockade, it returned to port never to challenge again. German submarines continued to prey on British and other ships, with tremendous losses to the British Merchant Marine and Navy. An estimated 60 percent of the British Fleet was torpedoed, but the British and Americans retaliated with depth charges and a gigantic shipbuilding effort. By the summer of 1918, Allied forces were inflicting serious losses on the German Army and by the end of October had driven them from France. An armistice was signed on November 11, 1918, signaling Germany's defeat.

On the Eastern Front, the initial successes of the Tsar's armies were followed by crushing defeats in August and September 1914, at the hands of Germany, and Russia was forced to fall back. A German and Austrian offensive in 1915 pushed the Russians back even further, but the following year Russian general Brusilov's victories on the Eastern front brought Romania into the war on the side of the Allies. After that, however, a decline in Russian military fortunes occurred, much of it ascribed to the incompetence and corruption of the Tsar's regime. This precipitated the end of imperial Russia. In the winter of 1916–1917, dissatisfaction and unrest became general over all of Russia. In the spring, strikes by workers were followed by strikes by sectors of the army and a revolution that resulted in the Tsar's abdication. In November 1917 a second revolution brought Vladimir Ilyich Lenin and the Communist Party to power.

Some seventy years earlier, Marx had called his work the *Communist Manifesto* to distinguish his theories from those of "Utopian Socialism," and there can be little question that in both spirit and intellectual vigor the Marxist tradition was distinct from earlier prescriptions for improving the conditions of the poor and the working class. Marx's critique of capital is still read today, but it was his role as prophet that brought so much energy to the movement. Marx believed that economics was the only driving force of society. It had shaped its institutions and had created classes with antagonistic interests during the Industrial Revolution. He decried religion as an "opiate of the masses" that reinforced the enslavement of the working class. He created a framework of language and analysis to explain what he thought was inevitable: the overthrow of the capitalists by workers in a class war.

Neither Marx nor the other significant nineteenth-century utopian socialists lived long enough to see a state government embrace and try to give reality to their ideas. Communist revolutionaries led by Lenin took over Russia, not by a rising of the proletariat, but by an opportunistic political coup. They spoke of the creation of a Workers' Paradise, hailed technology as the path to making workers' lives less filled with toil, and transferred private property to the state. Marx intensely disliked utopian socialists, such as England's Robert Owen. Soviet Marxists were utopianists in their own right, and their revitalization movement included a totalitarian state that Marx, had he been alive, would probably not have supported.

When Georgian peasants failed to embrace the Workers' Paradise and agricultural collectives, Joseph Stalin, Lenin's successor, caused millions to starve. When a separatist movement developed in the Ukraine, Stalin sent the Ukrainian intelligentsia to Siberia and starved more millions of peasants. In pursuit of the perfectible socialist world, indigenous peoples east of the Urals were abused, dissenters were shipped to draconian gulags in Siberia, protests were ruthlessly and bloodily suppressed, and religious and traditional ethnic practices were outlawed. Russia's Workers' Paradise was to be a place with rules where the powers of the state would be exercised. "From each according to ability," they intoned, "to each according to need." But between those who produced and those who consumed stood the Soviet state and the all-powerful Communist Party, which had appropriated to itself the right to dispense brutality in the name of economic justice and to appropriate a healthy share of the wealth of the society.

Bibliography

Anderson, Benedict. *Imagined Communities: Reflections on the Origin and Spread of Nationalism.* London: Verso, 1983, 1986.

Gourevitch, Philip. *We Wish to Inform You that Tomorrow We Will Be Killed with Our Families: Stories from Rwanda.* New York: Farrar,

Straus & Giroux, 1998.

Heilbroner, Robert L. *Marxism: For and Against.* New York: W. W. Norton, 1980.

Hobsbawm, E. J. *Industry and Empire: From 1750 to the Present Day.* New York: Viking/ Penguin, 1968, 1987.

Hobsbawm, Eric. *The Age of Revolution: 1789–1848.* New York: Vintage Books, 1962, 1996.

Kipling, Rudyard. "The White Man's Burden," in *Rudyard Kipling's Verse: Inclusive Edition 1885–1918.* Garden City, N.Y.: Doubleday, Page & Co., 1927, 371–72.

Lucas, Henry S. *A Short History of Civilization.* New York: McGraw-Hill Book Co., 1943, 804.

TEN
European Expansion in North America

> Although the ideologists of conquest can no longer evoke administration for holy war or pseudobiology, they have yet one great and powerful system of myth among their resources. In it the Christian Caucasians of Europe are not only holy and white but also civilized, while the pigmented heathens of distant lands are not only idolatrous and dark but savage.
>
> Francis Jennings, *The Invasion of America: Indians, Colonialism, and the Cant of Conquest*

France and England struggled for domination as the early developments of the Industrial Revolution rose to threaten what remained of European feudalism. From 1756 to 1763, they engaged in what has been described as the first world war. England won, expelling France from India and New France, but the contest was far from over. The American Revolution offered France a chance at revenge, and French forces played a crucial role in the British defeat, especially at Yorktown, but this involvement helped to drive France closer to bankruptcy.

By the mid-eighteenth century some European colonies in the Americas had become prosperous and even cosmopolitan. Philadelphia rivaled many European cities in population and sophistication. The colonization of the Western Hemisphere offered certain parallels to that of ancient Greece in that the colonies eventually took on personalities of their own, independent of that of the mother country. An example of how this kind of colonization would play out was the American Revolution.

Although the seventeenth century was a turbulent one characterized by civil strife, England had been able to lay the foundations of empire. Various European countries adopted distinct strategies for colonizing new regions. The English strategy often included searching for lands for settlement that offered a climate similar to England's, so that the colonies could easily be used as safety valves for religious strife in the motherland as well as for economic exploitation. The list of English colonies grew long and diverse: Jamestown (1607), Plymouth (1620), Massachusetts Bay Colony (1630), Maryland (1634), Hartford (1636), New York (1664), Carolina (1665), and Pennsylvania (1681) and other colonies demonstrated a growing North American presence.

In North America, the early part of the eighteenth century was relatively prosperous for the French colonists. The economy experienced steady growth. Shipbuilding flourished, and forges at Saint-Maurice provided iron for stoves fashioned in Quebec. The centerpiece of New France's economy, however, remained the fur trade. The Indians employed as trappers became part of the European market economy.

The French differed from the other colonizing nations in their relations with the Indians. In their discourse with Indians, the English rarely acknowledged that they intended to enclose the land and displace the original occupants. Spain worked to reduce Indians to serfdom. The French not only fraternized with Indians, they adopted a clear policy of blending the two races. Even with this generally friendlier attitude, however, French-Indian relations sometimes turned violent. In 1729 a French commandant ordered a Natchez town to move from a spot where he intended to build a settlement. The Indians, unaccustomed to such arrogance and unwilling to move, massacred the garrison. The French then entered into an alliance with the Choctaw and, with about 700 allied warriors, overran the Natchez and destroyed them. Despite this and other evidence of ferocity toward Indians, France's colonies generally cultivated good will, treating Indian peoples as possible trading partners and potential converts to Catholicism.

There was considerably more Indian-white conflict in the English colonies. In 1711 the Tuscarora attacked settlers on the Roanoke, killing an estimated 137. The Virginians struck back with devastating effect, and the Tuscarora appeared on the verge of extinction. Some Seneca (members of the Iroquois Confederacy) were present at a peace conference in Pennsylvania, where they heard the story, and they introduced the plight of the Tuscarora at the Five Nations Iroquois Grand Council. The Tuscarora were shortly thereafter admitted to that body and, in 1722, were formally recognized as the sixth nation in a treaty made with English colonists. Henceforth the Iroquois would be known as the Six Nations Iroquois Confederacy.

Despite the frequency of violent conflicts, whites from the English colonies sometimes "went Indian." Many white immigrants who had agreed to a period as indentured servants to pay for their passage were worked mercilessly under near-slave conditions long beyond the agreed period of indenture. Some of them, mostly young people, were captured by Indians or ran away and ended up living with Indians. The children were brought up by the Indians; both children and adults were adopted, trained in the Indian customs, and often married into the Indian nation. When given the chance to leave and rejoin the whites, a significantly high percentage of these people chose to stay with the Indians. Captured Indians who were raised by whites, on the other hand, almost never chose to stay with them when they had a chance to rejoin their nation (Axtell 1985, 302–327). Benjamin Franklin observed:

> When an Indian Child has been brought up among us, taught our language, and habituated to our Customs, yet if he goes to see his relations . . . there is no persuading him ever to return. . . . When white persons of either sex [have] lived a while among them, tho' ransomed by their Friends, and treated with all imaginable tenderness . . . in a Short time they . . . take the first good Opportunity of

escaping again into the Woods, from whence there is no
reclaiming them. (Labaree 1959, 4:481–482)

In the first half of the eighteenth century, France and England both
looked for ways to gain advantage in the competition for empire in
North America. When Roland Michel Baron became governor of
New France in 1747, he embarked on a plan to revitalize the
colony by establishing a French presence in the Ohio River Valley.
His successor, Celeron de Blainville, led an expedition into that
country to claim it for France in 1749, and French colonists soon
established a post in what is now western Pennsylvania at the
confluence of the Allegheny, Monongahela, and Ohio Rivers—the
site of present-day Pittsburgh. They called it Fort Duquesne.

Members of the English Parliament saw an opportunity to
seize valuable French properties and markets in Canada (Hobsbawm 1968, 49) and began agitating for a military expedition to
accomplish that goal. They rationalized that the Iroquois were
subjects of the British Crown—an assertion the fiercely independent Iroquois denied—and that to invade the Ohio Valley was to
invade British territory. The British called on General Edward
Braddock to carry out the military campaign to expel the French.
Braddock, who had been quashing rebellion in Scotland, landed in
North America and immediately provoked resentment. He housed
his troops in residences in Boston, a practice that exposed the wives
and daughters of Boston colonists to the presence of men the local
citizens considered uncouth ruffians. He also commandeered what
he needed in the way of wagons and horses. He eventually set off
for Fort Duquesne with an army and orders to build a road to the
Ohio country. Clearly one objective of the campaign was to annex
territory and open up Indian country in Ohio and beyond to
English land speculators and settlers.

Braddock's march required several months of preparation and
involved a difficult wilderness campaign of a type for which he and
his army were unprepared. They cut a road across the Allegheny
Mountains and were approaching Fort Duquesne when he met
with Iroquois and allied Indians, who inquired about his inten-

tions. He replied that he was going to expel the French. Whose land, the Indians asked, was being fought over? Braddock replied that where the blood of English soldiers stained the ground, that was English soil. The next day the Indians had disappeared. Braddock had earlier expressed confidence that disciplined English troops could easily defeat French irregulars and Indians, and that in any event, Indians were notoriously bad shots. He was wrong on both points. On July 9 his forward column of 1,459 officers and men was ambushed by 254 French and about 600 Indians. Braddock's army was routed, suffering one of the worst defeats in British military history. Braddock was killed. Cannon and other military supplies, which would be used by the French in the ensuing war, were abandoned by English soldiers fleeing in panic.

If England was to defeat France, it was clear it would not be done casually in a single campaign. After William Pitt the Elder became war minister and began to direct the war in North America aggressively, the English won a series of victories. Fort Frontenac, Carillon, and Duquesne fell in 1758. Louisbourg and Quebec were captured the following year, Montreal in 1760. At the end of the war France had lost its most cherished North American possessions. England now laid claim to all of the continent east of the Mississippi, including Florida. An era of colonial conflict had ended, and the British Empire, hardly more than 150 years old, had become the world's dominant imperial power.

During the time France and England vied for power, the Indian nations west of the English colonies played an important role as key players in the balance of power. With the defeat and disappearance of New France, that role quickly evaporated. The Seven Years' War (1756–1763) was the beginning of the end of Indian independence, but the English followed a policy of restraint toward them and did not claim that Indian rights were extinguished when the French lost the war. English settlers and landowners soon encroached into Indian country, however, and disputes grew increasingly bitter.

The Indians of the Ohio region grew increasingly angry with their reduced role, and many viewed encroachment into Indian country, especially western Pennsylvania, as evidence of the threat to their existence. Probably with some French collaboration, they rose in rebellion in 1763 under Pontiac, a previously obscure leader. Pontiac and his allies coordinated an effort to expel the English and quickly attacked and seized a number of English forts. It was a major and, for the most part, effective campaign and one of the most important Indian wars in the struggle for North America. Even some Seneca joined Pontiac, attacking and destroying an English force along the Niagara escarpment at a place called Devil's Hole. In 1764, however, English arms and English diplomacy, led by the able Sir William Johnson, began to prevail.

Indian military skills were well respected among the English, and Indian ambushes were a form of warfare that was difficult for the English to combat. At Bushy Run, some twenty-five miles east of Pittsburgh, however, an English force defeated an Indian ambush. It was an important battle in British military history, since they had rarely been able to defeat Indians in similar encounters.

In 1763, as a concession to the Indians to end the war and to sustain the valuable fur trade, the Crown declared a "Proclamation Line" along the Appalachian Divide, with a promise that white settlers would not be allowed to encroach on Indian country. The promise to protect Indian land rights would eventually become a major point of contention among wealthy American colonists who saw potential profits in the sale of this land.

Daniel Boone was among those who led the colonization of the Kentucky region in 1769, and a bitter and largely undeclared war ensued between Kentuckians and Indians for more than a generation. There was intermittent hostility from 1763 until the War of 1812 as Indians fought to drive the invaders from their country.

Significant changes in the relationships between England and its North American colonies had been ignited by the expulsion of the French from North America. For most of the century, England had not vigorously enforced its trade laws, but now Parliament passed a series of acts intended to step up economic exploitation of its colonies. Included were acts that forbade colonists to manufacture products that would compete with English manufacturing. Colonies were expected to provide raw materials and markets for the mother-land, not finished products in competition with England. Colonists were allowed to sell raw materials to and purchase finished products only from England. They were not allowed to purchase goods from Spanish or French colonies, which were favorite sources of sugar, molasses, and other commodities. American colonists, especially those who were merchants or aspired to be manufacturers, saw these laws as unfair limitations to their freedom.

Shortly following his coronation, King George III gave author-ity to tax collectors in Boston to search for and seize goods that had avoided custom duties and to begin enforcing tax laws stringently. The new role of the English Navy, now that it was relieved of the duty of monitoring and menacing the French Navy, was to enforce these regulations on the high seas. American colonists had long ignored these kinds of rules and had traded where they pleased. The colonists, the Bostonian merchant class at which the regulations were aimed, seethed at the rules and taxes. American patriots seized British tax ships and staged the Boston Tea Party, during which colonists dressed as Mohawks dumped 342 chests of tea from ships into Boston Harbor. These expressions of anger, which verged on sedition, set the stage for open rebellion. In 1775 armed resistance flared in New England, beginning with a small battle at Concord.

The most successful Indian agent in the British service was Sir William Johnson, who served as the superintendent of Indian affairs in the north. He was an immigrant who had befriended Indians in the Mohawk Valley, had children by a Mohawk woman named Mary Brant, and had built a significant estate—Johnson Manor—in the Mohawk Valley. His life had been devoted to his complex relations with the Six Nations Indians (the Mohawks were the eastern-most nation of that confederacy). Johnson had been involved in both military and diplomatic missions most of his adult life. As the clouds of war gathered, however, and at a most dramatic moment, Sir William Johnson collapsed and died, and the Mohawk Valley Indians lost an important ally. This group, numbering about 500, was the smallest of the Six Nations. Their lands lay (and still lie) east of the 1763 Line of Demarcation, and were slowly being encroached upon by Americans, most of whom were loyal to the revolutionaries.

Their neighbors, the Oneida, were at the same time seeing their lands under pressure from and falling into the hands of colonists loyal to the Crown. As the violence grew more intense, most of the Mohawk joined the British cause, and most of the Oneida joined the side of the Revolutionaries. The Iroquois Confederacy saw warriors of its nations fighting on both sides. The confederacy itself had declared neutrality in the war, stating that it was a civil war among English people in which the Indians had no part.

Armed rebellion escalated into armed revolution in 1776 after Americans issued the Declaration of Independence. Although both sides at first issued statements that they would not recruit Indian fighters, American Revolutionaries had violated that rule at the Battle of Boston early in the war. The British soon found themselves in Indian country recruiting Indian mercenary units. During the winter following the Declaration of Independence, the Onondaga Nation, capital of the Six Nations Confederacy, was hit by a disastrous epidemic that left ninety dead, including many of their principal chiefs. At a critical moment, the Onondagas were forced to announce they were unable to host confederacy meetings.

The sentiment for neutrality was strong among the warriors. Cornplanter, a Seneca and one of the important warrior chiefs, argued forcibly against joining the British. The latter, meanwhile, called assemblies at which they appealed not only to the warriors but also to the women, especially among the Seneca, offering gifts of ostrich feathers, bells, kettles, blankets, and other goods. When the British invited the Indians to observe as they attacked Fort Stanwix and defeated the Americans, a large delegation went along, including many Seneca. At the siege, the British were unable to capture the fort. They suffered delays, and meanwhile the Americans were able to complete the fortifications. The British Army failed to bring siege cannon capable of demolishing them. An American army under Brigadier General Nicholas Herkimer was dispatched to lift the siege. A battle ensued at Oriskany at which a number of Iroquois Indians were killed. At this battle Oneida

Indians fought for the Americans. It was the first time in memory Iroquois Indians had been on opposite sides in a battle.

By every standard and expectation of the day, the British should have won the war. The Americans were undisciplined and, for the most part, inexperienced in the arts of war. It is probably accurate that, at the beginning, about 20 percent of the colonists were devoted to the revolution, an equal number solidly behind the Crown, and the rest passionate about neither side. The Americans appointed the most popular and able military leader in the colonies, George Washington, who performed miracles keeping his troops' morale high and pushing forward through very difficult times. Throughout much of the war, the American forces lost the pitched battles. Washington, however, utilizing a great talent for managing people, kept his army in the field and wisely avoided engaging in any battles that could provide the British with a definitive victory.

Indians rendered the frontier unsafe and forced large numbers of Americans in the Mid-Atlantic region to abandon their farms, eventually causing serious hardships and food shortages. The Oneida were critical in providing Washington's troops with food during a disastrous stay at Valley Forge. As the war ground on, the American forces learned to fight and even evolved tactics that were to become familiar in European warfare. The British military was accustomed to wartime conditions in Europe, where the peasantry was, for the most part, unarmed. Americans, however, were a predominantly rural people who were usually experienced hunters. They possessed excellent firearms—the Kentucky rifle was superior to the British musket—and were excellent marksmen. As the war progressed, militia attacks on the British Army became a major factor. The American force, fighting on its home turf and often employing tactics it had learned during the Indian wars, had become a match for the most feared fighting machine in the world, the British Army. Still, valor alone couldn't carry the day, and they needed help to win.

King George III would eventually be seized by madness, but before that happened—or at least before it was conclusively diagnosed—his policies affected England's war effort. Some members of Parliament felt that George III was overstepping the bounds of the monarchy and trying to reverse the results of the Glorious Revolution. They viewed his actions as a usurpation of parliamentary power, and some Whigs actually cheered news of American Revolutionaries' victories over British armies.

George III appointed an old crony, the Earl of Sandwich, to oversee the affairs of the British Navy. Some English historians blame Sandwich for the loss of the war because, they say, he failed to pay attention to the job, spending much of his time at the gambling tables. Indeed, he is said to have invented the food item that bears his name so his gambling would not be interrupted by the need for nourishment and he could play and eat at the same time.

The British Navy had long been dependent on New England forests for masts and timbers for ,their warships, and with this supply cut off, existing masts rotted. No one—certainly not the Earl of Sandwich—solved this problem. It was one of the few times in modern history that the French Navy was temporarily stronger than the British Fleet.

In 1783 France, again at war with England, joined the Revolutionary cause and sent ships and troops to North America to cut off British General Cornwallis' retreat to the sea. The British Fleet gave chase but was caught in a storm in the North Atlantic that broke many masts and scattered the ships. Cornwallis was trapped between the French Fleet and the Revolutionary Army and was forced to surrender. There were, of course, other important factors responsible for England's defeat. Even a superior military force was not assured victory against a well-armed and mostly well-fed population with a strong determination to resist. England had lost the war and, as significantly, the monarchy had lost considerable prestige.

The premier statesman for America was Benjamin Franklin, and he had befriended the British prime minister. When the peace treaty was signed, the British failed to mention the rights of its loyal Indian allies and allowed the Americans to claim lands well to the west of the Appalachians, an outcome most observers did not expect. The Americans were, for good reasons, elated and came to claim these lands as a right of conquest.

The Revolution had brought great change in the way people thought about freedom and democracy. The idea arose that the American experience was the embodiment of progress and promised the future perfection of human societies. When advocates of liberal democracy spoke of freedom, they were not speaking primarily of freedom of the individual from control by the state but of freedom to buy and sell in a marketplace unregulated by the state.

The ideology of progress, however, has political implications. Things will change, but in fact will not always get better for everyone. At the end of the war, the new United States was deeply in debt. A plan emerged to address this debt by using Indian lands to compensate soldiers owed money for their services and to raise funds to pay other debts. Thomas Jefferson and others believed that when white settlements encroached on Indian lands, the ensuing loss of game animals would force the Indians to move further away. Congress was very confident that Indians would sell their lands and move west as settlements came closer to Indian country. Congress acted on this belief when, before actually securing title to the Indian land in question, it passed the Northwest Ordinance of 1787, which designated lands in Ohio as available for purchase and settlement. The land was to be sold by conferring purchasing rights on individual members of Congress who were land speculators. They would then sell the land to middlemen and individual buyers. The speculators and buyers would certainly benefit, but the Indians were expected to sell at a low price and were not given a choice.

When the Shawnee, Miami, and allied Indians were told the land had been conquered during the Revolution, but that the Americans would pay them for it, the Indians refused to sell. Officially the policy of the new United States was simply to purchase the land, but messages to the local agents carried the veiled threat that the Indians were to sell whether they wanted to or not. Urged on by the British, who had built forts in the area that the Indians could use for defense, the Indians absolutely refused to sell. Armed force was authorized in an attempt to change their minds. A few years later Thomas Jefferson gave a utopian spin to the takeover of land, burying dispossession and what today we might term human rights abuses under high-minded rhetoric:

> I have observed this march of civilization advancing from the seacoast, passing over us like a cloud of light, increasing our knowledge and improving our condition. . . . And where this progress will stop no one can say. Barbarism has, in the meantime, been receding before the steady step of amelioration; and will in time, I trust, disappear from the earth. (Sheehan 1973, 25–26)

The Indians, however, could not be trusted to disappear without some assistance. The 1787 Northwest Ordinance committed the United States to the acquisition and development of lands not ceded by the Indian nations that occupied those territories. It was the intention of the U.S. government to identify tracts to be sold and prices to be paid. There was no provision for the possibility that the Indians might not wish to sell. Congress sent instructions to governor of the Northwest Territories, Arthur St. Clair, in 1787 to scout out Indian attitudes toward their proposals to determine whether they were "hostile" to forced sales. If so, St. Clair was to convene a general treaty so that peace and harmony might ensue. The obvious subagenda was that if Indians did not sell, peace and harmony would not ensue. The strategy did not work. Indians attacked squatters and squatter settlements and made travel into their country very dangerous.

In 1789 Josiah Harmor organized 1,400 combatants, mostly militiamen, to invade Indian country to intimidate them. That did not work either. Harmor was defeated in 1790 by a small confederacy of Shawnee, Miami, and their allies. More than 180 of Harmor's forces were killed and more than 30 wounded, while about a third of the packhorses were lost, along with a considerable store of equipment. Rather than intimidating the Indians, Harmor's campaign had given them great confidence. St. Clair returned to carry on the war. His force was surprised early on the morning of November 4, 1791. Of 1,400 men, 632 were killed and 264 wounded. It was a complete rout, the worst defeat at the hands of Indians in the history of the U.S. military.

St. Clair's defeat convinced President Washington that nothing less than a professional army would be needed. Reliable armed enforcement was necessary to force Indians to sell land and insure safe conditions of settlement for whites. Another motivation for a regular army lay in the need to put down tax rebellions among whiskey producers. These were major reasons the United States abandoned the Articles of Confederation and adopted the U.S. Constitution. Under the new document the central government became much stronger, the U.S. Army was founded, and the new United States embarked on a century of armed military conquest known as the Indian Wars, the object of which was the seizure of Indian lands from the Appalachians to the Pacific. The Indian Wars would formally end in 1890 on the rolling hills of South Dakota near the village of Pine Ridge, at a place called Wounded Knee, following the slaughter and dispossession of dozens of Indian nations.

Following St. Clair's defeat, the Indians of the Western Confederacy (which included the Shawnee, Delawares, Wyandottes, and several other groups) insisted the Americans abandon their settlements and move to the east and south of the Ohio River. Washington and Congress claimed it would be impossible to uproot any established settlements but were willing to make concessions to the Indians, including guarantees of fair treatment, fair payment for lands, and guarantees against further American encroachments into their country. British military agents dreamed of a buffer zone in the form of an Indian country between the United States and Canada and took steps to frustrate peace efforts.

By 1792 General "Mad" Anthony Wayne was in the field with a trained army. He established Fort Defiance at present-day Defiance, Ohio, and from there set out to engage the Indians who were fighting under Chief Turkey Foot. After two years of fighting, the Western Confederacy was defeated on August 29, 1794, at a place where a cyclone had destroyed an area of forest. It was called the Battle of Fallen Timber.

> [A]n Ottawa commander acted prematurely, leading his
> men in a charge against the advanced guard of 150
> mounted Kentucky militia, who panicked, broke, and
> incited the front line infantry to do the same. . . .
> [Wayne] rallied his men—in part by the effective expedi-
> ent of shooting those who ran—and ordered an attack on
> the Indians' line. . . . Two regiments under the command
> of Colonel John Hamtrack attacked vigorously, mainly
> with bayonets. (Axelrod 1993, 129)

During the years when the United States was not actively trying to
seize Indian lands, racism toward Indians was at a low ebb. By
1796, however, the year the young President Andrew Jackson
appeared in Congress and announced his presence by denouncing
the Cherokees and the previous administration's policy, attitudes
toward Indians were definitely hardening.

A young Shawnee leader named Tecumseh came to prominence early in the nineteenth century. Said to be a superb orator,
he had been compared with the young Henry Clay. He became a
spokesman for Indians in the Ohio. His brother, Tenskwatawa, was
known as "the Prophet." The brothers worked tirelessly to persuade
the Indians of all tribes to unite in resisting the pressures of American settlers and the U.S. government and to discard white
customs. Tecumseh would later become something of a myth
among American writers, who would find in him many qualities
they thought they saw in themselves. He was a complete Indian
patriot, known for his courage and integrity, and was undoubtedly
one of the greatest Indian political and military leaders the United
States was to encounter. He encouraged his people to take up agriculture, become economically independent, and reject violence
except as a necessity of war. He had hoped to establish an Indian
territory in the Ohio Valley and to unite the Indian nations in that
area, but he was killed on October 5, 1815, at the Battle of the
Thames during the War of 1812.

Other Indians became embroiled in the War of 1812, fighting for their lands under the British flag. In the south, during

the winter of 1813–1814, three American armies converged on the Creek Nation, whose homelands consisted of most of present-day Alabama. The Creek warriors, called the Red Sticks, fought bravely and desperately with spears and bows and arrows and for a time drove back the invaders, including Andrew Jackson. The beginning of the end came for the Creek Nation on the Tallapoosa River at Horseshoe on March 27, 1814, where their army of warriors was practically annihilated, only a few wounded surviving.

The United States fought four wars with nation-states during the nineteenth century. Three of these were wars of expansion and the other was the Civil War. The War of 1812 with Britain was fought partly because the British Navy kidnapped American sailors and forced them to serve on British warships. But an equally important motive for the war was to push the British out of the Northwest Territories and to end British collaboration with the Indians in the Ohio and Great Lakes regions. The war was an ill-chosen adventure that pitted the United States against a significantly superior British military. Since England's main military forces were engaged in fighting Napolean, however, the Americans managed to avoid disaster. The war ended in something of a stalemate. Thereafter Britain withdrew from forts in the disputed territories and ceased or at least dramatically diminished collaboration with the Indian nations there.

The Indian Removal Act of 1830, a legislative directive for what today we term ethnic cleansing, required all Indians east of the Mississippi to cede their lands and migrate to the western plains. By 1831 the federal policy was firmly in place, and the fate of the Indians was now in the hands of the individual states. Indians were subjected to what was to become a lengthy period of outright fraud and misrepresentation. Documents were misrepresented to the Indians before they signed them. Purchases were made fraudulently by bribing Indians to impersonate other Indians who were the legitimate owners. Fraud, politics, and a policy of dispossession took from the Creek people their lands and forced them into exile in Indian country in Oklahoma.

The Cherokees suffered a similar fate. In 1832 a constitutional crisis tested whether the courts might protect Cherokee rights. In a landmark case, *Worcester v. Georgia*, the Supreme Court under Chief Justice John Marshall rendered a decision that seemed to recognize the rights of the Cherokee Nation. President Andrew Jackson, who had signed the Indian Removal Act, is reported to have said, "John Marshall has made his decision; now let him enforce it." The defiance of the Supreme Court by the president opened the door to continued persecution of the Cherokees by the state of Georgia.

Everywhere in Cherokee country the Indians were robbed of their livestock and driven from their homes. The removal of the Cherokee from Georgia is known as "the Trail of Tears." The Cherokee were evicted by a contingent of 7,000 U.S. Army soldiers and driven by forced march to what is now Oklahoma, during the fall and winter of 1838–1839, in bitter weather with inadequate supplies of food. The soldiers refused to slow or stop so that the ill and exhausted could recover. The resulting loss of life on the Trail of Tears was appalling. Grant Foreman, author of *Indian Removal*, estimated that of 18,000 who went on the Trail of Tears, 4,000 died in stockades or along the road.

Some Seminoles refused to leave their homelands in Florida, and the U.S. Army engaged in a seven-year war against them. There were atrocities on both sides, and it was the bitterest episode in U.S. Army history of Indian wars to that time. Some 1,500 soldiers were killed, and the cost of the war was a staggering $20 million. The conflict was never resolved. Osceola, a chief of the Seminole, was captured under a flag of truce, but the surviving Seminole kept fighting from the Florida swamps.

Around this time (1837–1863) an Apache war chief, Mangus Coloradas, waged war against white men after some of his people were attacked and slaughtered for their scalps because of a Mexican bounty. He and his son-in-law Cochise waged a generation-long fight, slaughtering whites and virtually driving them from southern New Mexico and Arizona.

When gold was discovered in California on February 2, 1848, thousands of miners flooded into northern California. To say there was a lawless element among these miners is an understatement. The miners engaged in an orgy of abuse of Indians, marked by casual murders, kidnapping, and rape. Indeed, the attitude at the time was that killing Indians, even Indians who had done no harm, was a sport. Similar episodes of genocide would occur in Tasmania near Australia and in Newfoundland and in remote corners of Brazil and other South American countries well into the twentieth century, but the history of the destruction of the Indians of California by white miners and settlers is one of the darkest pages of United States history. A white man who killed an Indian, no matter how outrageous an injustice the act might be, was not punished. The Indian population of California plunged.

The military conquest of the Indians was planned and systematic and resulted in dramatic population declines among all the Indians so encountered. California was admitted as a state in 1850, and it almost immediately implemented a horrific Indian policy. Indians were subjected to virtual slavery, especially the women, who were procured for the use of the miners. The original Indian population for California was estimated at 150,000. By 1890, only 17,000 were alive.

The rest of the Pacific Northwest was also under great pressure because of the flood of Americans seeking gold and land. Even U.S. military personnel were perplexed because the usual sequence of events was that the army was sent in to protect the settlers, the settlers committed grave crimes against the Indians, the Indians resisted, and the army was used to conquer the Indians. Once defeated, the Indians were required to give up most of their lands.

By 1860, white populations dominated both coasts, but in the rush for land and gold in California, Oregon, and Washington, they had bypassed a vast area in the center known as the northern Great Plains. The Dakota Indians in Minnesota had signed treaties and had tried to live in peace with their white neighbors. By 1862, however, they had become dissatisfied with their reservation, an area 10 miles wide and 150 miles long along the Minnesota River, and they resented having been swindled out of a large percentage of their original lands. They usually hunted buffalo, but that year they delayed the hunt, waiting for the rations that were part of their treaty settlement. The annuity was late in arriving, and now they had neither annuity nor buffalo meat. On August 4 they rioted, invading a warehouse containing food. The riot turned into a war, and before it was finished the Sioux had killed 800 settlers. The U.S. military retaliated, rounding up the rioters and dispatching most of them in a mass hanging.

Two years later, American militiamen under former Methodist minister Colonel John Milton Chivington attacked a Cheyenne camp under Chief Black Kettle on November 29, 1864. "I have come to kill Indians," Chivington said, "and believe it is right and honorable to use any means under God's heaven to kill Indians." Black Kettle had signed a treaty of peace with the United States. When the soldiers approached, he ran up a large American flag on a pole in front of his tipi. It was a horrific event. Little children were gunned down, babies killed in their mothers' arms, a lieutenant killed three women and five children and scalped them. A little girl was shot down when she emerged from a pit carrying a white flag. It was called the Battle of Sand Creek. Chivington's men killed 105 women and children and 29 men.

General George Tecumseh Sherman was among the famous Indian fighters. "We must act with vindictive earnestness against the Sioux, even to their extermination, men, women, and children," he said. But a war against the Sioux went badly for the United States, which responded by making extensive promises at a treaty at Fort Laramie in 1868. Among these promises was a guarantee of the right of the Indians to hunt buffalo as long as the numbers permitted. Sherman objected to this clause, commenting that the best thing would be to invite all the sportsmen of the United States and Britain to a buffalo shoot. This was, in fact, U.S. buffalo policy. Americans shot down some 70 million buffalo by 1876. In the space of a decade an enormous demographic and ecological change swept the northern Great Plains. Suddenly all the buffalo were gone, all the people who had lived there up until then were gone—rounded up on reservations—and following the planting of crops, all the grasses native to the region were gone or dying out.

That year, as the United States was approaching July 4 and celebrating its one-hundredth anniversary—a hundred years of expansion and imperialism, George Armstrong Custer led a contingent of cavalry into Little Big Horn country, where Custer and his Seventh Cavalry were wiped out by Sioux, Cheyenne, and allied Indians. White Americans were shocked and clamored for revenge. At that time many Indians left their reservations to join a legendary Sioux leader, Crazy Horse, who had sworn to try to drive the whites from the sacred Black Hills. The war that followed was a disaster for the Sioux and their allies. Driven onto reservations, they sank into despair. In 1877 a Ute Indian from Idaho by the name of Wovoka announced a series of visions and declared that if the Indians would dance the Ghost Dance, all the buffalo and the dead ancestors would come to life and their days of glory would return. The new religion was adopted by many Indians, but none embraced it so fervently as the Sioux, for whom it became the center of one of the most remarkable revitalization movements in world history. In 1889 a group of Sioux following Minneconjou chief Big Foot were confronted by soldiers at Wounded Knee Creek on what is now the Pine Ridge Indian Reservation. The Sioux were ready to do battle, believing that their ghost shirts would protect them from the white man's bullets. As the soldiers tried to disarm the Indians, a shot was fired and the army opened fire, killing 150 mostly unarmed Indians, and wounding 50. It was the final significant armed encounter between Indians and the U.S. Army.

Bibliography

Axelrod, Alan. *Chronicle of the Indian Wars: From Colonial Times to Wounded Knee.* New York: Konecky & Konecky, 1993.

Axtell, James. "The White Indians." In *The Invasion Within: The Contest of Cultures in Colonial North America.* New York: Oxford University Press, 1985.

_____. "The White Indians of Colonial America." In *The European and the Indian: Essays in the Ethnohistory of Colonial North America.* New York: Oxford University Press, 1981.

Carranco, Lynwood. *Genocide and Vendetta: The Round Valley Wars of Northern California.* Norman: University of Oklahoma Press, 1981.

Churchill, Ward. *Indians Are Us: Culture and Genocide in Native North America.* Monroe, Me.: Common Courage Press, 1994.

Cook, Sherburne F. *The Conflict Between the California Indian and White Civilization.* Berkeley: University of California Press, 1976.

Foreman, Grant. *Indian Removal: The Emigration of the Five Civilized Tribes of Indians.* Norman: University of Oklahoma Press, 1932.

Hobsbawm, E. J. *Industry and Empire: From 1750 to the Present Day.* New York: Viking/Penguin, 1968, 49

Jennings, Francis. *The Invasion of America: Indians, Colonialism, and the Cant of Conquest.* New York: Norton, 1976.

Labaree, Leonard W. *The Papers of Benjamin Franklin.* New Haven, Ct.: Yale University Press, 1959.

Sheehan, Bernard W. *Seeds of Extinction: Jeffersonian Philanthropy and the American Indian.* Chapel Hill: University of North Carolina Press, 1973.

Svaldi, David. *Sand Creek and the Rhetoric of Extermination: A Case Study in Indian-White Relations.* Landham, Md.: University of the Americas Press, 1989.

Sword, Wiley. *President Washington's Indian War: The Struggle for the Old Northwest, 1790–1795.* Norman: University of Oklahoma Press, 1985.

ELEVEN
Slavery, Abolition, and Racial Violence in America

> Whatever their treatment of slaves, most planters worked consistently to make them submissive and deferential. While the lash was the linchpin of his regime, the slaveholder adopted several practices to assure the slave's submissiveness. A master started early trying to impress upon the mind of the young black the awesome power of whiteness: he made the slave bow upon meeting him, stand in his presence, and accept floggings from his young children; he flogged the slave for fighting with young whites. The ritual of deference was required at every turn: the slave was flogged for disputing a white man's word, kicked for walking between two whites on a street, and not allowed to call his wife or mother "Mrs."
>
> John W. Blassingame, *The Slave Community: Plantation Life in the Ante-Bellum South*

The discussion about how best to organize governments, support the development of national economies, and create a more perfect world failed, for the most part, to acknowledge the role slavery would play in creating the wealth that became the foundation of much that would follow. The pursuit of the ideal has been a major factor in what has been called the "searchlight" view of history, which is somewhat visible in the way writers of American history have treated slavery, reconstruction, the rise of terrorist organizations to intimidate African Americans, and black nationalism. There has been a tendency among American historians to tell the story of the evolution of contemporary society by selecting those events that most impacted the story of the pursuit of a national ideal, and many such histories are highlighted and retold mostly within that context. The result typically is that the stories of people who are not seen as active in the pursuit of the ideal (and who are in fact only marginally engaged in that pursuit) are either not told or are largely limited to the period in which the struggle over ideals reaches a crisis.

Some of the earliest discussions of whether or not slavery is a good thing begin with the Greek philosophers, especially Aristotle, who thought that slavery of the peoples subjugated by Greek armies accorded with the natural order of things. The enslaved people, believed to be inferior by nature, were needed to free the upper class of Greek society from manual labor and give them time for higher pursuits, particularly the study of philosophy.

Slavery was common during the days of the Roman Empire, when the Greeks themselves were often enslaved. It declined following the collapse of Rome and was revived to some degree with the Arab conquests. The terms Slav and Slavic derived from Arab enslavement of Eastern Europeans. During the eleventh century Arab expansion swept westward across Africa, and Arab customs of slavery took root. When the Portuguese began to traffic in volumes of slaves around the middle of the fifteenth century, it was Islamic slavers who supplied them. Muslims were known to take Christians as slaves, and the pope had declared it legal to make slaves of Muslims on the grounds that the purpose was to convert them to Christianity. Because the earliest black slaves to reach Portugal were Muslims, it was legal to enslave them under Christian law.

For about two centuries, Europe and the Atlantic Islands took almost all the slaves flowing from Africa. Beginning in the mid-sixteenth century, increasing numbers were shipped to the Caribbean, Brazil, and North America. Altogether, between 1492 and 1771, more Africans than Europeans were brought to the New World. Although there were others engaged in slavery, English, Portuguese, Dutch, and French slavers supplied most of the slaves who provided the labor that made the American colonies of the southeastern seaboard sustainable (Roberts 1997, 529). Slavery, together with the dispossession of indigenous peoples throughout the Western Hemisphere, unquestionably played an important role in the evolution of the modern world economy as well as produced a legacy of inequality and bitter race relations, which remain significant problems, particularly in North America.

The early slave trade was among the most brutal chapters in human history. Young healthy slaves sent to Caribbean sugar plantations lived an average of seven years after arrival. Later, in the American South, plantation owners tried to project an image of happy slaves who were better off as slaves than they would have been as free men, but even under the best conditions slavery was harsh and dehumanizing. Slaves lived in very poor and crowded housing conditions. They were forced to work long hours, often not finishing until after dark, and they were responsible for their own subsistence needs. The food was bad; health care was limited for the most part to what they could provide for themselves. Family members were often sold to other slave owners at the whim or economic needs of the master. Slave women were often sexually exploited, coerced, or raped by their masters or their master's children, and the children they bore their masters were likely to continue to live as slaves. Above all, slavery was about submission based on race. Every moment of a slave's life was lived with the consciousness that any sign of resistance to absolute subjugation could be met with torture, mutilation, or death. Any attempt to escape carried the risk of the same reprisals.

Slavery was a form of human exploitation that carried within it the inevitability of revolts. There were slave rebellions, the most famous of which was in Hispaniola, then under French rule, in 1791. The rebellion was successful, and the rebels established the first black republic in the Americas in 1804, restoring the island's original Indian name of Haiti. The Haitian Revolution inspired fear of similar revolts among slave owners in the United States and did little to increase respect for the rights of African-descended peoples outside Haiti.

The Enlightenment produced ideas about the dignity and equality of humankind that inspired a movement among European and European-descended peoples, who began to question the morality of the institution of slavery. The earliest abolitionist society in the United States was founded in Philadelphia in 1775, and other such societies multiplied in the North after that. During a time when the idea of slavery was becoming increasingly unpopular in European countries, the United States was the only emerging industrial nation whose national boundaries embraced an agricultural region in which slavery was an integral part of the economy. Nevertheless, the United States joined Great Britain in outlawing the international slave trade in 1807. This was a significant move because Great Britain, Holland, and the United States all benefited greatly from the trade in human lives, and as numerous historians have claimed, profits from the slave trade provided some of the capital that created the Industrial Revolution. Although the international slave trade was illegal, smuggling of slaves to the United States continued until around 1863.

For almost two centuries, tobacco had been king in the South, even though tobacco prices were subject to wild fluctuations and the trade sometimes fell into conditions similar to a depression. Tobacco experienced its first success in the English colonies as a commercial crop in Virginia. It required very fertile soil and depleted that soil quite rapidly. Crop rotation required large amounts of land for profitable production. It is said that a planter needed about twenty acres to support each slave, although a single person could work little more than three acres. Land could be planted for about three years but required twenty years to regain its fertility. By the time of the American Revolution, Virginia had every potential acre under cultivation and was growing all the tobacco it was possible to grow.

Tobacco prices fell during the Revolution, recovered a bit, but fell dramatically during the French Revolution. Although the plantation owners experienced hard times growing tobacco, luck was with them. In 1793 Eli Whitney invented the cotton gin, a machine that could quickly and cheaply strip the seeds from raw cotton, and American industrialization picked up momentum. Cotton began to replace tobacco and after 1815 was America's most valuable export crop. By 1820 the South was a cotton kingdom that stretched from South Carolina to the Mississippi. The expulsion of the Cherokee and other Indian nations of the Five Civilized Tribes in the early 1830s opened a vast area of fertile land in Alabama and Mississippi, greatly expanding the number and profitability of cotton plantations and generating greater demand for African and African-descended slaves.

As profits from slave labor grew in the South, the institution of slavery grew more and more distasteful to the non-slave-owning north. Rhode Island had made slaveholding illegal in 1774, Vermont in 1777, and Pennsylvania in 1780. Slavery was illegal under the federal Northwest Ordinance of 1787. The slave revolt in France's Haiti in 1791 caused Americans to cease importing slaves from the Caribbean. The failure of Napoleon to recapture Haiti was a factor in his decision to agree to the Louisiana Purchase and give up the French territory that would comprise most of the area of the Gulf states. With the Louisiana Purchase, a large territory was opened to the expansion of the South's slave economy.

Although anti-slavery sentiments were rising, the issue of slavery was not an intensely emotional one even in light of the fact that three slave rebellions shook the South between 1800 and 1831. Indeed, it was not much raised between the American Revolution and the war with Mexico. In 1820 the Missouri Compromise admitted Missouri as a slave state and Maine as a free state and maintained the balance of senators at twelve free and twelve slave states.

War with Mexico changed the balance between slave and free states. Soon after gaining independence from Spain in 1821, Mexico agreed to an Anglo colonization in Texas led by Stephen Austin. In 1833 General Antonio Lopez de Santa Ana came to power in Mexico, and in 1836 Anglo settlers in Texas declared Texas an independent nation. Texans withstood a nine-year military struggle, until Texas was annexed by the United States in 1845. Mexican anger about this annexation continued, and in 1846 the

United States became embroiled in a dispute with Mexico about the location of the Texas border.

A secret envoy had been sent to Mexico in March 1846 with an offer to purchase California and New Mexico for $30 million. Mexico refused to negotiate, and war was declared. The Mexican military was little match for the U. S. Army, and Mexico surrendered in September of 1847. Under the terms of the Treaty of Guadalupe Hidalgo, Mexico ceded Utah, California, western Colorado, Wyoming, New Mexico, Nevada, and Arizona for $15 million.

The war with Mexico not only vastly extended U.S. territory; it also intensified the question of the future of slavery. Would the new states formed from these territories be free or slave? The issue was brought to the fore in 1850 with the Kansas-Nebraska Act, a compromise move that launched a policy of congressional non-intervention and allowed the residents of Kansas and Nebraska to decide on the issue of slavery for themselves. It worked poorly because pro- and anti-slavery forces rushed into these territories, especially Kansas, and started what turned out to be a preview of civil war. The violence of 1856 gave rise to the phrase "Bleeding Kansas." Soon after the 1850 compromise, the Underground Railroad, a clandestine network of free black people and white abolitionists, began to assist slaves fleeing from the South to reach sanctuary in Canada and the northern states in defiance of the Fugitive Slave Act. The Republican Party, a major development in national politics around abolition, was formed in 1854.

In the Dred Scott decision of 1857, the Supreme Court offered full protection for the institution of slavery. Scott, a slave who had once lived in a free state, brought suit arguing that his residency in a free state should have set him free. The Supreme Court disagreed, saying that Scott, as a slave, was not a United States citizen, could not bring an action in a federal court, and that the Missouri Compromise of 1820 was unconstitutional. This was only the second time the Supreme Court had declared an act of Congress unconstitutional. On this occasion, the Supreme Court found the Compromise unconstitutional because it denied a slave owner's Fifth Amendment rights to his or her property. The decision placed property rights squarely above human rights by implicitly defining slaves as non-persons in the eyes of the law.

As the debate over the morality of slavery heated up, Southerners retreated behind a wall of rhetoric that included religious permission to maintain slaves, assertions about the biological and cultural inferiority of black and dark-skinned peoples, and a discussion, difficult to understand today, about how the Southern white race and the Northern white race had distinct origins. (It was asserted that Northerners were descended from Anglo-Saxons, Southerners from Norman invaders. There was no historical, cultural, or biological evidence for this claim.) These issues produced a legacy of thought about black and white that still influences American religious and public life. The rationalizations intended to defend the economy and to give a framework to the moral order of the South produced the foundation for a racist, right-wing religious movement.

No single event or issue can be said to have caused the American Civil War. The cultural gap between the North and the South widened. Tensions increased with the publication of Harriet Beecher Stowe's anti-slavery novel, *Uncle Tom's Cabin*, and personal testimonies of slaves about the humanity of the black people and the inhumanity of the slave culture. Abolitionists became increasingly aggressive and militant, and it became clear that the South would not be able to maintain the deadlock on the slavery issue indefinitely because more free states were certain to join the Union. The agricultural South needed markets for cotton, and the industrial North needed a cheap supply of cotton for its mechanized mills, which utilized free labor. These economic realities intensified conflicts over trade and tariffs, states' rights versus the power of the federal government, and slavery.

A major part of the North's economy involved the production of grain for market. The mechanization of agriculture featured the McCormick reaper, a machine that made it possible for far fewer farmers to produce much more grain than ever before. Mechanized agriculture rendered slave labor obsolete in the North and gave the North a distinct advantage. Even England, in the end, needed

American wheat as much or more than it needed American cotton. In the South, large plantations depended on slave labor and on getting the best price for cotton, some of which was sold to England. Although Southern planters enjoyed the benefits of the cotton gin, too few of them were engaged in food production, a choice that would have repercussions for the South during the coming conflict.

Regional economic competition and ideological differences were played out in national politics. When Abraham Lincoln won the presidency, Southern states ceded from the Union and formed a confederacy of their own. Although the North had advantages in terms of industrial strength and numbers, the two sides were surprisingly well balanced in military strength. The war brought tremendous losses to both sides, and it is probable the South underestimated the resolve of the North to maintain the union. With the Civil War came the weaponry that would bring warfare into the twentieth century. The military inventions made possible by the Industrial Revolution contributed to the carnage of the war in significant ways, because very accurate firearms and powerful cannon were capable of inflicting horrible casualties. The ancient strategy of sending thousands of soldiers onto the battlefield without effective cover compounded the loss of life. In one three-day engagement at Gettysburg, fifty thousand men died, a number roughly equal to total losses in the Vietnam War a century later. The Civil War introduced the ferocity of modern warfare—the relentless pursuit of the enemy without the customary pause in hostilities to collect the dead and wounded. This characteristically modern strategy is most clearly exemplified in General Ulysses S. Grant's conduct of the Wilderness Campaign.

The South was weakened because of its lack of adequate agricultural production. Southern armies were sometimes near starvation, while the Union was able to provide its soldiers with a steady if somewhat monotonous supply of bacon and biscuits. Late in the war, when Union forces were becoming fatigued, blacks joined the Union Army. By war's end, 186,000 black soldiers had served the North, and more than 38,000 of them died, the clearest evidence that blacks had fought for black liberation from slavery. By the end of the war, the South was making slaves serve as soldiers, promising them freedom at war's end in a move reminiscent of the British offer of slave emancipation near the end of the American Revolution.

The Emancipation Proclamation, officially ending slavery, went into effect January 1, 1863, but after the war things went badly for black people. Under President Andrew Johnson, African Americans had few rights in the eyes of the law. They could not testify against whites in court. If they quit their job they could be sued for breach of contract. If caught without a job, they could be arrested for vagrancy or some similar offense and fined $50, an enormous sum. If unable to pay the fine, they could be hired out in servitude under a system that more than slightly resembled the slavery from which they had been "freed." President Johnson repeatedly vetoed Congress's Reconstruction legislation and blocked the passage of the Fourteenth Amendment, which guarantees the basic civil rights of all citizens, by convincing every Southern state except Tennessee to reject it.

Incidents of violence broke out in Memphis and New Orleans that can best be characterized as white-on-black riots. The New Orleans incident was a police riot, during which dozens of blacks were murdered. Immediately after the war, the Ku Klux Klan (KKK) was initially organized as a social club by Confederacy veterans. In time, however, it became a kind of cultural revitalization movement that claimed to be preserving the honor of white women (especially against unfounded allegations of black male lust), family values, and Christian virtue while in fact preserving white privilege. The KKK would eventually merge its ideals of racial purity with a version of American nationalism that claimed to find its principles in Protestantism and spawned hatred of Jews, Catholics, and nonwhites, especially blacks.

Although it is not customary in American discourse to think of it that way, American racism on this model has deeply idealistic roots. It claims that everything believed to be perfect—the white race, white civilization, the purity of white womanhood—is under attack by people who are not white, not Protestant, and not "true"

Americans. The idealists who embrace these racist concepts cannot compromise their beliefs without abandoning the certainty those beliefs provide. They therefore feel justified in doing whatever is necessary to protect and advance their ideals, including murder, intimidation, lynchings, castrations, mutilations, and a variety of other forms of terrorism that were widely tolerated in the South. Beginning as a secret terrorist society, the KKK created a mass organization that utilized strange rituals, cross burnings, costumes reminiscent of the Inquisition, and the trappings of a grand fraternal organization as a recruitment strategy. Following the Civil War, the KKK lynched and brutalized blacks and white sympathizers, effectively preventing the newly enfranchised blacks from voting.

Landowners created the sharecropping system, which served to keep former slaves on their plantations as tenant farmers living at a bare subsistence level. This system, combined with the use of convict labor (also mostly black), relegated rural Southern blacks to a permanent peasant status. Later, blacks were denied political participation through discriminatory laws: poll taxes set too high for poor blacks to pay, literacy tests designed to disqualify undereducated blacks, grandfather clauses requiring the prospective voter to produce proof his grandfather had voted, and another disqualifying procedure called the "understanding test." Even the legal gains blacks had made following the Civil War were soon eroded. In 1883 the U.S. Supreme Court declared the 1875 Civil Rights Act, which had never been enforced, void. In 1896 the Supreme Court, in *Plessy v. Ferguson*, upheld the doctrine of "separate but equal," which legitimized segregation in public places and institutions.

Whatever its rhetoric about race, sex, or biology, racism in America directed against black people was heavily tinged with the reality of collective economic self-interest. Not only were blacks to be exploited as cheap labor, they were to be denied any access to the tools to compete with whites for privileges in American society. The racist agenda was carried out through every "legal" means Southern legislatures could devise, and through tolerance and even encouragement by white law enforcement of white violence toward blacks—including public lynchings. During the 1890s, one black was lynched almost every two days, and very few people were ever prosecuted or convicted of these crimes. Although some common white criminals (along with, no doubt, some innocent people) were victims of street violence during the period 1900–1910, of 846 lynchings in the United States, 754 were of blacks. In 1904 a riot occurred in Springfield, Ohio, during which a black man was lynched and black homes burned. In 1906 white mobs rioted against blacks in Atlanta, Georgia, and in Brownsville, Texas. In 1908 two prominent blacks were lynched in Springfield, Illinois, after a white woman claimed she had been raped by blacks. In 1917 a huge riot broke out in East St. Louis during which hundreds were hurt in gunfights and other violence. Some two dozen riots took place in the summer of 1918 in Washington, D.C., Texas, Nebraska, and Illinois. Riots in Chicago lasted thirteen days and left at least 38 dead and 500 hurt.

These centuries of capture, transportation to a new land, and relentless slavery produced revitalization movements among African and African-descended peoples in the Western Hemisphere. The Christian religion provided a utopian vision that sustained many slaves in a situation in which there was little hope for a better future on earth. Haiti was the first independent black nation in the Western Hemisphere, and an early black sea captain, Paul Cuffe, first attempted to establish a black American colony in Africa between 1811 and 1815. It was not until more than a century later, however, that Marcus Garvey, a Jamaican, founded the Universal Negro Improvement Association and a black nationalist movement in the United States. His movement developed enterprises such as restaurants, hotels, and a steamship line, and was the first of a series of black revitalization movements that would later include Elijah Muhammad's Nation of Islam and spokespersons for black rights and dignity from Martin Luther King, Jr., to Malcolm X.

The KKK enjoyed a revival in 1915, and, during the decades that followed, anti-Semitism grew in the United States as well. By 1923, KKK membership had reached a reported 2.3 million; and there were a handful of KKK congressmen and senators elected to national office. The KKK attempted to seize the Democratic and Republican Parties in 1924, and the next year 40,000 klansmen marched down Pennsylvania Avenue. White-on-black racism and racial violence paralleled the white-on-white racism that was swelling in Europe and would culminate in the most dramatic, but certainly not the only, horror of the first half of the twentieth century—the Holocaust.

Bibliography

Berlin, Ira, Barbara J. Fields, Steven F. Miller, Joseph P. Ridge, and Leslie S. Rowland, eds. *Free at Last: A Documentary History of Slavery, Freedom, and the Civil War.* New York: New Press, 1992.

Blassingame, John. *The Slave Community: Plantation Life in the Ante-Bellum South.* New York: Oxford University Press, 1972, rev. 1979, 160.

Coombs, Norman. *The Black Experience in America.* New York: Hippocrene Books, 1972.

Delbanco, Andrew. *The Portable Abraham Lincoln.* London and New York: Penguin Books, 1993.

Douglass, Frederick. *Narrative of the Life of Frederick Douglass, An American Slave.* London and New York: Penguin Books, 1982.

DuBois, W. E. B. *Black Reconstruction: An Essay Toward a History of the Part Which Black Folk Played in the Attempt to Reconstruct Democracy in America, 1868–1889.* New York: Harcourt, Brace, 1935, 1976.

Jones, Jacqueline. *Labor of Love, Labor of Sorrow: Black Women, Work and the Family from Slavery to the Present.* New York: Basic Books, 1985.

Myers, Robert Mason, ed. *The Children of Pride.* New Haven and London: Yale University Press, 1984.

Roberts, J. M. *The Penguin History of the World.* New York: Penguin Books, 1976, 1997.

Stowe, Harriet Beecher. *Uncle Tom's Cabin.* New York: Bantam Books, 1981.

Williams, Eric Eustice. *Capitalism and Slavery.* Chapel Hill: University of North Carolina Press, 1961, 1994.

White, Deborah Gray. *Aren't I a Woman?: Female Slaves in the Plantation South.* New York: Norton, 1985.

Zinn, Howard. *A People's History of the United States.* New York: Harper & Row, 1980, 1990.

TWELVE
Road to
Holocaust

> The inescapable conclusion from a consideration of
> [Nazi] history is that these racist claims are a front . . .
> They are camouflage. For practical guidance in the world
> of affairs, we should do well . . . to go behind the racists'
> slogans and look squarely at the conflict they are trying
> to foment.
>
> Ruth Benedict, *Race, Science, and Politics*

Four great events dominate the history of the West in the twentieth
century: World War I, the Great Depression, World War II, and the
fall of the Soviet Union. Defeat at the end of World War I left a
Germany with deep internal divisions and a sense of alienation and
injustice at the hands of the Allies. The Depression provided an
opening for the rise of Hitlerism and the remilitarization of
Germany, which made the move for conquest in the east possible
and sparked World War II. World War II gave birth to the conditions of the Cold War that continued until the fall of the USSR.

World War II delivered a profound shock to Western ideology.
Germany was a fully accepted member of the circle of what was
thought of as civilized nations. It had been a pioneer in the study
of Greek history, and the degree of doctor of philosophy was first
granted there. According to the expectations of the Renaissance,
such a people should be incapable of unrestrained barbarism—but
the experience of World War II is proof that a people educated in
the Western tradition can be capable of genocide. World War II

challenged the West's expectations about progress and civilization and its relationship to morality. Historians, scholars, and philosophers were left mystified. The pope would later describe the Nazi movement as "pagan" (thus dissociating it from Christian Europe), but that is hardly an accurate description. Nazism was a revitalization movement, complete with its own vision of utopia, its rationalizations for conquest and plunder, and an ability to disarm ordinary people's sense of morality and to plunge an entire nation — indeed, segments of collaborating European nations—into an orgy of violence and murder.

The United States was the world's leading economic power when World War I broke out, and Germany was Western Europe's most populous and wealthiest country. The European nations allied against Germany borrowed heavily to support the war effort, and much of this debt was owned by the United States. At the end of the war the United States had invested more than $9 billion in Europe (compared to $2.5 billion before the war), and the American economy was more than ever tied to the European economy. In terms of its impact on the land and people, the war was the greatest catastrophe to befall the West since the great plagues. Germany alone suffered around 2 million fatalities, and perhaps twice that number were maimed or seriously wounded. In November 1918 the Spanish influenza ravaged the battlefields and circled the globe. By 1920 it had accounted for up to 20 million fatalities.

World War I had a deep impact on the outlook of Europeans, many of whom sensed a decline in European civilization. The amount of destruction is difficult to overstate. The number of young people killed during the war, especially young men, created a serious shortage in potential leadership in the coming decades. The system of nation-states had been founded in a complex environment that included competing economic interests, supported by the value of their currencies and the potential of armed force. This system had broken down in an orgy of destruction that seemed to defy rational explanation. A kind of utopian vision emerged after the war that found the conditions for world peace to lie in universals: free trade, democratic governments, international cooperation, and diplomacy.

Somehow these principles were expected to cancel many long-standing patterns and habits: governments that acted from self-interest at the expense of other countries or even their own citizens; ancient hatreds rooted in violence and conquests; imagined rights of nationals under foreign flags; and rising nationalism. Another factor came into play: the machine gun and the tank had changed forever the prospects for civil disobedience and local rebellions against central authority. In the past, towns and cities erected barricades and defied central governments to protest real or perceived injustices. Tanks and machine guns destroyed that potential and created the possibility of real dictatorships. An age of totalitarianism followed the war.

Perhaps the most important thing about World War I is that in some important ways it ended with things left unsettled. With the exceptions of the expansion of Poland and the disintegration of Austria-Hungary into several small East European states, little had changed in terms of the geopolitical map. Great changes did occur inside these countries, including the virtual disappearance of the old order of nation-states ruled by dynasties and aristocracies. There were two victories during the fighting. First, Germany had decisively defeated Russia, removing it as a world power for at least a generation and creating conditions that made possible a socialist revolution in that country, which ended the power and wealth of the Russian aristocracy. Russia's removal from the scene, however, signaled a significant shift in the balance of power that had defined European stability. Second, Germany was defeated, but not unconditionally. The Allies were exhausted and accepted an armistice rather than the kind of total victory that American General John Pershing favored. The armistice would prove to be a long cease-fire. Astute observers of European history hold that World War I was a kind of civil war among European powers and that World War II was a continuation of the first war.

France, which emerged from the war understandably nervous about security issues, wanted reparations from Germany and assurances that there would be no more invasions. The Treaty of Versailles, which ended the war, required Germany to pay huge reparations. Combined with the debt load owed by other European countries—much of it to Britain and, in turn, to the United States —the reparations created an almost impossible economic deadlock. British economist John Maynard Keynes thought reparations were morally indefensible and economically foolish, and even Winston Churchill described them as "idiocy."

Reparations meant demanding Germany either pay in goods or in money. Paying in goods would have been economically ruinous to the countries receiving the goods because it would have put their own workers and factories out of production. Germany had no money except that which it could borrow, and most of that would come from the United States. The first reparations payment of 132 billion gold marks came due in May 1921, and left Germany with two options. Either it could refuse to pay (as ultra-nationalists urged), or it could pay for a while and try to negotiate new and more realistic terms. Germany borrowed the money and made a first payment in August 1921, but, unable to raise more cash, paid in kind until early 1923, when the Weimar government announced payments must cease.

France, Belgium, and Italy retaliated by occupying the Ruhr. In response, the German government helped workers and industrialists bring production to a halt and printed more and more money, until the mark was virtually valueless. American economists stepped in and proposed plans that included returning the Ruhr to Germany, a two-year moratorium on reparations, and loans to help restart production. The central concern of Europe, sometimes called the "Germany problem," was that Germany continued to have the largest population and economy in the region and the potential to be the dominant military power.

Meanwhile, during most of the 1920s the economy in the United States was booming, fueled by a postwar optimism that led to excessive speculation. People bought on credit and borrowed record amounts from banks, and the stock market boomed. The economy had slowed by the spring of 1929. When there was a loss of confidence and a credit squeeze, demand fell, prices dropped, and goods piled up in factories. On October 24, 1929, the stock market crashed in the greatest economic disaster in the history of the West. Within three years the stock market lost about 80 percent of its value. By 1932 more than one-quarter of the work force was idle and manufacturing had fallen to 54 percent of its 1929 output. By 1933 almost 45 percent of American banks had failed.

Once the Great Depression was under way, things grew rapidly worse in almost every sector. Americans recalled their overseas investments to cover debts at home, draining gold reserves from foreign countries, especially Germany.

On June 17, 1930, the United States, in what is widely believed to have been a mistake, tried to protect domestic production by passing the Smoot-Hawley Tariff Act, which raised import duties to 50 percent, effectively prohibiting imports. With the American market shut off to European economies, the Europeans had no way to get the gold they needed in order to meet their obligations. On May 31, 1931, Kreditanstalt of Vienna, a respected bank, collapsed. The next month the United States announced a one-year moratorium on government war debts. In the ensuing year, the European countries agreed to cancel their claims for German reparations payments if the United States would cancel their war debts, but the United States refused.

Each of the countries of the world reacted to the crisis in ways they deemed best for their own situation and not in the interest of reclaiming the world economy. The United States passed laws forbidding even individual loans to foreign countries that were not making their debt payments. France and Germany cut wages, triggering social unrest. In Germany the Nazi Party made gains in the Reichstag, and in France the leftist Popular Front won the national election in 1936. By 1932 Germany had been virtually cut off and reacted by shunning world markets and concentrating on self-sufficiency and trade in marks with the smaller states of Eastern Europe. The Nazi government implemented a managed economy with such success that by 1936 Germany had escaped the Great Depression and was rebuilding its war machine. The Depression provided an opening for the rise of Hitlerism and remilitarization of Germany, which made the move for conquest in the east possible.

There is no consensus among economic historians about the causes of the Great Depression. Some blame the tariffs and the subsequent contraction of international trade; others blame wild speculation in the stock market, a contraction of the money supply, or a decline in the capacity of consumers to purchase goods and services. Each of these explanations leaves significant unanswered questions. Why did the Depression happen when it did under the conditions it did? Why was it so severe, and why did it last so long? And why have similar conditions in the past not resulted in the same kind of catastrophe? These questions continue to be debated. Two facts do emerge: the free market did not correct itself and solve the problems, and, in the 1930s, massive government intervention in the form of deficit spending and other corrections was making a positive difference.

Germany surrendered to end World War I because the German elite and the military did not want to risk losing power, as they would by agreeing to an unconditional surrender. In fact, the German masses no longer supported the elite.

A corporal in the German Army, Adolph Hitler, was radicalized by Germany's humiliation at the end of the war and worked tirelessly at rebuilding the German nation. He thought that the struggle between capitalism and socialism was a major cause of the lack of unity in Germany, and he set out to create a system that he considered to be neither capitalist nor socialist. Although the results of his effort and the fact that he was so willing to use murder on a massive scale to achieve political ends have caused Hitler to be demonized, his ideas were influenced by mainstream Western thought and have left a legacy that is unlikely to disappear soon.

Hitler sought to mobilize the German people around an idea of nationalism that would be more powerful than internal social contradictions and would forge a powerful, focused, and strident Germany. There had existed for a thousand years in Europe a fear and hatred of the Jews, which continued to be strong among the German people. The terms of the peacetime conditions were universally despised in Germany, and Hitler promoted his belief that Germany had lost the war because its power was subverted by Jewish bankers and businessmen.

Hitler despised socialism, which he believed was the invention of Karl Marx, a Jew. Hitler denounced the socialist ideal of an international brotherhood of labor, which many German workers embraced. He disbanded the unions, believing the movement would undermine his efforts to build German nationalism. Linking the loss of the war with both Jewish internationalist socialism and Jewish bankers, Hitler came to believe in the existence of an international conspiracy secretly led by Jews that not only was responsible for Germany's loss of the war but intended to subvert the potential of the German nation. He concluded that the history of the world was the story of the competition for hegemony not among classes but between "races," and he thought that the way this competition was played out was through warfare. Hitler's ideas about race did not contradict the ideology of scientific racism that had dominated Western thought during the nineteenth century, but his racism was consciously political, as he makes clear in a letter to a supporter:

> I know perfectly well that in the scientific sense there is no such thing as race, but you, as a farmer, cannot get your breeding successfully achieved without the conception of race. And I as a politician need a conception which enables the order which has hitherto existed on historic bases to be abolished, and an entirely new and anti-historic order enforced and given an intellectual basis. . . . With the conception of race National-Socialism will carry its revolution abroad and recast the world. (Thornton 1966, 6)

Hitler became obsessed with the idea of an international Jewish conspiracy against the German (or Aryan) race. Capitalizing on the fact that the German people felt unjustly victimized by the terms of the peace, Hitler offered a vision of a revitalized Germany that would build on the culture of its ancestors and create a utopian society he designated the Thousand Year Reich. Hitler's government would become the most popular in German history. His revitalization movement was enthusiastically embraced by the German people for two reasons: it offered redemption by blaming others for German failures and proposed a plan for future glory.

The fact that this vision was not realistic—that Germany was very unlikely to be successful in a war against most of the world's industrial nations and that leaders of Nazism were aware of this—was characteristic of the way revitalization movements of this type are played out. That it was able to recruit ordinary German citizens to commit acts of murder and genocide is also consistent with revitalization movements in which the members are so convinced of the justice of their cause that they feel no criminality in their behavior. Quite the contrary, many of them were proud of what they were doing. Speaking of ordinary Germans in the Nazi military, Daniel Goldhagen wrote, in *Hitler's Willing Executioners:*

> They repeatedly showed initiative in killing and did not shirk their assigned tasks, though they could have without punishment. They gave priority to the killing of Jews and even acted with cruel abandon. Their dedication to the genocidal slaughter was such that they persisted in it despite [its] gruesomeness. . . . Much of the killing was also personalized, in that the men often faced their victims one on one. Frequently, they were facing children. (1996, 238)

This type of movement has been capable of creating its own martyrs and of carrying its followers into great danger. It is also capable, when conditions are right, of creating mass murderers. Throughout the decade of the 1930s, Hitler ceaselessly repeated his ideas about Germany's rightful place in the world, about the need of the German people for more space to live in, about racial purity and the role of the Jews in humiliating Germany during the war, and about what must be done. The German people (and other white supremacists) shared his obsession.

Hitler was not interested in overseas markets, international trade, or the free market economy; and although he did what he had to do to obtain the support of the army and Germany's elites, he was not primarily a servant of their interests. Hitler remained purposefully vague about his thoughts on many subjects, but his goal of building a unified German nation led him to believe that economic competition between classes was counterproductive, and his thinking did not idealize the market economy or the Workers' Paradise. He was not a strongly religious person and probably did not believe in God. What he believed in was his own vision of "nature," a particular nationalism-serving idea that asserted that in a world where subversive forces could not interfere, the German people would create a master race by letting their "nature" take its course.

He preached about the greatness of the German *volk*—its history, its art, its genius. As seen through an intensely nationalist and visionary lens, the volk was imagined to exist in some historic or social reality. The restoration of the volk became a sort of religion of nationalism.

When German students of the eighteenth century had cried "Down with Tyrants!" they referred to the Holy Roman Emperor Charlemagne, who had slaughtered their forebears in Saxony nine hundred years before. The new movement of students, teachers, and workers who helped forge Hitler's great cultural propaganda machine promoted the myth of Germans victimized by Jews and labored enthusiastically to create a volkish culture out of a mythic and idealized past (Mosse 1964, 153).

This was a reaction to the conditions that had created a demoralized and despairing Germany. It offered a dream of a revitalized people with a mission to become the most perfect nation morally, biologically, and militarily. Hitlerism was one of the most intense revitalization movements of all time in terms of its ability to hypnotize a modern, technologically advanced nation into advancing a cause of unspeakable evil. Versions of it continue to inspire paranoia about international Jewish conspiracies to dominate the world. Hitler's "alternative" to socialism and capitalism was National Socialism, a form of totalitarianism devoted to racially based nationalism. In speeches he mesmerized German audiences like no orator before or since, because he was telling them exactly what they most yearned to hear: that the German people were ultimately the greatest people on earth but that their greatness had been stymied by a world conspiracy of enemies—pacifists, socialists, foreign capitalists, and others, all led by Jews. Under the hand of a strong leader, a *fuhrer*, they could rise up to seize this greatness. The vast majority of the German people crowded under Hitler's banner, a black swastika in a white circle on a red background, Hitler's contribution to twentieth-century art.

It was not difficult for many Germans to extend these ideas to what was then known about biology. It was perfectly logical that a superior people should lead the world (the Greek philosopher Plato had offered the thought that the smartest people should run governments), and that selective breeding could produce perfect human specimens with the capacity to solve all humankind's problems. Before this could happen, it was clear to those inspired by this movement that there were a lot of inferior humans taking up German space and natural resources that should ideally be dedicated to the Hitlerean project. It has been estimated that as many as one million "racially defective" Germans were sterilized. Furthermore, the Master Race would need more room than was available in Germany—*lebensraum* or "living room"—and in Hitler's eyes such land lay to the east. As conquerors have always done, Hitler used "inferior" peoples— those he designated as "non-Aryan"—for menial work and especially for slave labor under conditions that would eventually kill them. This burden fell especially on Poles and other Slavic peoples, who, historically speaking, were as Aryan as the Germans. (Jews and Gypsies were used for slave labor but more often directly exterminated.) The pattern of a utopian construction rationalizing conquest and the use of forced labor by peoples deemed inferior, as we have seen, was not at all unknown in the West.

Hitler thought that capitalism was a decadent way of life and in decline, and that the great ideological competition to his ideas lay in another great movement, socialism. Socialism was strongest at that time in Russia, and Russia had been defeated by Germany during the last war. But Russia, which had been an agrarian giant at the beginning of the century, now embraced an ideology that included the presumption that industrialization was destined to relieve workers of the drudgery of their existence. The Russia of 1939 was a very different country from the one that had collapsed in 1917. Although it is impossible not to condemn Stalin and the treatment of people in the Soviet Union during the 1930s, Russia's move toward industrialization was a major factor in its ability to resist and repel the German invasion when it came.

Hitler tried to stage a coup in 1923, but was instead arrested and spent thirteen months in jail, where he wrote his most famous book, *Mein Kampf.* He went on to head the National Socialist German Workers' (Nazi) Party, and his chance came with the 1930 election. The Weimar Republic had not coped well with the appeal of communism, and relations with the West had also failed. This dismal situation was reflected in the elections, which brought 77 seats to the Communist Party and 107 to the Nazi Party.

The Nazis came to power promoting the argument that the Great War had seen the German people united as never before and that they had been "stabbed in the back" by defeatists in the Weimar government. The July 1932 elections brought 230 Nazis to the Reichstag, and on January 30, 1933, Chancellor Hindenberg was obliged to appoint Hitler chancellor of Germany. Hitler quickly used the Reichstag to establish a totalitarian dictatorship and within two years had outlawed all other political parties. In early 1934 Hitler signed a nonaggression pact with Poland, which served to stabilize Germany's relations with France and England while Germany rearmed. As Hitler seized power at home, England lapsed into a mentality that favored appeasement and avoidance of war at almost any cost, while the United States carried out a policy of isolationism.

Civil war broke out in Spain in 1936 with a military revolt led by Francisco Franco. Hitler and Italy's Mussolini sent supplies and military aid to the future dictator, while the democracies did little to help the democratically elected government of the Spanish Republic. Stalin provided material support but sent agents who murdered people they identified as enemies of the Russian state, and this served to undermine the credibility of the Republic. The Republic fell in 1939.

In March 1936 Hitler occupied and fortified the Rhineland, while the rest of Europe watched but took no action. In May Italy completed the conquest of Abyssinia (Ethiopia). The League of Nations remonstrated, but stood idly by. In November Italy and Germany created the Rome-Berlin Axis, and Germany signed an agreement with Japan.

During these interwar years, Germany perfected the tactics and technologies that emerged during World War II into something they called *Blitzkrieg* or "lightning war." It involved massive attacks using tanks, bombers, and paratroopers and was to prove stunningly effective.

Shortly after Hitler came to power in 1933, the persecution of Jews was under way. Jewish property was confiscated, and by 1935 Jews lost German citizenship. Intermarriage with Germans was forbidden. On November 9, 1938, Nazi thugs smashed Jewish property during the "night of broken glass" *(Kristallnacht)* and destroyed practically every synagogue in the country. Most Jewish wealth was confiscated and Jews were rounded up and placed in concentration camps. By 1939 Jews were required to wear a yellow Star of David badge on their clothing and were forbidden to own property, use the telephone, go to parks or other public places, attend public school, engage in business, or use public transportation. The Nazis soon found allies in western Europe willing to extend the pogrom of the Jews: Romania, Hungary, and German-occupied Czechoslovakia passed anti-Jewish laws. Eventually, as Germany conquered and occupied Western Europe, most countries, including France and Switzerland, passed restrictive laws aimed at Jews.

In 1938 the Nazis engineered the annexation of Austria and two weeks later demanded autonomy for the Sudetenland, a German-speaking province of Czechoslovakia. Czechoslovakia began mobilizing its army, and Hitler paused until September, when he met with England's prime minister, Neville Chamberlain. Hitler demanded that Czechoslovakia allow German annexation of the Sudetenland. After a few days England and France persuaded Czechoslovakia to submit, only to find the demands had escalated and Germany now wanted immediate occupation of the territory.

The leaders of Germany, Italy, France, and England met on September 29, 1938, in Munich, and Hitler was given everything he had asked for: about a third of Czechoslovakia, including industrialized regions. One of France's major military allies following World War I was now practically a German dependency. Germany invaded and annexed most of what was left of Czechoslovakia in early 1939 and seized the seaport of Memel from Lithuania. Next, Italy annexed Albania, and by late summer the head of the Nazi party in Danzig was demanding that Poland surrender Danzig to Germany. Hitler prefaced these moves by signing an agreement with Russia, which included a promise that the latter could take some Polish territory and have a free hand in Latvia, Estonia, and Finland. Hitler invaded Poland on September 1, and France and England declared war two days later.

Poland collapsed in less than a month, and Hitler next attacked Denmark, taking the country in one day, April 9, 1940. Norway fell next, and in May, the Netherlands and Belgium fell. The German Army pressed forward and trapped the French and British forces at Dunkirk. They were evacuated to Britain by a flotilla composed of great numbers of civilian vessels. Germany continued its attack, and France surrendered on June 16. For a year, from June 1940 to June 1941, Germany launched air attacks against Britain, which the latter rallied to withstand. Winston Churchill called this period Britain's "finest hour."

In June 1941, Germany assembled the largest contingent of armor ever seen in the world and unleashed a blitzkrieg against Russia. Germany expected a quick victory in the east, and its armies moved rapidly at first, but Russia proved a much more difficult foe than expected.

Hitler had threatened earlier that if there was another world war and Germany found itself facing a united opposition of the world's most powerful countries, as had happened during World War I, the Jews, the people he held responsible, would pay. German forces quickly conquered huge territories across Eastern Europe that were the homeland of much of Europe's Jewish population. At first some Ukrainians welcomed the Germans as liberators from Russian oppression. As German arrogance and brutality became apparent, Ukrainian resistance mounted. Early German victories slowed and German casualties increased.

Germany now was faced with dealing with large numbers of civilian captives, mostly Slavs and Jews. Slavs were rounded up and sent to concentration camps to become slave laborers for the German war effort. Although historians have searched unsuccessfully for decades for a document with Hitler's signature ordering the slaughter of Jews, there can be no doubt he gave such orders. Jews were rounded up and marched to the edge of towns, where they were systematically shot. Ordinary Germans who were accountants, teachers, or bricklayers in civilian life marched innocent people—men, women, and children—to trenches and systematically killed them. Whole towns disappeared. How ordinary Germans could undertake the task of shooting babies and little boys and girls in cold blood (and people of every generation within a whole population) has been the subject of considerable discussion since then. When the army grew weary and disgusted with this task, the German high command devised other, less personal, ways of killing: carbon monoxide pumped into vehicles en route to burial sites and, finally, death camps. This was the Holocaust, an extraordinary episode in the history of nationalism, racism, and the drive for plunder, conquest, and world domination. It was a testimonial to the power of revitalization movements even among contemporary peoples possessed of a classical Western education.

Bibliography

Benedict, Ruth. *Race, Science, and Politics.* New York: Modern Age Books, 1940.

Goldhagen, Daniel Jonah. *Hitler's Willing Executioners: Ordinary Germans and the Holocaust.* New York: Alfred A. Knopf, 1996.

Hitler, Adolph. "Mein Kampf." In Benjamin Sax and Dieter Kuntz, eds., *Inside Hitler's Germany: A Documentary History of Life in the Third Reich.* Boston and Toronto: D. C. Heath & Co., 1992.

Mosse, George L. *The Crisis of German Ideology: Intellectual Origins of the Third Reich.* New York : Grosset & Dunlap, 1964.

Thornton, M. J. *Nazism 1918–1945.* New York: Pergamon Press, 1966.

THIRTEEN
World
War II

> In a world full of hatred, death, destruction, deception, and double-dealing, the United States at the end of World War II was almost universally regarded as the disinterested champion of justice, freedom, and democracy. American prestige would never be as high again.
>
> Stephen Ambrose, *Rise to Globalism: American Foreign Policy Since 1938*

World War II changed the way a generation thought about the world. It was an exercise in devastation almost beyond recounting, a disaster so immense that many reasonable people, especially in Europe, seriously thought the survival of Western civilization was at risk. At its end, in the European theater alone, some 60 million people lay dead, Europe's production capacity was in ruins, and many of its cities were virtually destroyed. Little wonder that as the war came to an end, most of the leadership of the Western world were of one mind that nothing like this should ever happen again. Out of the ruins would come ideas about how to rebuild.

The Grand Alliance that joined forces in 1942 to combat Hitler has sometimes been called the Strange Alliance. The three main figures were the Soviet Union's Joseph Stalin, Britain's Winston Churchill, and U.S. president Franklin Roosevelt. They were an odd union because Britain was the world's leading colonial power, the USSR was the only communist superpower, and the United States was the world's leading capitalist power. The three powers all had vital interests in containing Germany, which had become, at that moment, the world's leading military power. Japan bombed Pearl Harbor on December 7, 1941, and the following month Churchill arrived in Washington to discuss strategy. Although Americans were largely united in a war effort against Japan, there was some reluctance to go to war with Germany.

Churchill wanted to attack the periphery of the empire of the Third Reich, as Hitler had dubbed Nazi Germany. His strategy called for use of resistance forces and bombing raids to wear the Germans down, and to let Russia maintain the only front against Germany's army and to take most of the casualties. The United States Chief of Staff, General George Marshall, was opposed to this strategy because he thought the Red Army would probably collapse, thus affording Hitler total victory on the European mainland. If that happened, any attempted invasion would face the full might of the German military. He proposed an immediate build-up of forces in England in preparation for a massive invasion. There were both practical and political problems with Marshall's strategy. Roosevelt wanted to engage the Germans quickly so Americans would feel a sense of commitment to the war effort in Europe rather than waiting a year or more. Unless the Allies took some kind of aggressive action on the ground soon, Russia would be left holding the only significant front against Germany, and Roosevelt insisted this should not happen.

The plan that was adopted essentially combined both strategies. Germany would be ringed and bombed as Churchill desired, but the Allies would attack Germany's allies under France's collaborationist Vichy regime in North Africa. This was approved by Churchill because it was consistent with Britain's objective of re-establishing a presence in the Mediterranean. It was approved by Russia because it opened a second front, although not the second front on the Continent as they wished. It satisfied Roosevelt because it meant that U.S. ground forces would be engaging the German Army in combat. Both Dwight Eisenhower and Marshall were sharply critical of this strategy, however; and, in the long run, their reservations were well founded. American and British successes in Morocco and Algeria led to those areas being used as staging grounds for campaigns into Sicily and Italy. Much of the Allied war effort was concentrated on this Mediterranean front, which produced victories that looked good on the map but did little to diminish German power or its grip on central Europe.

Believing that most of the French forces under the Vichy government disliked the Germans, the Allies thought the war in North Africa might be made easier by a lack of commitment on the part of the French troops. The Americans, for their part, were reluctant to fight the French. Charles de Gaulle had fled France and established the Free French Government in exile in Britain but, despite much urging, few French officers or units defected to the Free French Army. As the preparations for the invasion were nearing completion, French Admiral François Darlan opened independent negotiations from Algiers. Darlan was a bitter opponent of the British and had written some of the Vichy government's anti-Semitic laws; but when he was offered a position with the Free French and the title of governor general of French North Africa, he signed a cease-fire and took the job.

This early foreign policy victory was bittersweet indeed, because Darlan represented fascism to the Allies. The settlement raised the issue of how far the Allies would go in the name of military expediency. Would this mean that when they attacked Italy, perhaps Mussolini, the fascist dictator, could cut a deal? The problem was resolved on Christmas Eve 1942, when Darlan was mysteriously assassinated by a cadre of French officers. To this day, no one knows how this came about, who ordered it done, or why. French General Henri Geraud succeeded Darlan, but Charles de Gaulle, with help from his British sponsors, soon joined Geraud, and by the end of 1943 displaced him completely.

In January 1943, Allied leaders met in Casablanca. Roosevelt was deliberately vague about his long-range plans for Europe except in stating that the goal of the war effort was the unconditional surrender of Germany and its allies. The Russians were understandably suspicious. What kind of governments would succeed the fascists? It was clearly understood that following a surrender there would be occupation governments under the Allied military forces, but what then? Roosevelt carefully avoided engaging in the bickering that would result from any attempt to answer the question, and he kept his attention focused on the war effort.

Most of that year Anglo-American military operations concentrated on Italy, but events on that front moved slowly. In July Rome was bombed. The fascist governing council overthrew Mussolini and in short order changed sides, offering to join the Allies against Germany. The Allies accepted, and the "reformed" Italian government remained in power. Thus the same people who were in power before the war and during the alliance with Hitler were to remain in power under the Anglo-American occupation. Stalin at first objected because the Russians were left without a voice in this arrangement, but he soon acquiesced because it created a principle that whichever country liberated an area from German influence would now have the right to dictate what kind of government would be established there. Stalin had plans for Eastern Europe that would work nicely in this environment.

In January 1944 Eisenhower took over command of the Allied Expeditionary Force and the planning of the massive cross-channel invasion that would directly strike German-occupied Europe through southern France. From that moment on, Allied military planning in Europe proceeded with a single-minded purpose: defeat of Germany's military machine. With the war now going in the Allies' favor, the British were primarily interested in the long-term postwar results and wanted to limit Russian influence in Europe. They urged that forces be sent to the Balkans to undercut the Soviet position in that region, and they wished to seize Berlin before the Red Army arrived. At that time the American leadership was not concerned about the USSR's future role in Europe and wanted to concentrate on the short-term objective of crushing the German military as quickly as possible. Roosevelt was firm in his replies to the British that the United States intended to establish a front in Western Europe and could not divert troops to other locations in the east. Roosevelt was seeking a balance of power. Since the United States clearly dominated the war effort (by this time,

Britain's contributions to the Allied effort were down to about 25 percent), the American strategy prevailed.

The year 1944 marks a watershed in world history because it is clear that from that point on the United States succeeded Great Britain as the dominant economic and military power. Almost half of the world's industrial production was, by that time, centered in the United States, and 45 percent of all military goods were American made. Of all the great ships afloat in the world, two-thirds had been manufactured in the United States.

The invasion at Normandy, code-named OVERLORD, was launched on June 6, 1944. It was a massive undertaking that involved some 6,000 airplanes, 5,000 boats, and 175,000 troops from twelve nations. It was a display of both unity and military coordination, and a testimony to Eisenhower's talents for large-scale organization.

The advance across Western Europe was filled with drama and intrigue. Eisenhower and the Americans designed an advance with American and British forces moving cautiously eastward along a broad front in a methodical well-planned military operation. Britain's General Bernard Montgomery wanted to take the risk of rushing eastward to meet the Red Army as rapidly and as far to the east as possible. But Eisenhower was in charge, and things went according to his plans. In the early spring of 1945, Allied forces moved across the Rhine. Montgomery wanted air support and supplies to make a push to reach Berlin before the Red Army, but it was not to be, and military historians generally doubt it was even possible. Churchill wanted British forces to capture Berlin to counter Red Army claims that it had been the major victor in the war. The Russian army, which in fact was a major factor in the defeat of Nazi Germany, was first to enter Berlin.

On the Pacific front, the Japanese leadership viewed all Europeans as intruders in Asia and the Americans as the most powerful and dangerous of all; this view was rooted in the history of Japanese/Western relations. Japan was determined to drive the European powers from positions of dominance in Asia. As early as 1871 Japan had sent delegations to Europe and the United States to negotiate an end to Western judicial and other privileges that had been negotiated in previous treaties. In 1879 Japan annexed the Ryukyu Islands against Chinese protests. In 1894, Japan sent troops to crush a rebellion in Korea (traditionally within the Chinese "sphere of influence"), and the Sino-Japanese War erupted. China was quickly defeated and forced to make significant concessions, including granting to Japan the kind of economic privileges enjoyed by Western powers.

In 1900 a Chinese revitalization movement called the Boxer Rebellion mobilized peasants to expel Westerners from China but inadvertently provoked a Western military invasion, ostensibly to rescue Christian missionaries and other foreign nationals. The Japanese Army played a major role in this invasion. China was forced to make reparations to the invaders, and Japan used this money to subsidize steel production the following year. The Yawata Iron and Steel Works greatly expanded Japan's heavy industry and announced it as an emerging industrial nation. As Japan industrialized, its population grew but its food production did not, and the country became more and more dependent on international trade and credit to pay for needed food and other imports. Rural Japan experienced increasing economic pressure from foreign competition and remained tradition-bound and poor. The silkworm industry provided some capital but was dependent on international trade. A panic in 1927 and the collapse of the American market in 1929 caused significant misery.

Russia entered an alliance with Korea, and in 1904 Japanese ships attacked the Russian Fleet, thus initiating the Russo-Japanese War. Japan was successful at arms but the war was costly in lives and treasure. Russia made significant concessions and the war altered the balance of power in Asia; in 1909 Japan annexed Korea. During World War I, Japan's aggressive demands of China for economic and political power fueled anti-Japanese Chinese nationalism. Following the war, in an attempt to limit Japanese imperial ambitions, the Western powers entered into a Five-Power Naval Limitation Treaty that restricted Japanese naval presence to three battleships to every five for Great Britain and the United States.

Japan and Germany would emerge as distant allies during World War II, but there were parallels in their feelings about the nations that would emerge as the Allies. To begin with, there was resentment of a perceived lack of full respect for Japan in its dealings with European nations vis-à-vis its imperial ambitions in Asia. The Japanese were also troubled by a sense of cultural and military domination by the West. When the United States passed the discriminatory National Origins Act of 1924, which excluded Asians from immigration to the United States, the action was perceived as an insult and was taken by militant factions as evidence of the futility of cooperation with the West. There was also a significant and deep ethnocentrism that translated into a feeling of Japanese superiority, not unlike the sense of racial superiority emerging in Germany at the time.

Japan's urban prosperity had brought significant cultural westernization to some parts of the society, but Japan remained a premodern society, with a mere 20 percent of its work force engaged in industrial production. Economic hard times brought criticism about corruption in the government and a chance for conservative forces in the army to move to dominate politics. Japan had a parliamentary form of government that incorporated universal male suffrage and a constitutional emperor. The military, however, had succeeded in making itself independent of civilian control by 1931. With the collapse of foreign markets during the Great Depression, Western tariffs that excluded Japanese products and made it difficult to import enough food, and the rejection of Japanese and Chinese applications for racial equality in the League of Nations, many Japanese began to accept the argument that the only recourse was the use of force.

At this time there arose an ultranationalist movement in Japan that rejected Western influence and attempted to preserve what was seen as the essential Japanese spirit. The movement supported military intervention on the Asian continent and opposed party politics as "un-Japanese." The ultranationalists spawned a small terrorist movement that assassinated some business and government leaders. The most powerful opposition to parliamentary government in Japanese society, however, involved junior military officers, many from rural areas, who did not trust their leaders, knew little about political economy, and were contemptuous of urban society.

The next phase of Japanese military aggression was launched in 1931, when the army occupied Manchuria. In the political unrest that followed, assassinations occurred as well as compromises by the government that strengthened the role of the army in governance and especially in foreign policy.

Some historians date the beginning of World War II to the Japanese invasion of China in 1937. The war was devastating to China and has been called the "Asian holocaust." Japan occupied all the important coastal areas, brushed aside Western protests, and turned its attention to the resources of other areas of Southeast Asia, especially Indonesia and Indochina. Japan's challenge to Western, and especially U.S., hegemony in Asia convinced many in Japan that war was inevitable and that the only question was under what circumstances it would be ignited. The Chinese, meanwhile, united to face the Japanese invasion. Knowing that Japan could only obtain the necessary materials for the conquest of China with U.S. cooperation, the United States imposed an embargo on oil exports and all other trade with Japan in October 1941.

The decision to go to war with the most powerful industrial nation in the world was not a rational one. No reasonable Japanese —no doubt including some of Japan's highest military commanders—would have expected Japan to win such a war. The inspiration for this action came from ultranationalists whose enthusiasm for what they saw as Japan's destiny to rule Asia, its racial superiority, and its need to uproot decadent Western influences overwhelmed rational judgment.

When Japan attacked Pearl Harbor on December 7, 1941, American anger turned toward this antagonist across the Pacific and not, in the early stages, toward Nazi Germany. Japan achieved stunning successes early in the war. The attack on Pearl Harbor had destroyed much of the American Pacific Fleet, and Japan soon invaded Indonesia and the Philippines and was threatening Australia. Asia was much farther than Europe—about twice as far—and presented huge logistical problems for the American military effort. The United States devoted about 40 percent of its war effort to fighting Japan, but it was a very different war. No American military commander wanted to get mired down in a war on the Asian mainland, and while the U.S. Navy necessarily engaged the Japanese Navy, American ground troops did not engage the mass of Japan's army. The American war in the Pacific was fought on small islands and great oceans and in the air over the water.

American conduct of the war in the Pacific was influenced by several other factors. Roosevelt opposed the old-style colonialism of Great Britain and the European powers, which before the war had closed or limited markets and sources of raw materials to the United States, and he had spoken out against colonialism. The United States had pledged independence to its largest colony, the Philippines, a pledge it kept in 1946. As a matter of military reality, the United States would not have been able or willing to maintain a standing army large enough actually to occupy Asia and would not have been willing to risk American troops in a protracted ground war there. The United States was unwilling to commit to much more than the military defeat of Japan. U.S. policy, therefore, encouraged the dismantling of European empires in the region and counted on the rise of friendly "democratic" regimes in the postwar period to keep communist expansion in check.

The American effort was divided into two spheres. In the southwest Pacific, operating from Australia, General Douglas MacArthur planned a campaign through the Netherlands East Indies and the Philippines and on to Japan. Admiral Chester Nimitz was in charge of the Navy in the central Pacific and was based in Hawaii.

During the war the United States sought to unite the forces of Mao Tse Tung and Chiang Kai-Shek against Japan, and American support continued to flow to Chiang despite poor results. Mao was mistrusted by Stalin and Roosevelt, but the Chinese Nationalists led by General Chiang had a well-deserved reputation for corruption. In the end, only a full American occupation of China would have saved Chiang's regime, and the United States was not willing to commit millions of soldiers to a ground war in Asia. By 1949 Mao's communist forces prevailed and Chiang and his Nationalist forces retreated to the island of Taiwan and exile.

Roosevelt suggested that Indochina be snatched away from France and placed under joint receivership, a proposal Stalin found attractive. It is probable that Roosevelt took this step because of a personal dislike of Charles de Gaulle. Britain alone objected to this transfer of a colonial possession from France. After the war this policy changed and France regained its former possessions, only to be plunged into the Vietnamese war for independence. Some decisions, entered hastily at the war's end, were to have serious repercussions, especially the division of Vietnam and Korea into communist and noncommunist states.

By spring 1945, the United States was confident it would soon possess an atomic bomb of enormous destructive power. Germany collapsed and was occupied in the spring, but the Japanese Army was largely intact and its Air Force boasted some 12,000 planes. Japanese fighter planes were arguably technologically superior to American fighter planes. Although Japan had lost the territories it had gained in the war, it was far from conquered. American strategists made an effort to bring the Red Army into the war with Japan, hoping to hasten the surrender of the demoralized Japanese Army. In the early summer of 1945, it was clear that the only way to defeat the Japanese Army was to fight it. American generals hoped that if anyone undertook that task, it would be the Red Army.

The first successful secret test of the atomic bomb came in July, and the U.S. government's attitudes changed immediately. It was no longer necessary to invite the Russians into the war with Japan. The bomb would do the trick, and there was great public pressure on the president to end the war. Japan demanded guarantees that Emperor Hirohito would not be punished as a war criminal, an idea that had much popular support in America. The Allies refused to make any guarantee, Japan refused to surrender, and President Truman ordered the military to drop the bomb. The first atomic bomb was dropped on Hiroshima on August 6, 1945. The second was dropped on Nagasaki on August 9, 1945.

Americans would later question the motives behind the bombing of two Japanese population centers with little importance as military targets, and there would be speculation that the United States dropped the bomb to impress the Soviets. There is significant evidence, however, that the United States dropped the bomb because it no longer adhered to the rules of civilized warfare regarding civilian populations and because popular fear and hatred of the Japanese was very intense.

The United States could have won the war without dropping the bomb but, given the remaining strength of the Japanese Air Force, especially in fighter planes, the price would have been high. The bomb ensured that Russian influence in Asia would be much less than it would have been had the Red Army fought and defeated the Japanese Army. Thus the bombs were dropped to save American lives, but also to ensure American interests in Asia in competition with Russia. Racism also played a role, as did the almost incomprehensible brutality of the war. The Americans had engaged in attacks on civilian populations in Europe that had no discernible military objectives, including bombings of German cities. Millions of Jewish people had been murdered. Millions of Russian people were dead, as were millions of others throughout Europe. World War II can be remembered because of the triumph over fascism, but its toll in human life and its assault on the human spirit should not be forgotten.

Roosevelt, Truman, Churchill, and others felt they were charged with saving Western civilization, an idea that had a certain racial characteristic because it meant, in practical terms, continuing to promote the white man's hegemony over the other peoples of the world. The leaders who had selected themselves to preserve Western culture had acquired in the course of this war a version of depraved indifference to human life. It could be argued that dropping atomic bombs on two Japanese cities were the first acts of the Cold War, because the bombs were aimed as much at Russian ambitions in the region as at the Japanese determination to continue the war.

Bibliography

Ambrose, Stephen. *Rise to Globalism: American Foreign Policy Since 1938.* New York: Penguin Books, 1971, rev. 1995.

Boling, David. *Mass Rape, Enforced Prostitution, and the Japanese Imperial Army: Japan Eschews International Legal Responsibility.* Baltimore: University of Maryland Law School Press, 1995.

Davis, Glenn. *An Occupation Without Troops: Wall Street's Half-Century Domination of Japanese Politics.* Tokyo: Yenbooks, 1996.

Fritzsche, Peter. *Germans into Nazis.* Cambridge, Mass.: Harvard University Press. 1998.

Herzstein, Edwin Robert. *The Nazis.* Alexandria, Va.: Time-Life Books, 1980.

Irving, David. *The War Path: Hitler's Germany, 1933–1939.* New York: Viking Press, 1978.

Mueller-Hillebrand, Burkhart. *Germany and Its Allies in World War II: A Record of Axis Collaboration Problems.* Frederick, Md.: University Publications of America, 1980.

Peres, Louis G. *The History of Japan.* Westport, Conn.: Greenwood Press, 1998.

Rees, David. *The Defeat of Japan.* Westport, Conn.: Praeger, 1997.

Tanaka, Yuki. *Hidden Horrors: Japanese War Crimes in World War II.* Boulder, Colo.: Westview Press, 1996.

Wetzler, Peter. *Hirohito and War: Imperial Tradition and Military Decision Making in Prewar Japan.* Honolulu: University of Hawaii Press, 1998.

FOURTEEN
Pax Americana

In all the world, only the United States had a healthy economy, an intact physical plant capable of mass production of goods, and excess capital. American troops occupied Japan . . . while American influence was dominant in France, Britain, and West Germany, the industrial heart of Europe. The Pacific and the Mediterranean had become American lakes.

> Stephen E. Ambrose, *Rise to Globalism: American Foreign Policy Since 1938*

In July 1944, seven hundred world leaders met in the shadow of Mount Deception in New Hampshire, near the nonexistent village of Bretton Woods, to create a strategy to insure the stability of the world's currencies. They met to address the problems that had produced the currency collapses and worldwide depression of the 1930s, and the ideas that drove the meetings were consistent with previous ideas about the pursuit of the ideal:

[S]cores of dissertations, books, monographs and articles have been written about this almost alchemical scheme to organize the irrational cravings of man and nations. . . . But the devil is in the details, after all: there is no New Hampshire village called Bretton Woods. . . . The village of Bretton Woods was an invention of a hotel promoter of the Gilded Age (Millman 1995, 64).

It was thought that the best minds in the world would be capable of devising a rational plan to stabilize currencies and halt the kinds of economic stresses that had led to war and, therefore, could end warfare, at least among the major industrial nations. Such an economic order, driven by reason instead of passion or nationalism, could create universal prosperity. The existence of the atomic bomb appeared to signal an end to armed conflict between states that would possess the capability for total annihilation.

At war's end the United States possessed about two-thirds of the world's gold, and the U.S. dollar became the standard of international currency. American economists urged free trade because it was in America's interest to do so. Because the United States had relatively few overseas possessions, it was opposed to the European system of overseas colonies, which essentially denied these markets to American firms. Britain preferred a system of imperial preference that provided special trade privileges among members and former members of the British Empire, and the continuation of the vestiges of the colonial economy. Even if the European countries had not been exhausted by war, the old form of colonization was probably too expensive to maintain with British or French troops stationed overseas. The United States wanted to do away with such arrangements and with colonies, and to create a world market. American ambitions under the conditions prevailing at the end of the war were, in the long run, irresistible.

World War II had been the most destructive event in world history. The institutions that were created during this period—the General Agreement on Tariffs and Trade (GATT), the World Trade Organization (WTO), the World Bank, and the International Monetary Fund (IMF)—were designed to regulate trade and the world's money supply, and to help stabilize national currencies, in order to avoid economic disasters like that which occurred in 1929. In 1945 the United Nations was created to avoid the disasters of warfare caused by diplomatic meltdown. During the final stages of the war, the Red Army drove toward Berlin and the Soviet Union was left in possession of Eastern Europe. In 1949 communist revolution in China was about to enjoy success against the pro-Western

Nationalists of Chiang Kai-Shek. Communism thus expanded dramatically in the wake of war, but most of these countries had little industrial base and little if any proletariat. The Chinese Revolution came about at the hands of peasants. Postwar communism focused on being anti-imperialist and could be seen as a kind of reaction to the expansion of European hegemony during the nineteenth and early twentieth centuries.

The first meeting of the United Nations was held in London in 1946, but the organization was moved to New York the same year, when John D. Rockefeller donated $8.5 million for a site. Winston Churchill delivered his famous "iron curtain" speech, which some associate with the beginning of the Cold War. The Cold War was to be a contest not only between nations—the Soviet bloc and its allies and the capitalist countries—but also between two versions of the pursuit of the ideal. One of the peculiarities of such a pursuit in Western history is that in many such contests, the contestants believe there can be no compromise. One version or the other must triumph, at least in the eyes of the most fervent ideologues on each side.

France and Britain withdrew from Lebanon and made way for the founding of the state of Israel in 1948. The United States founded the School of the Americas, which came to be known by its detractors as the School for Assassins and by some of its students as the School of Coups. Throughout history, people who possess a version of what is ideal for humankind give themselves permission to deny others choices inconsistent with their own. The School of the Americas did not become famous for its support of democracy.

> [I]t has much more to do with counterinsurgency than democracy, with fighting dirty wars than peacemaking. . . . SOA graduates in El Salvador, Honduras, Colombia, Bolivia and elsewhere throughout Latin America have stained the soil and have been linked so consistently and perversely to human rights abuses, dictatorial rule, torture and disappearances that the School of the Americas is finally being scrutinized. (Nelson-Pallmeyer 1997, 4)

Henceforth U.S. foreign policy would focus on avoiding deploying American troops abroad as much as possible by supporting a military culture in Third World countries, which could be used to overthrow local civilian governments that interfered in any way with American interests. This was the military foundation of neocolonialism. In this way U.S. hegemony and U.S. corporate economic interests abroad would be maintained, while projecting a plausible deniability of responsibility for atrocities committed overseas by Indonesian or Guatemalan or other local forces at American urging and with American support.

In 1947 General George Marshall became Secretary of State and proposed the European Economic Recovery Program, which came to be known as the Marshall Plan. The Plan meant that the United States would aid in rebuilding industrial countries. Most aid to nonindustrialized countries would be military in nature and designed to promote "stability," a euphemism meaning resistance to political changes that might challenge economic exploitation by the industrial countries. Little aid to the poor countries was provided to create a locally owned industrial base or economic production to supply local markets. The idea was to create markets in the poorer countries for goods manufactured in the industrialized countries, while foreign investment in an export crop industry provided profits to American corporations. In time the policy evolved to promote the use of cheap labor to produce goods intended for export. Implicit in this model was the expectation that the status quo would be maintained by military regimes loyal to this kind of neocolonialism. Such a plan on a global scale could not be expected to work in each and every case, but it worked often enough.

India was proclaimed independent in 1947 and partitioned into India and Pakistan. The same year Congress passed the National Security Act, which unified the armed forces and created the National Security Council and the Central Intelligence Agency. In March, President Harry S. Truman addressed the House of Representatives and asked for aid for Greece and Turkey, both struggling with indigenous left-leaning insurgents. This policy of U.S. involvement in internal struggles of foreign countries became the Truman Doctrine, which was designed to oppose practically all political change outside Eastern Europe, with U.S. intervention disguised as "aid." The directive was marketed as intervention into the struggle between "freedom" and "totalitarianism" but often resulted in political and military support for some of the world's most repressive totalitarian regimes. In 1948 the religious leader and statesman Mohandas Gandhi was assassinated. Right-wing strongman Syngman Rhee became president of the Republic of Korea. Israel came into existence, with David Ben-Gurion as its first premier; and the Cold War escalated when the USSR blocked highway traffic to Berlin. In 1949 Vietnam became a state, and apartheid was established in South Africa. The following year Senator Joseph McCarthy initiated his search for communists in the U.S. government, and Congress passed the McCarran Act establishing severe restrictions against communists.

In 1950 President Truman adopted National Security Council Policy Paper 68 (NSC68), one of the most important documents of the Cold War. It advocated a huge military buildup, intended to induce political changes in the Soviet system without resorting to all-out war. NSC68 estimated that the United States could devote 20 percent (about $50 billion) of its gross national product to an arms race without destroying the economy. To sell this huge rearmament campaign to Congress, however, required some kind of crisis. In April, a newly elected South Korean Assembly, composed of a significant number of leftists, pressed for reunification of Korea, even on North Korea's terms.

On June 25, 1950, North Korean forces crossed the 38th parallel and captured the capital city of Seoul, South Korea. The Korean War expanded when the Truman Doctrine was extended to Asia, thus redefining American military commitments, as opposed to revolutionary struggles, in the Philippines, Indonesia, Formosa, and Vietnam. President Truman announced a policy of "containment" on June 30 and, because the South Korean Army was retreating in what amounted to a rout, he directed ground forces to the Asian mainland. The United States entered the Korean War without the required declaration of war by Congress. When it

appeared American forces (with UN sanction) would be able to
drive the North Koreans back to the border with China, the United
States announced that its goal was no longer "containment" but
had been broadened to "reunification," a term that meant military
conquest of North Korea. On October 7, U.S. troops crossed the
38th parallel into North Korea, and three days later China warned
that if the Americans continued north, China would enter the war.
General Douglas MacArthur's advance northward was dramatically
reversed when Chinese forces ("volunteers") virtually drove UN
forces out of North Korea. In November, Truman threatened to use
atomic bombs in China.

In early 1951 Truman implemented NSC68 with its $50
billion defense budget and greatly expanded U.S. military presence
around the world. This initiated a permanent relationship between
the military and the industrial complex, which supplied ever-larger
and more expensive weapons systems in a never-ending arms race.
In Guatemala, Jacob Arbenz Guzman became the democratically
elected president and proceeded to appropriate 225,000 acres of
land from the United Fruit Company. This event was interpreted
as contradictory to U.S. foreign interests and as evidence of
expanding socialist influence. In December 1952, Truman
approved sending $60 million to France for use in its war against
insurgents in Vietnam.

General MacArthur advocated all-out war in Korea. His forces
drove the communists beyond the 38th parallel by March 1951 and,
while Truman tried to negotiate a peace, MacArthur sabotaged the
effort by crossing the 38th parallel. MacArthur then challenged the
power of the president to set foreign policy by issuing a statement
calling for all-out war, an act that prompted Truman to fire him.

Truman had set the foundation for the next five decades in
U.S. foreign policy to contain communism all over the world,
with huge military expenditures and a global military presence
intended to protect and advance American economic interests
under an umbrella of rhetoric about defending freedom. The
armistice ending the war was signed on July 27, 1953, months
after General Eisenhower was inaugurated president. Some

Republicans were pointedly disappointed because the peace meant a return to the policy of containment and an abandonment of the idea of conquest. Eisenhower urged France to agree to grant independence to Vietnam and thus abandon its colony, an idea that met French opposition. Eisenhower wanted to redefine the struggle in Vietnam from one of colonial independence to a struggle against communist expansion.

President Eisenhower could be inconsistent in his enthusiasm for militarism and the impact of the Cold War on the poor:

> Every gun that is made, every warship launched, every rocket fired signifies, in the final sense, a theft from those who hunger and are not fed, those who are cold and are not clothed. (Ambrose 1993, 132)

Far more was spent by all sides on weaponry intended to produce either political stability or to defeat or wear down the enemy than was spent on food and support for the poor. Even in years when there were food surpluses, as is true today, people went hungry. Hunger resulted because people did not have the money to pay for food. It is a product of inadequate distribution of wealth. Nothing makes that clearer than military budgets, as Eisenhower suggested.

In 1954 the St. Lawrence Seaway Project, the largest waterway project in U.S. history and one of many such "public works" facilitated during the Eisenhower administration, was approved. Also in that year, in *Brown v. Board of Education of Topeka*, the Supreme Court ruled that public school segregation by race is unconstitutional; and the Senate voted to censure Joseph McCarthy, thus ending the worst part of the McCarthy era.

The CIA conspired with the Guatemalan military to oust Guatemalan President Jacob Arbenz Guzman in 1954 in an action that set into motion a contest between revolutionary movements and military dictatorships, resulting in the death of some 150,000 Guatemalans over the following decades. On May 7, French forces were decisively defeated at Dien Bien Phu. In July, the Geneva Accords were signed, dividing Vietnam into North and South.

In 1956 Gamal Abdel Nasser was elected president of Egypt. The West announced it would not assist in financing the Aswan Dam, and in retaliation Nasser seized the Suez Canal. British and French nationals evacuated Egypt, and on October 31 Anglo-French forces bombed Egyptian airfields. A week later the United States and the USSR intervened to call a truce, and UN forces cleared the canal. The following year, six countries signed the Rome Treaty creating the Common Market.

Alaska became the forty-ninth state and Hawaii the fiftieth in 1959. As America continued to expand, race issues and Cold War pressures remained troublesome. In 1958, Governor Orval Faubus closed public schools in Little Rock, Arkansas, to thwart desegregation. The schools were reopened ostensibly as private schools beyond the reach of desegregation. Meanwhile, Egypt and Sudan joined to create the United Arab Republic with Nasser as president, and the USSR granted a loan to construct the Aswan Dam on the Nile. Fidel Castro, who was conducting a guerilla war in Cuba, escalated the war effort. Fulgencio Batista, Cuba's president, fled to the Dominican Republic in 1959, and Castro soon appropriated U.S.-owned sugar mills and closed gambling casinos, some of which were owned by organized crime figures based in the United States.

In 1960 the United States admitted to aerial reconnaissance over the USSR when a U-2 spy plane was shot down, and American pilot Gary Powers confessed the purpose of his mission. That year the United States continued to protest Castro's appropriation of Cuban properties deemed those of American citizens. Adolph Eichmann, former head of Nazi Germany's Gestapo, was arrested. The 1960 election produced the historic TV debates between Democratic Party candidate John F. Kennedy and vice president and presidential candidate Richard Nixon. Kennedy was narrowly elected.

It was 1961 before the UN condemned apartheid, the same year the United States broke off relations with Cuba and launched a devastating economic blockade against that island nation. Cuban exiles, with covert help from U.S. agencies—most notably the CIA, attempted to overthrow Castro in an ill-fated invasion of the island that ended in a battle at the Bay of Pigs in April of 1961. Castro's forces crushed the attack. A week later President Kennedy took responsibility for the fiasco, but relations continued to be strained within the Kennedy administration around the role of the CIA in this affair. The Cold War intensified when the USSR constructed the Berlin Wall to stop East Germans from fleeing to West Berlin. Adolph Eichmann was found guilty in a well-publicized Jerusalem trial and hanged the following year.

The United States established a military council in Vietnam in 1962 and discovered Soviet missile bases under construction in Cuba. Following the U.S. implementation of a naval blockade of Cuba, there ensued a very tense period of negotiations during which the United States and the Soviet Union moved as close as they would ever come to the brink of nuclear war. Soviet leader Nikita Krushchev agreed to withdraw the missiles from Cuba and the blockade was ended. Ahmed Ben Bella became premier of Algeria following a bitterly fought war for independence from France. Uganda and Tanganyika also became independent. Decolonization was uneven and sometimes involved bloody revolutions, but there were many instances in which European nations simply allowed their colonies independence. France was particularly unwilling to release some of its colonies peacefully.

Following riots and violence by police and whites in Birmingham, Alabama, in 1963, some 200,000 "Freedom Marchers," blacks and whites led by civil rights leader Martin Luther King, Jr., descended on Washington, D.C., demanding civil rights. On November 22, John F. Kennedy was assassinated in Dallas, Texas, and shortly thereafter the man accused of killing Kennedy, Lee Harvey Oswald, was killed by nightclub manager Jack Ruby on American television.

Kenya gained independence in 1963. In 1964 Zanzibar united with Tanganyika to form Tanzania. Its first president was Julius Nyerere. Northern Rhodesia became the independent country of Zambia, and Nyasaland became the independent Malawi. Jack Ruby was found guilty of killing Lee Harvey Oswald (and died in prison of cancer in January 1965). The United States claimed one of its destroyers was attacked off the coast of North Vietnam, and in reprisal U.S. forces attacked North Vietnamese bases, in a serious escalation of U.S. involvement in the Vietnam War. Martin Luther King, Jr., was awarded the Nobel Peace Prize that year, and Yassir Arafat was elevated to leader of the guerilla movement Al Fatah.

The African nation of Gambia achieved independence in 1965. Ahmed Ben Bella was deposed as president of Algeria. Malcolm X, a Black Muslim leader who spoke eloquently but bluntly about racism in America, was assassinated in New York City by members of the Black Muslim movement. Violence broke out in Selma, Alabama, and Martin Luther King, Jr., led a demonstration of some 4,000 from Selma to Montgomery, Alabama, to deliver a petition. One of the worst race riots in U.S. history erupted in the Watts district of Los Angeles, producing 35 dead and 4,000 arrests. The war in Vietnam continued as North Vietnamese jets shot down American jets, and there were student demonstrations in Washington protesting the bombing of North Vietnam. Terrible violence occurred in Indonesia after six generals were murdered on September 30. Pro-American General Suharto launched a campaign that resulted in the removal of President Sukarno, the establishment of a military dictatorship, and the deaths of hundreds of thousands and possibly more than a million people, mostly landless peasants. At least 750,000 people were arrested and many were held without trial for years.

In 1966 Botswana achieved independence. Israel and Jordan engaged in a brief war in 1967 in the Hebron area. Indira Gandhi, Nehru's daughter, became prime minister of India, and protests against the Vietnam War continued in the United States and abroad. A military coup in Ghana sent President Kuame Nkrumah into exile and British Guiana became the independent country of Guyana. The United States bombed Hanoi. Conflict intensified between Israel and Syria, and General Moshe Dayan became defense minister of Israel. During the Six-Day War of 1967 between Israel and three Arab nations—Egypt, Jordan, and Syria— Israel defeated Egypt in the Sinai and annexed East Jerusalem, the West Bank, and the Golan Heights. Ernesto ("Che") Guevara, a hero of the Cuban Revolution, was killed in Bolivia. Some 50,000 people demonstrated against the Vietnam War at the Lincoln Memorial in Washington, D.C., and Martin Luther King, Jr., led an anti-Vietnam War march in New York City. Another anti-war march was staged in San Francisco. There were race riots in Cleveland, Newark, and Detroit.

An American intelligence ship, the *Pueblo*, was captured by North Korean forces and charged with being in North Korean waters in early 1968. (In December the crew was released after the United States admitted encroaching into North Korean waters, an admission almost immediately repudiated.) Senator Robert Kennedy, brother of John F. Kennedy, announced his intention to run for president of the United States, and President Lyndon Johnson announced he would not seek another term of office. Martin Luther King, Jr., was assassinated at a Memphis motel, and Scotland Yard arrested James Earl Ray for the crime in London. Ray was extradited to the United States for trial and was later convicted of King's murder. Senator Robert Kennedy won the Democratic Party primary in California and was assassinated immediately after giving a victory speech. Sirhan Sirhan, a Jordanian, was arrested, charged, and convicted of the murder. Vice President Hubert H. Humphrey won the Democratic nomination for president at a convention marked by anti-war riots and police violence in Chicago. Richard Nixon, with a promise to end the Vietnam War, won the election by the narrowest margin in a presidential election since 1912.

In 1969 violent fighting erupted in Northern Ireland; famine broke out because of civil war in the African land of Biafra; and Yasir Arafat became chairman of the Palestine Liberation Organization. In the United States public attention was focused on the trial of the so-called "Chicago Eight," indicted for leading the demonstrations at the previous year's Democratic Convention. They accused the police of initiating a riot and were found not guilty. The first U.S. troops were withdrawn from Vietnam. Senator Edward Kennedy's car plunged off a bridge into a pond on Chappaquiddick Island, killing passenger Mary Jo Kopechne.

That year also saw more protests against the Vietnam War. During one week, U.S. casualties in Vietnam exceeded one hundred fighting men. Two U.S. Army members were indicted in a massacre of a village of Vietnamese civilians at Mai Lai. Fred Hampton, chairman of the Black Panther Party in Illinois, was killed with others in a predawn police raid in Chicago that would, over time, become very controversial because activists would characterize the government's repression as terrorist in nature. Arab commandoes hijacked three jets headed for the United States in early 1970. Although the United States continued to withdraw troops from Vietnam, student protests also continued. Four students were killed by National Guard troops at a demonstration at Kent State University in Ohio. A Marxist leader, Salvador Allende, was elected president of Chile.

In 1971 the United States bombed Vietcong supply routes in Cambodia, and large-scale bombing in North Vietnam was used as a strategy to force the North Vietnamese to the negotiating table. Fighting spread to Cambodia and Laos. Idi Amin became the dictator of Uganda that year; and Henry Kissinger made a secret visit to China to prepare the way for President Nixon's plan to open diplomatic relations with that communist country. The first segments of the *Pentagon Papers,* leaked to the press to expose official misinformation about the Vietnam War, were published in the *New York Times.* Violence worsened in Northern Ireland, and Algeria announced seizure of majority control of French oil interests but promised restitution.

The United States returned Okinawa to Japan in 1972, and Bangladesh became a sovereign country. Norwegian voters rejected membership in the European Common Market, but Ireland, Denmark, and Britain were admitted. Terrorists seized Israeli Olympic athletes in Munich and eventually eleven hostages were killed, nine in a gunfight between the kidnappers and the West German police and army personnel. In the Philippines, Ferdinand Marcos assumed dictatorial powers after declaring an emergency involving a communist revolution; and Ceylon became a republic and changed its name to Sri Lanka. President Allende of Chile nationalized large businesses. In September 1973, his government was overthrown by a military coup during which Allende was killed. In March columnist Jack Anderson reported that major U.S. businesses and the Central Intelligence Agency collaborated in the coup to overthrow the Allende government. The Chilean right-wing military junta initiated a period of terror during which torture and "disappearances" were used to repress any dissent.

Violence between Catholic and Protestant factions in Northern Ireland continued, and Britain imposed direct control. Five men were arrested at Democratic National Committee Headquarters in the Watergate apartment complex, in Washington, D.C., and Democrats charged the break-in was orchestrated by the Committee to Re-Elect the President (CREEP), thus initiating the "Watergate scandal." On the eve of the presidential election, a demonstration by Native American activists at the Bureau of Indian Affairs building became an occupation and was featured on front pages of newspapers around the world. The American Indian Movement and other activist groups were protesting U.S. treatment of Indians and the misuse of Indian lands and resources. The United States mined Vietnamese ports, including Hanoi Harbor, but the Vietnamese peace talks continued in Paris. On the eve of the election, Henry Kissinger, Nixon's secretary of state, announced: "Peace is at hand." Nixon was reelected in a landslide.

Another Arab-Israeli war broke out in 1973, with significant casualties on both sides. The Arabs were effectively pushed back on the battlefield, but assembled a coalition to punish the Western nations and Japan for support of Israel by cutting off a significant part of its oil exports and causing serious shortages in some countries. The Shah of Iran nationalized all foreign-owned oil companies in Iran. Secretary of State Henry Kissinger and President Nixon launched a policy of "détente," which opened conversations with the Peoples Republic of China and extended conversations with the USSR, in the mistaken belief that these countries could dictate terms to Hanoi that would allow U.S. forces a dignified exit from Vietnam.

A protest against U.S. land-use policies and interference in internal politics in Indian country precipitated a seventy-three-day occupation by Native Americans of the village of Wounded Knee, South Dakota, site of a massacre of Indians by the U.S. Army in 1890. The Watergate scandal led to forced resignations within President Nixon's staff. John Dean, a member of that staff, gave testimony implicating the president. Nixon appointed a special prosecutor, Archibald Cox, to pursue the matter, but fired him when Cox insisted Nixon produce previously secret White House tapes of conversations about Watergate. Attorney General Elliot Richardson resigned. The Nixon White House produced tapes with curious "gaps," and serious talk of impeachment began. Meanwhile, Vice President Spiro Agnew resigned after pleading no contest to charges of tax evasion, and Gerald Ford, a Republican representative from Michigan, was named to replace him.

A cease-fire agreement between the United States and North Vietnam was signed, but fighting continued. The Nobel Peace Prize was awarded to Henry Kissinger and North Vietnam's Le Duc Tho. The latter refused it. Losses in the Vietnam War included 937,562 North Vietnamese and Vietcong combat deaths, almost one million wounded Vietnamese civilians, 415,000 killed. American losses included 45,948 combat deaths, 10,298 non-combat deaths, 303,640 wounded. Estimated total cost of the war to the United States: $109.5 billion. The war illuminated a serious schism in American society and did much to elevate public skepticism about official reports and versions of the conflict, as well as official justifications for the war. This loss of credibility, coupled with disillusionment, would continue to be a significant element in American life long after the war's end.

The conflict in Northern Ireland was played out in England in 1974, when the Tower of London and the Houses of Parliament were bombed. Golda Meir resigned as Israel's premier and Yitzhak Rabin was named to head the cabinet. Greek-led rebels overthrew the government of Cyprus, but Turkey invaded and occupied much of the island that had been under Greek control. Portuguese Guinea was granted independence as Guinea-Bissau, and Granada gained its independence. A serious drought and famine spread through parts of Africa.

Costs of fuel rose dramatically as oil-producing nations boosted prices and economic growth slowed in industrial nations. President Nixon was forced to agree to pay $432,787 in back taxes, and a grand jury secretly named him as a co-conspirator in the Watergate burglary. The Supreme Court unanimously agreed that Nixon was required to turn over additional tapes to the special prosecutor, and the House Judiciary Committee drafted three articles of impeachment for consideration by the full House. Nixon resigned August 9. Gerald Ford became president and chose Nelson Rockefeller as vice president. Ford granted Nixon a pardon for whatever role he may have had in the Watergate affair and also granted limited amnesty to war resisters, draft dodgers, and deserters.

War erupted in 1975 in Ethiopia when the province of Eritrea tried to secede, and famine soon followed. Saudi Arabia's King Faisal was assassinated by a nephew, who was beheaded. Khmer Rouge insurgents seized the Cambodian capital of Phnom Penh and forced urban residents into the countryside; as many as a million civilians are believed to have died in death marches and systematic massacres. The Suez Canal was reopened after being closed for eight years. South Vietnam and Laos fell to communist insurgents, and a Cambodian ship seized the U.S. merchant vessel *Mayaguez,* which was retrieved by U.S. forces. Fighting intensified between Christian and Muslim factions in Beirut. More countries created during the nineteenth-century European conquest were made independent: Sao Tome, Principe, the Comoro Islands, Papua New Guinea, Cape Verde, Mozambique, and Angola. Indonesia launched an invasion of the island and former Dutch possession of East Timor and began what many have described as a chapter of genocide against its people. East Timor is known to have significant natural gas and oil reserves in the Timor Gap. (An account of how the U.S. media treated the excesses and bloodletting of the Indonesian government is found in Chomsky 1993, 130–135.)

John Erlichman, H. R. Haldeman, and John Mitchell, powerful figures in Nixon's inner circle, were convicted in the break-in and cover-up of the Watergate offices and sentenced to two-and-one-half years in prison. Judge John Serica refused to reduce the sentences of E. Howard Hunt, Jr., or G. Gordon Liddy, both of whom were active members of the burglary ring. The Organization of Petroleum Exporting Countries (OPEC), raised its prices by 10 percent. The final surrender of U.S. forces in Vietnam took place. U.S. support for the Army of the Republic of Viet Nam (ARVN) had been so massive that by this time the defeated army was the fourth largest in the world. Some historians think that 1975 was the year in which U.S. dominance in world economic and political affairs, a position established at the end of World War II, began to decline. Vietnam represented a divergence from the preferred U.S. strategy, which included an aversion to ground war in Asia and support for military organizations overseas while limiting the use of American military force where the prospects for victory were uncertain.

Spain abandoned rule of the Spanish Sahara in 1976, and Morocco and Mauritania divided the country, ignoring an indigenous Saharan declaration of independence. North and South Vietnam were reunited, and Venezuela nationalized its oil industry. Pol Pot was appointed premier in Cambodia. Rioting and violence against apartheid continued in South Africa, and an independent Republic of Transkei, one of South Africa's black homelands, was declared. Fighting escalated in Lebanon as Palestinian guerillas and Lebanese Moslems battled Syrian troops and Christian militias. The Parti Quebecois won a majority of seats in the Provincial Parliament, and René Levesque, leader of the PQ, became premier of Quebec. Thailand's government was overthrown in a military coup. The United States celebrated its bicentennial, and Jimmy Carter was elected president.

Angolan forces invaded Sheba (once Katanga) Province and threatened Zaire's copper industry in 1977. Amnesty International, the human rights group that monitors prisoners of conscience and opposes state uses of imprisonment and torture against civilians, won the Nobel Peace Prize that year. Pol Pot was named Secretary General of the Communist Party of Cambodia. Egyptian President Anwar Sadat made a much-publicized visit to Israel, the first by an

Arab leader since Israel was founded in 1948. Rhodesia's prime minister Ian Smith announced that his government was prepared to negotiate a political settlement with the country's black majority.

President Carter granted pardons to almost all Vietnam-era draft resistors. When activists and intellectuals in Czechoslovakia published a human rights manifesto in West Germany, Czech police harassed and arrested them. The Carter administration charged Czechoslovakia with violations of the Helsinki Accords; and Russian writer Andrei Sakharov appealed to Carter to publicly oppose human rights violations in Eastern Europe. Meanwhile, equally serious human rights violations were common in many countries allied with the United States. The energy crisis intensified, and Carter declared that Americans must respond with "the moral equivalent of war" by reducing consumption of petroleum and petroleum products. The U.S. Department of Energy was established. G. Gordon Liddy, the individual credited with masterminding the Watergate break-in, was released from prison after almost four and a half years, the longest prison term of any Watergate figure.

In 1978 the Nicaraguan leftist guerilla movement known as the Sandinistas overthrew the government of right-wing dictator Anastasio Somoza. A revolutionary terrorist group known as the Red Brigades kidnapped and murdered former Italian Premier Aldo Moro. In Afghanistan, a military junta seized power. Zaire's Sheba (Katanga) Province was invaded by secessionist rebels with reported backing from Cuba and Angola, and the U.S. airlifted troops from Morocco and other African nations to help repel the invasion. In Guatemala a four-year reign of terror began when SOA-trained General Romeo Lucas Garcia came to power. Much of the violence was directed at Indians in the Guatemalan highlands. Israeli Premier Menachem Begin and Egyptian President Anwar Sadat shared the Nobel Peace Prize for their efforts to end Egyptian-Israeli hostilities and entered into an agreement, the Camp David Accords, at summit talks arranged by President Carter. The Solomon Islands and Dominica became independent countries. A military junta seized power in Honduras. Atrocities committed by the junta were reported in 1995:

The intelligence unit, known as Battalion 316, used shock and suffocation devices in interrogation. Prisoners were often kept naked and, when no longer useful, killed and buried in unmarked graves. Newly declassified documents and other sources show that the CIA and the U.S. Embassy knew of numerous crimes, including murder and torture. (Nelson-Pallmeyer 1997, 31–32)

The Shah of Iran declared martial law to end anti-government demonstrations, and the Iranian oil industry was idled by strikes. The Shah's government was widely criticized because of its use of repression, including its routine use of torture and murder to terrorize its citizens into submission, while the ruling families looted the country and lived in a luxurious style considered to be Western decadence by the masses and the Shi'ite clergy. The United States ratified the Panama Canal Treaty, and full diplomatic relations were created between the United States and the Peoples' Republic of China.

United States policy toward Third World countries experienced something of a crisis during this period, because in these countries many agencies associated with the business of state security not only condoned but advocated the use of torture. Their procedures differed from those of the Spanish Inquisition principally because they used electricity and drugs to elicit pain and information in addition to the ancient techniques. Although many countries used torture and death squads extensively, several had become particularly well known: Somoza's Nicaragua, the Shah's Iran, the military junta's Argentina, Pinochet's Chile, Marcos' Philippines, and military governments in Guatemala and El Salvador. These governments sometimes used implements of torture manufactured in the United States and practices taught to the local police and military agencies by American advisers in the United States or overseas. The use of torture by state governments became part of the constellation of causes of popular revolts in several cases, particularly the Philippines and Iran. Reports of these practices were widespread and became distasteful to Americans but were not actively discouraged in Third World countries until the Reagan administration. Although a few countries (Indonesia, Guatemala, and El Salvador) could claim success using draconian measures, including massacres, such countries were increasingly becoming pariahs in the international community and grew into an embarrassment to the United States during the Carter administration.

In early 1979 the Shah of Iran was driven from power following public demonstrations that resulted in considerable loss of life at the hands of the army and police. An Islamic republic was founded, at least in part as a rejection of the Western idea of the state and in an effort to seek different ways to legitimate authority. The new Iran, above all, consciously attempted to reject Western values. In July, Saddam Hussein came to power in Iraq. Southern Rhodesia attained independence as the Republic of Zimbabwe. In 1980 Islamic students stormed the American Embassy in Tehran, Iran, seized American embassy staff as hostages, and demanded the Shah be returned to face Islamic justice. In 1981, the president of Egypt, Anwar Sadat, was murdered by Islamic fundamentalists. U.S. officials initiated a program to destroy all pigs in Haiti, most of which belonged to peasants, to protect the American hog industry from an anticipated outbreak of swine flu in 1982.

That year, Soviet leader Leonid Brezhnev died. Israel invaded Lebanon and encircled the Palestine Liberation Organization fighters there. PLO fighters were evacuated by sea. A suicide bomb exploded in U.S. and French barracks outside Beirut, killing 241 American and 58 French soldiers. Lebanese president-elect Bashir Gemayel was assassinated, and the Christian Philange militia murdered more than 400 Muslims in Beirut's Sabia and Shatilla Palestinian refugee camps. Argentina invaded the Falkland Islands, claimed by Britain, and was repulsed. Argentina's military government collapsed. The Argentine military government was replaced by a democratically elected government in 1983.

Mikhail Gorbachev became the leader of the Soviet Union in 1985 at the age of fifty-four. He brought with him the terms *glasnost* or "openness" and *perestroika*, which was a call for economic and structural change. Brutal Haitian dictator "Baby Doc" Duvalier was driven from power in 1986 at a moment when an estimated 60 percent of the Haitian population existed on an income of $60 per year or less. American bombers attacked Libya in an attempt to punish Libyan leader Omar Qaddafi for his suspected support of anti-American terrorism. In 1987 Haiti experienced gruesome massacres when the army and paramilitary terrorists of the *tontons macoutes* attacked poor people. Martial law was declared in Poland as that country inched toward independence from the Soviet Union.

F. W. de Klerk became prime minister of South Africa in 1989, the same year the Iran-Iraq War ended and the Palestinian *intifada* began. The Polish Peoples' Republic was dissolved and replaced by the Republic of Poland. The movement for independence was led by Lech Walensa, an organizer of the labor union Solidarity; it was the first of the major changes resulting from Gorbachev's initiatives. After the revolution of 1989 in Russia, the USSR further disintegrated as various member states declared themselves republics.

Populist priest Jean-Bertrand Aristide was elected president of Haiti with 67 percent of the vote. He was the first popularly elected president of Haiti during the twentieth century. Ayatollah Khomeini, the Islamic fundamentalist who inspired the course of the Iranian revolution, died. Iraq invaded Kuwait, and within hours Kuwaiti military resistance collapsed. Nelson Mandela was released from prison in South Africa in 1990.

In 1991 coalition forces under American command assembled in Saudi Arabia and launched Desert Storm, a military attack that dramatically overwhelmed the Iraqi military in little more than a month with minimal losses to the coalition and significant losses to Iraq, but did not occupy Baghdad or topple Saddam Hussein. Iraq withdrew from Kuwait. A Kurdish rebellion in northern Iraq and a Shi'ite rebellion in the south were crushed by Iraq, which used poison gas and was accused of further brutality. Help for the Kurds, much hinted at by American agents there, was not forthcoming. A Costa Rican request to the United States for extradition of American rancher John Hull, charged with murder in the La Penca bombing, which killed six people, was turned down at the same time American forces were violating Panamanian sovereignty while searching for and seizing dictator Manuel Noriega. U.S. officials circulated a thick notebook of allegations of human rights abuses under Haitian President Aristide, something they had never done during the much more brutal Duvalier regime. In September a military coup overthrew Aristide. A civil suit in a U.S. court found Guatemala's School of the Americas-trained General Hector Gramajo responsible for the rape and torture of U.S. teacher Diane Ortiz, a nun kidnapped on November 2, 1989. He was ordered to pay $47.5 million in damages, but he ignored the order.

In the summer of 1991, an attempted coup by Russian communists failed, and the USSR was formally dissolved. One reason Russians favored this step was the widespread belief that the motherland was subsidizing the republics, the cost of these subsidies was too high, and the only thing holding these countries inside the Soviet state was military force. U.S. ambassador Jack F. Matlock, Jr., explained:

> [Gorbachev's] top financial advisors complain angrily to their American colleagues how heavy the burden of responsibility was for them in Eastern Europe. "Can you believe that we spent—absolutely wasted—between twenty and twenty-five billion dollars on Eastern Europe since World War Two, providing them with a military umbrella and selling them oil below market rates?" one such advisor told an American. "You Americans thought we were imprisoning them, and then we looked around one day and found that we got no benefits and that we were the prisoners." (Halberstam 1991, 19.)

The American system of keeping Third World countries in orbit through a system of international debt and indigenous military forces had triumphed over the Russian system. There were many additional reasons for this collapse, but this was one cited by many in Russia at the time. The dominant competition of the twentieth century was not merely between capitalism and communism but included broad elements of reaction to the expansion of Western economies to many parts of the world in a process of military globalization that evolved into American-led economic globalization. In the communist world and among some unaligned countries as well, Western economic globalization helped to stimulate nationalism that took the form of anti-Western governments and policies. If history is a guide, economic globalization can be expected to provoke reactions against foreign ownership of local assets and global economic policies that infringe on local prerogatives just as exploitative projects have done in the past.

The Soviet Union was an empire of a type that would have been understood by Caesar or Constantine or Charlemagne. It was maintained by a permanent military presence in essentially foreign lands. When the tanks and troops were withdrawn, the Soviet system collapsed (Matlock 1995, 193). Russians were not popular among the people in these lands, and the feelings were, to some extent, mutual. In a century that saw the nineteenth-century Age of Empire recede, the Soviet Empire outlived its usefulness. Information/propaganda about prosperity in the West, ecological problems, a failing economic system, and the economic drain of the arms race may have been contributing factors, but in the end the decision makers in the Kremlin, especially Gorbachev, decided not to use the military to keep the empire intact. Russia did not have the option of switching to Western-style empire building, which recruited subject nations and created elites and military establishments within them poised to overthrow local governments that failed to cooperate with the needs of international (Western G-7) capital.

Yugoslavia dissolved as a nation-state and Serbia and Croatia went to war in 1991. Manuel Noriega was sentenced to forty years in an American prison for involvement in the drug trade. The Irish Republican Army bombed 10 Downing Street, address of the offices of England's prime minister. Neo-Nazis rioted against foreigners in Germany, and journalist Terry Anderson, held hostage in Lebanon for seven years, was freed. South Africa rescinded its apartheid laws in 1991. Rajiv Gandhi, son of Indira Gandhi of India, was killed by a bomb while campaigning.

In 1992 President George Bush barred ships that visit Cuba from coming to the United States. Following the ouster of the Sandinista government, peasant farmers on twenty-one farms were attacked by Nicaraguan security forces and the land was returned to former owners, half of whom were members of the Somoza family. Latvia, Lithuania, and Estonia became independent nations. Russian leader Boris Yeltsin and U.S. president George Bush agreed to further weapons reductions.

In November 1992, William Jefferson Clinton was elected U.S. president. War erupted in Bosnia and Herzegovina, which were formerly parts of Yugoslavia, and Serbian nationalists practiced "ethnic cleansing" with rape and murder. Americans and allied forces became bogged down in Somalia's civil strife; Yitzhak Rabin became Israeli prime minister; and rioting occurred between rival Hindu and Muslim mobs after Hindu fundamentalists burned a mosque. President Alberto Fujimoro of Peru assumed dictatorial powers, and the leader of the terrorist organization Sendero Luminoso, Abimael Guzman, was captured. Egyptian terrorists attacked foreign tourists.

Willem de Klerk and Nelson Mandela shared the 1993 Nobel Peace Prize for establishing a constitution that would bring "fundamental rights" for all South Africans. Opponents of Boris Yeltsin staged a rebellion that was quickly quelled. Israel attacked Hezbollah in southern Lebanon and terrorists bombed the New York Trade Center. The North American Free Trade Agreement was ratified. Pablo Escobar, escaped drug lord, was killed in Colombia, and more than 100 of 246 Colombian officers cited for war crimes were discovered to be graduates of the School of the Americas.

President Clinton's hopes for health care reform in the United States were defeated in 1994. Israel and the Palestinian Liberation Organization signed a peace accord. African National Congress leader Nelson Mandela became president of South Africa. American forces occupied Haiti, and Aristide returned as president.

With the collapse of the Soviet Union, the United States emerged as the surviving superpower but with an uncertain definition of the limitations of its capacity to project its will. Military solutions, certainly, were not unlimited. Two ground wars in Asia since World War II had proven unproductive and unpopular, and successive small-scale interventions were rarely deemed successful. At the same time, the strategy of supporting local solutions to local problems was not universally successful and no clear alternative had presented itself.

Bibliography

Ambrose, Stephen E. *Rise to Globalism: American Foreign Policy Since 1938.* New York: Penguin Books, 1971, rev. 1993, xiii.

Chomsky, Noam. *Year 501: The Quest Continues.* Boston: South End Press, 1992.

Cohn, Gary, and Ginger Thompson. "Unearthed: Fatal Secrets," *Baltimore Sun,* June 11-18, 1995.

Halberstam, David. *The Next Century.* New York: William Morrow, 1991.

Matlock, Jr., Jack F. *Autopsy of an Empire: The American Ambassador's Account of the Collapse of the Soviet Union.* New York: Random House, 1995.

Millman, Gregory J. *The Vandal's Crown: How Rebel Currency Traders Overthrew the World's Central Banks.* New York: Simon & Schuster, 1995.

Nelson-Pallmeyer, Jack. *School of the Americas: The Case for Closing the School of the Americas and for Fundamentally Changing U.S. Foreign Policy.* Maryknoll, N.Y.: Orbis Books, 1997.

Wilentz, Amy. *The Rainy Season: Haiti Since Duvalier.* New York: Simon & Schuster, 1989.

FIFTEEN
Conclusion

History is not simply a record waiting to be unpacked and examined, but a series of emerging texts subject to revision and reinterpretation, each built on previous work. The record of history should tell us important things about the world we live in and the trends we are experiencing in a way that helps us understand the context of the events. It is often said that we are condemned to repeat the history we do not understand, and it often appears that we do not understand it. Is not our inability to understand founded on errors of perception—prejudices—woven into the fabric of the body of "knowledge" passed to us by previous generations? Even if we are conscious of this pattern of prejudice, is it possible to write about the past as though we are not invested in its outcome and are unaware of our reflections in its mirror?

For the most part, contemporary historians have proceeded from the presumption that modern people are different from and superior to those who came before—especially those designated as "primitives." Distortions and incomplete and even dishonest renderings of the past are found in many modern accounts of ancient peoples and contemporary "primitive" peoples; these accounts serve to reinforce the sense of difference and to distance moderns from unflattering legacies of the past. Contemporary image makers, especially people in the entertainment industry, have often tended to represent these people as somehow less human than twentieth-century people, but stone age peoples, whom anthropologists describe as "hunter-gatherers," developed vigorous and successful cultures by any reasonable definition of success. Accounts by some modern observers have documented the complexity of the social and spiritual cultures of contemporary stone age people—an indication that earlier hunter-gatherer peoples also generated complex cultures that contributed to their survival and ability to adapt.

They did not, however, write history. Attempts by the earliest civilizations to record history come down to us mostly as pottery markings and carvings on stone monuments. Great civilizations such as those that arose in Mesopotamia left such records. It is worth noting that those who commissioned those historical records were the classes or leaders who held power, usually the military elite of the culture. Until fairly recently, across most cultures of the world, only the elite classes could read and write, and therefore they alone were capable of leaving a record. Since those who set down the events naturally prioritize them according to their view of what is most important, historical accounts tend to be distorted by the bias and interests of the class in power. It is not necessary to judge this kind of admittedly necessary distortion as either good or bad; we need only acknowledge that it exists. We might also remember that virtually our entire "knowledge" of the past comes from this source and that the elites who are recording the facts are unlikely to report them in patterns unflattering to their class.

Lightning strikes the earth hundreds of times every day but produces fire only rarely, and those fires seldom burn very far from the point of impact. Over the centuries, however, some fires can be expected to be significant. When conditions are right, fires can burn huge areas and conceivably change the world they touch forever. Revitalization movements—movements to create conscious change in the culture inspired by visions, revelations, or challenging circumstances—have appeared among human populations in history in a manner resembling lightning fires. A few such movements—especially those originally inspired by utopian beliefs or the pursuit of the ideal—continue to shape today's world.

The Greek philosopher Socrates became dissatisfied with the extreme skepticism and nihilism of the Ionian philosophers of his day, especially around the issues of knowledge and ethics. Countering the Sophist view that nothing can be known for certain, Socrates founded a school of thought based on the belief that, through vigorous reasoning, it is possible to know such things as truth with great certainty. He believed that there exist universal truths that can be discovered through reason and that these truths will guide humanity toward the ideal of a more perfect society.

It is probable that the tradition of Greek philosophy—from Socrates to Plato to Aristotle—would have languished in obscurity in Greece and been lost to history except that Alexander the Great was not only an enthusiastic student of Aristotle but also one of the greatest military geniuses of all time. His project of conquest created an empire stretching from the Indus Valley to North Africa and thus spread Greek culture beyond the city-states to a wider Hellenistic world. Conquest carried Greek culture far and wide. Of all things Greek, the most critical for Western civilization across the millennia was the pursuit of the ideal, originating with Socrates. This idealism was to become a foundation of Western thought; and its underlying assumptions, which give absolute and exclusive value to Western thought, continue to shape the contemporary world.

Utopian ideologies can be either secular or spiritual in nature, but the most powerful and lasting revitalization movements have been based on belief in the supernatural. Initially an attempt to find relief from the heavy boot of Roman oppression, the movement of the followers of Jesus of Nazareth predicted a coming age that would be ushered in by supernatural forces and would create a veritable Kingdom of God on earth. Like all such movements, early Christianity adopted survival strategies when its prophesies failed to materialize. Once established, the institutions that represented the utopian vision of the Kingdom of God—the Roman and Greek Churches—took steps to strengthen and fortify their control, particularly over any deviation in matters of doctrine and belief. The survival strategies of institutions that inherit utopian legacies can become intensely repressive in nature, policing behavior and even thought in order to maintain their control. In the Christian establishment these strategies produced repression, excommunications, the search for heretics, the Inquisition, witch-craft trials, and the ruthless use of torture, executions, and even mass slaughter—all in the cause of advancing a religion that once claimed itself committed to principles of peace.

In the eleventh century Roman popes called upon the secular heads of Europe to subordinate themselves to the Church and to engage in a war of European expansion in the name of Christianity. The Crusader movement implanted the idea throughout Christendom that it was legitimate to spread Christianity through conquest, Crusader culture dominated European thought and behavior for at least four centuries. The idea of spreading Christianity by the sword would underlie the themes of conquest and religious war in Western civilization into the twentieth century and arguably to the present.

Secular revitalization movements have tended to be as intolerant and violent as those rooted in religious institutions. The rise of French nationalism in the age of Napoleon celebrated the supposed glories and superiority of French culture and urged that the ambitions of the French nation entitled that nation to the resources and loyalty of other nations. This formula for conquest and empire building enabled people to rationalize as "in the national interest" acts that otherwise would have been considered barbaric. This kind of thinking produced nationalist and ultranationalist movements that shared the enthusiasm, a reckless disregard for human rights, and a capacity for destructive behavior exceeding anything seen in the past. These movements left a legacy of nation-states that claim to have a special place in history or a special configuration of national personality that is in competition with its neighbors—a competition that brooks no compromise and is therefore often settled by violence. At the end of the twentieth century this form of nationalism has spread to remote corners of the globe.

The life work of Karl Marx is an illustration of the power of ideas. The English philosophers of the sixteenth and seventeenth centuries had written in support of capitalists; the French and American Revolutions had supported the interests of the bourgeoisie, and Marx wrote in support of the proletariat. Marxism became a revitalization movement that viewed history in the context of an economic contest between classes and, with a certainty characteristic of people writing within the tradition of the pursuit of the ideal, left little room for negotiation or compromise. Aggressively Eurocentric, his writings embraced elements of the theory of progress that found expression during the Enlightenment and gave rise to one of the most powerful revitalization movements of the modern era. By mid-twentieth century nearly one-half of the human population was living under regimes that designated themselves Marxist.

The Industrial Revolution had not only created new classes, it also stimulated a period of European expansion and the subjugation of peoples across the globe who tended to equate European domination with capitalist expansion. When the theories of communism and socialism merged with nationalism, many of these countries "nationalized" foreign assets, created a repressive state apparatus, and for the first time settled into a period of defiance of Western hegemony.

The history of Europe has been characterized by a series of ideas and movements that rationalized warfare. In medieval times, wars were fought among cultures defined by religion. During the early stages of the Industrial Revolution, nationalism arose and wars became contests based on the competing interests of "nations." Karl Marx proposed that the fundamental contest was among classes. Adolph Hitler proposed that the contest was between races. Each of these tendencies continues to be nurtured in some form or another by significant numbers of people. They are, in essence, the dark legacies of Western civilization, and each has provided extensive rationalizations for the perpetuation of organized violence. The embers of those movements continue to glow, waiting to be reignited when the right conditions appear.

Revitalization movements, whether religious or secular in inspiration, tend to incorporate a form of idealism that is intolerant of those who do not share the group's beliefs or identity. Tolerance—the willingness to accept that there may be other ways of being in the world that are different from but no less legitimate than one's own—cannot coexist with this view, since legitimizing those seen as "other" destroys the exclusive legitimacy of the movement and the privileged identity of its followers.

Movements that recruit people who have little power are often met with force and repression, and result in destruction of the followers, as in the case of the Jonestown Massacre and the Ghost Dance of the Great Plains Indians a century ago. Revitalization movements undertaken by a group that can mobilize a military force or even a mob have been behind most if not all of the acts of genocide in Western history. Such events have actually increased in the twentieth century. The slaughter of the Tutsi by the Hutu in Rwanda, the extermination of European Jews by the Nazis, and the genocide practiced against Armenians by Turkey in 1915, and more recently against ethnic Albanians by Serbian nationalists, are examples of what we now term "ethnic cleansing." Although genocide is not necessary to forced displacements, massacres and wholesale murder have been common.

It is clear that revitalization movements are not disarmed by the "civilizing" influence of a Western education or exposure to Western culture. The people doing the slaughter in Rwanda were reacting to nineteenth-century versions of European scientific racism imported into their culture, and most of them were from the Christian community. Nazi Germany was, of course, among the countries most steeped in Western tradition. The ethnic cleansing of Muslim Albanians by Christian Serbs revives an old Western "tradition" of religious intolerance.

Capitalist advocates have a long history of a version of the pursuit of the ideal that urges there is only one correct answer to every question. The moral claim of the theory is that ways of being in the world will be invented and tried and then, when people see the choices, they will choose the one best for them. Unless people find meaningful options that are culturally affirmative and meet their physical and spiritual needs, however, they can be expected to attempt to achieve their goals through their own methods and to employ considerable energy and sometimes inhumane tactics to do so.

The intolerance of many world economic leaders for self-sufficient local economies suggests that only one form of economy—

global capitalism—will be allowed to survive. This is a formula for creating conditions that could easily heighten nationalism, increase pressure on already destitute populations, and provide fertile ground for future and unpredictable revitalization movements. Such movements may be unavoidable, but it is unwise to create conditions that have historically given them birth. We live in a world in which weapons of mass destruction will soon be within reach of peoples in diverse cultures across the globe. The combination of weapons of mass destruction and mass movements that render people blind to what would otherwise be obvious dangers can be expected to lead people to take actions that can only lead to disaster.

In the process of creating cultures, peoples borrow consciously and unconsciously from peoples of other cultures, who in turn borrow from them. Whenever two peoples meet, there is an intense exchange of ideas and other cultural elements such as language and customs. Contemporary Western culture, for example, has borrowed foods, medicines, plant knowledge, words, customs, artifacts, music, stories, ideas, and attitudes from many cultures of the world. It is not the creation of particular "Western" peoples—Europeans. It is, rather, a descendant of many cultures. The thinking that characterizes Western revitalization movements, as we have seen, cannot include the contributions of many cultures as essential elements in Western culture. The white supremacist and the Eurocentric philosopher believe that modernity is essentially an invention of the European mind, that all useful creativity flowed from that single source. In the same way that an individual who believes in the coming Kingdom of God is drawn to believe in a theory of progress—that the world is on a journey that will take it closer and closer to the Kingdom—the Eurocentric philosopher must also believe that the genius of the culture is carrying it and humankind into a continually improving future.

It is not difficult to understand that few contemporary students are attracted to the study of the history of Western philosophy because it is a discouraging study of a series of bad ideas that have gone wrong. There have been no powerful new ideas in Western culture for several generations. Because philosophy has limited itself to ideas that find their way into Western discourse through a traditionally Western path, and people from other cultures have not historically had access to that path, Western philosophy has not had the benefit of the ideas of people of other cultures. That is and has been changing for some time, however. Philosophy, anthropology, and history all have advocates for pluralism within their disciplines.

Some of history's darkest moments have occurred during times when people have been confronted with ideas they found enormously attractive. These powerfully attractive ideas propelled peoples into adventures that brought them into conflict with others. The result—whether the annihilation or near annihilation of the other or of themselves—have too often been tragic. The potential for such projects to be reenergized, or for new projects to be invented, exists in every culture in the world. They are most likely to appear among a distinct people who feel oppressed or unjustly denied their rightful place in the world and are often played out with dangerous or deadly behaviors. Oppression and the perception of injustice are no less common today than in any previous century. Indeed, there is evidence that they may be on the rise.

The antidote to these kinds of movements is to defuse intolerance. Philosopher Isaiah Berlin points to this need in his calls for pluralism. But pluralism, at the end of the twentieth and beginning of the twenty-first century, is unpopular in most of the world's societies because it goes against the perceived interests of religious establishments, ethnic and racial groups, and power elites. Nationalists see it as threatening to their beliefs and ability to wield power. Many religious leaders see tolerance as a threat to their system of beliefs. People who embrace combinations of nationalism, religious intolerance, and racial distinction tend to be alienated from all other peoples. To the degree a people or nation can be taught to respect the principles of pluralism and tolerance, the prospects of militias committing slaughters and armies participating in wholesale ethnic cleansing are dimmed. To the degree that pluralistic thinking is not respected or practiced such events await opportunity. To this, history is our witness.

Index